BOL BAM
Approaches to Shiva

Scharada Dubey was born in Jabalpur, Madhya Pradesh, and showed an early aptitude for writing, winning First Prize in an essay competition conducted by the Royal Commonwealth Society across the Commonwealth countries for her essay on the Indian farmer in 1973–1974, when she was still in school in Mumbai. She graduated from St. Xavier's College, writing articles for various magazines and newspapers, and working briefly in the publishing industry. She has also briefly lectured in Sociology after her post-graduation, first in Mumbai, and then at Stella Maris College, Chennai.

She began writing stories for children as Scharada Bail shortly after the birth of her daughter in 1986, and these appeared regularly along with other articles for children in the Young World section of *The Hindu*. She won the Travelogue category of the National Competition for Writers of Children's Books conducted by the Children's Book Trust on three consecutive occasions. These prize-winning entries were then published as her first three books, *Footloose on the West Coast, Malwa on My Mind* and *A Necessary Journey*.

Scharada has worked on reports for Doordarshan, shooting short films on Narikuruva gypsies, indigenous dog breeds, and regional cuisine, among other topics. From 2000 to 2002, she travelled extensively in India, supported by a grant from the India Foundation for the Arts, Bangalore, researching the lives of toymakers who make and sell their toys on Indian streets. Her essay on these men and women, called *The Bits and Pieces Artists*, came second in the Outlook-Picador Non-Fiction Contest in 2000.

She has published several titles after that, including *Portraits from Ayodhya: Living India's Contradictions*, and profiles of the Presidents and Prime Ministers of India, all published by Westland.

She is also a popular practitioner of Tarot. She now lives in Pune.

BOL BAM

Approaches to Shiva

Scharada Dubey

TRANQUEBAR

Tranquebar Press
An imprint of westland ltd

61, Silverline Building, 2nd floor, Alapakkam Main Road, Maduravoyal, Chennai 600095

No. 38/10 (New No.5), Raghava Nagar, New Timber Yard Layout, Bangalore 560026

93, 1st Floor, Sham Lal Road, New Delhi 110002

First published in TRANQUEBAR PRESS by westland ltd 2013
Copyright © Scharada Dubey 2013

ISBN: 978-93-83260-53-9

Typeset by PrePSol Enterprises Pvt. Ltd.

To
Shiva the most compassionate,
who blesses me in ways I only dimly understand
and
the millions of poor pilgrims across the country
who have taught me the meaning of devotion…

Disclaimer

This book is not the product of extensive scholarship of the Hindu religion, nor is it based on any detailed or thorough knowledge of Hindu philosophy. It has not been authorized or blessed by any religious authority of any sect or community. The author does not claim to be speaking on behalf of millions of Hindus in India or elsewhere in the world. All views expressed are the author's own, or of the interviewees encountered during pilgrimages and other journeys. All descriptions of Hindu beliefs and traditions are from observations of everyday practices in different parts of the country, unless attributed to specific texts and sources.

Contents

Acknowledgements

My journey towards *Bol Bam* started years before writing this book, and is still continuing, in many significant ways. It is, therefore, inevitable that a great many people have contributed to it in no small measure.

I remember with gratitude Anmol Vellani and the India Foundation for the Arts, who first trusted me to write a book of narrative non-fiction based on my travels and interviews, and supported me with a grant that resulted in *The Toymakers: Light from India's Urban Poor*. Some of the journeys for that book have been described in this one, from a different perspective. I am thankful to a legion of my friends and family who supported me with encouragement and enquiries, suggestions and patient listening. In Bhopal, my cousin Colonel Atul Mishra and his wife Anu, and Colonel Milind Chaudhary and his wife extended warm solidarity. Brigadier Shailesh Tinaikar and Seema Mahale Tinaikar have cheered me on at every step, besides offering me warm hospitality in Jalandhar. Chitra and Ramesh Shastry in Vadodara provided another haven between destinations, and Usha Purohit brought camaraderie to our all-female journey to Somnath.

It is hard to list all those who shared my enthusiasm for temples and deities during my life in Chennai, but those years are undoubtedly when I first felt the desire to write a book like *Bol Bam*. Thanks are due to Ranvir Shah and Prakriti Foundation for bringing out my Hanuman poems in 2005, several of which have been quoted in this book. Sushila Ravindranath, Mathangi Srinivasamurti, Uthra Srinath, Lalita Kannan and Rohini Rajavel brought companionable moments to my last decisive trip to Tamil Nadu in December 2011. Kalyan Arun shares my love for Thiruvannamalai and helped locate a vital link. Srini Subramanian nurtured my spirituality in unexpected ways. I remember a dear friend and neighbour, Shanta Krishnamurthy, for showing me what Tuesday afternoon and *pradosh* worship of Shiva was all about, and Sandhya Sridhar will well understand this.

My grateful thanks to Dr Kalpana Dube and her daughter Aditi for saving me from complete isolation and despair during the years I spent in Lucknow, and to Jaya Chauhan and Shivashish Singh for some precious companionable moments. Girish Tiwari helped re-establish my Varanasi connection. Jaya Santhanam's frequent enquiry during this phase also brought comfort. Thanks are due to Rajiv Maliwal for being consistently concerned about my predicament of the moment.

I thank Geeta Hosmane, Jennifer Rodrigues, Sharmila Ranade, Sunando Kundu and others who warmly welcomed me in my new life in Pune, and enabled me to bring this work to conclusion by steadfastly giving me the time and space to write, when we would all rather have been kicking up our heels.

Most of all, my heartfelt gratitude and deep love to my children Shivani and Shishir Bail, who have accompanied me on so many of the journeys in this book, my mother Madhu Dubey for her belief and the path it showed me to God, my sister Suhasini Kirloskar and brother-in-law Sudhir Kirloskar for their unstinting support, and my brother Rohit Dubey for his appreciation and encouragement.

Westland Tranquebar and Renuka Chatterjee continue to be part of my journey and I feel honoured to be on their list. Thanks are also due to Kanishka Gupta of Writer's Side, who has consistently believed in my work.

My thanks to all the interviewees in this book, whose views and insights have made it what it is. Particular thanks are due to Shri Subodh Prasad, Indian Police Service, Senior Superintendent of Police at Deoghar, who enabled me to understand what women face every day of their lives in so many parts of the country.

Finally, my thanks to all companions in faith, and even the sceptics and critics who pick up this book and go through its contents. What better gift can I hope to receive than the engagement and attention of readers?

Scharada Dubey
Pune, March 2013

Introduction: The Problem of Faith

Our names often reveal the faith our parents and forefathers practised, and it is their actions that lay the foundation for how we approach it in our own lives. Of course, the first appearance of faith in our adult selves is in a form of branding, as one of the ingredients of our identity. 'Hindu, Muslim, Sikh, Isai' we often intone in our patriotic songs, naming the four dominant religions practised in India, and our names offer a clue to the particular faith that claims us as one of its own, or that we can claim to represent as significant for us. But beyond this superficial branding, whether we do indeed follow in the footsteps or dictums of a particular faith depends a lot on the way our parents approached matters at home. Which is not to say that it's a simple equation of temple-going parents producing pious children. In fact, visible symbols of religiosity in some families lead to children growing up with a counter-reaction to the whole question of religion. After all, if a man spends many hours doing puja, or is a pillar in his congregation at church, but gets drunk and beats his wife and children regularly, they can't be expected to have the kindest view of his faith. Like many other aspects dependent on the dynamics of the family, faith can produce some unexpected results.

My faith as a believing Hindu is rooted almost entirely in the way my mother professed and practised it in the years I was growing up.

I lolled around the house reading Enid Blyton and P.G. Wodehouse, Georgette Heyer or the then ubiquitous Mills and Boon romances to the background sound of my mother singing verses aloud out of Tulsidas' *Vinay Patrika* or *Ramcharitmanas*. I raised a host of pets, from squirrels, rabbits, parrots, puppies and finally, kittens and cats, with my mother making room for their accompanying dirt and clutter without invoking scriptural taboos or citing the daily puja as a reason for them to be kept at bay. She never insisted on any of her three children following any special routine of worship, but she would occasionally bring us closer to such matters by clever strategems — like one summer vacation when she made me read the *Ramcharitmanas* every day to 'improve my Hindi'! At other times, the presence of God in our home was underlined in the simplest of ways – no fruit or sweets, new clothes or books, or any shining item of use, freshly bought, was put into operation without enjoying a few moments '*Bhagwanji ke saamne* (In front of God)', which meant they were always first placed before the few small figures of deities my mother worshipped each day. If I was forming any definite idea of God in those days, it would have been as an inoffensive, broadly loving but unobtrusive presence, which we gathered up and carted along with all the rest of our possessions to the numerous cities we lived in, for my mother to set up and pay homage to in each new place. My mother's equation with her Bhagwanji certainly did not communicate any sense of fear to any of us, or make us, literally, God-fearing.

Any element of awe in relation to faith was derived from other sources, also within the family. My maternal grandmother, admonishing my cousin and me for helping ourselves too freely from jars of home-made goodies made especially for Diwali, or visitors, opened her eyes terrifyingly wide and told us how Bhagwanji punished greedy children. She also painstakingly taught me my first prayer, '*Sri Ramachandra kripalu bhajaman, harana bhava bhaya daarunam*' (Tulsidas) and the importance of unfailingly turning all one's worries to God at night before one slept, after one had prayed. I was encouraged thus to see God as the final authority on everything, one who could hand out a punishment or two, but who could also be appealed to through the simple expedient of nightly prayer.

My paternal grandfather, who clicked around the house in wooden, single-toed *khadaun* (footwear used by orthodox Hindus) from a very early hour in the morning, was the only one who brought in any sense of rules or decorum to be followed in the practice of faith. It was he who insisted that I join my brother and cousins (all of them years older than me) in reading a few *shloka*s from the Bhagavadgita every morning — we sat in a line on four chairs lined up against the wall, dutifully bent over. I remember my wet hair still dripping on the back of my neck, although it had, of course, been neatly combed. Doing anything connected with God only after a bath, sitting upright, learning difficult Sanskrit letters and adopting a pose of sheer concentration, all these were definitely instilled by my grandfather, who was addressed as Bade Bhaiya (eldest brother) by everyone in the house, including us, his grandchildren. From his disciplined daily routine to his discussions on philosophy with student visitors from the college where he taught, my grandfather represented the structure and system of faith, while my grandmothers, both of them, and my mother, represented the feelings. It was subtle, but unmistakable — the conditioning that women were the primary nurturers and protectors of faith in a family — but not its ultimate authority.

In comparison to my mother's daily and visible contact with her God, my father's relationship with Him was very ambiguous. He would, of course, visit the great temples with us, such as Tirupati, or arrange for us to go to the important and famous shrines when we were on holiday, like the Mangesh temple in Goa. But he was rarely seen with bowed head or closed eyes, never in supplication or surrender, and his confident, quirky smile, dark moustache raised at the ends, and complete rejection of any form of overt religiosity set him apart as a picture of devil-may-care masculinity. He must have had his own spiritual crises, of course, but these were presumably addressed through professional efforts and growth, the company of friends and alcohol. What made me cheer my father's slender attachment to faith was the fact that it made him a definite liberal, truly modern in many ways. He despised all caste and community based networking, for instance, and neither sought to ingratiate himself with others on the basis of his Kanyakubja Brahmin lineage, nor specially encouraged others to approach him in a similar manner. He was also eclectic enough in his choice of friends, music, food and fashion to accommodate mine and my siblings' youthful tastes and demands.

My mother kept pace with his modernity with no problem whatsoever. She was, and remains today, one of the truly modern, expansive, tolerant individuals I know, if a modern perspective is to be equated with a respect for all. It was another matter that her faith remained as fierce as ever as my parents entered middle age. As the glasses tinkled and snacks were passed around on the terraces of the fine homes where they attended parties, my mother could be spotted sitting calmly, half-smiling, her lips moving imperceptibly in silent prayer. She wore Chanel and Nina Ricci, lipstick and Kanjeevaram sarees, but didn't lose touch with the saint-poets that had nurtured her childhood — and mine.

I grew up as their child with the same blithe insouciance about many matters that must have characterized those delightful Edwardian men and women whose stories I was wont to read, courtesy Wodehouse. I was literally larking about, not a whit worried about my faith, or the lack of it, the religious identity I was born into, or the social complexities it represented, till I began experiencing the first challenges to it in young adulthood as a self-conscious college student. Suddenly, I was in company where it was cool to discuss Bertolt Brecht or Jean-Paul Sartre, Karl Popper or George Steiner, but confessing to a fondness for going to the Siddhi Vinayak temple on Tuesdays would have drawn very strange looks. I remember listening avidly in the college canteen to a friend describe the whole mind-versus-matter debate in the context of Hegel and Marx (all the time admiring his flashing brown eyes) and knowing with absolute certainty that artless little confidences about my family's relationship with Bhagwanji could never pass my lips.

Secularism (the anti-religion version), and the radical challenge to the might of the State and its repressive agencies posed the first awkward obstacles in my easy familiarity with God as a presence to be invoked. As I spent more time amidst friends, peers and those seniors I respected for their visible contribution towards civil and women's rights and the plight of poor and marginalized communities, I spent no time at all in prayer, nor did I then feel the need to. In the last few years of school, I had filled notebooks with stories and poetry exploring all manner of existential questions. But then, just a couple of years later, I was afraid to speculate on the nature of God for fear of sounding silly. If I had stayed true to the influences that shaped my life in those youthful years, I would either have become a significant revolutionary, with clearly visible work around a cause, or an aesthete with sophisticated tastes who could wax eloquently over the beauty of Chola bronzes without any personal connection to the deities they represented.

Instead, I took the plunge into messy domesticity and parenting, the beginning of my own family, complete with questions of what vision of God I would pass on to my children. My deepening acquaintance with Bhagwanji in this journey over the years has been described at various places in this book.

But I wouldn't have taken to writing this book at all, if I had not wrestled with the *problem* posed by faith.

By the time I had navigated my forties, the difficulties of being a believing Hindu in the twenty-first century had been borne in on me in a variety of ways. The identity politics of the

1990s, with the twin horrors of the Babri Masjid demolition in 1992 and the Gujarat riots in 2002 made it difficult to admit aloud with any pride that one was a Hindu. Even though, ironically, that was the exact slogan of the perpetrators of these horrors — '*Garv se kaho, hum Hindu hain* (Proclaim with pride that you are a Hindu)'. Instead, the aggressive posturing by self-appointed guardians of the Hindu faith actually made it appear less attractive than it had ever appeared in its timeless history. Professing a fondness for the deities and symbols of Hindusim after the emergence of the chauvinistic 'Hindutva' in the political arena became a virtual minefield, which the faint-hearted would do well to avoid completely.

In this context, even writing a book about faith, or seeming inordinately interested in pilgrims or pilgrimages is an odd choice for some of my friends. When I tell them I am writing about devotees of Shiva, I can sometimes hear a sharp intake of breath — for a few seconds I have been placed only shades away from Narendra Modi, chief minister of Gujarat during the riots of 2002, in the narrow bandwidth of their imagination. Then they profess to listen to my reasons for writing, and don't actually descend into argument (I am, after all, fifty, female and quite harmless!). But you can see that somewhere, I have entered very suspect territory in the way they conceive of 'secularism'. Ah, well. I will deal with more of that in later chapters. Right now, it's just enough to say that 'Hindutva' was a poison that made the most personal attachment to Hindu gods seem a political statement.

Later, the breakdown of my marriage to the father of my children, and my second marriage to a staunch atheist, posed other challenges. 'How have you lived a lifetime in a religion that celebrates a racist and supremacist approach to society, that confers respectability on injustice and inequality?' my partner asked, narrowing his eyes, and I was forced to search for suitable answers. Shadowy images in flashback emerged from the depths of my childhood memories. Alongside my paternal grandfather in his austere wooden khadaun, I remembered a wooden door set in the back of the courtyard of our home in Jabalpur, which was the only entrance permitted to the lady who cleaned the toilets. No one else ever used that door, and we were even discouraged from handling it. I recalled the smell of incense that always surrounded the small, brilliant, beautifully clothed figures of Krishna and Radha, kept on a special brass *singhasan* or throne, and lovingly tended to by my grandfather's sister. She always wore white sarees as a child widow, and her life, apart from the hours she spent teaching in a nearby school, was devoted to helping out in her brother's household, and showering great love and care on the '*Biharji*' on the brass throne. When I had gone to Brindavan in 2000, I had felt the shock of recognition seeing many women dressed similarly to Chhoti Jijji (younger sister) and, widows just like her, hanging on to life with the diminutive figures of their personal Bihariji or '*Thakurji*'. I may have lived in a happy bubble in my childhood, but these reminiscences in later life showed me that I had not been too far removed from some of the most shaming aspects of Hindu practice and belief — the untouchability of people who cleaned toilets, and the plight of child widows.

Such memories did make me pause and consider my attachment to the structure and practices of the faith that I had been born into — but could not quieten the messages emanating from my heart. As the years went on, I often experienced a complete dissolution of thought, a melting down in pure emotion, through the sheer mention of some of the names we use to call God. '*Keshava, Madhava, tujha naamaatre godava* (Keshav! Madhav! Your very names are sweet)' goes a popular Marathi song of the 1970s and '80s, and I perfectly knew what that meant, identifying with it whole-heartedly.

However, my struggles with faith were not confined only to the contradictions between head and heart, or the way I perceived Hindus and Hinduism. I tried to provide myself every opportunity for what I hoped was spiritual growth. The Art of Living, Vipassana and the global fraternity of Nichiren Daishonin's Buddhism — I joined each spiritual class and was diligent in the recommended practice for a period. Somehow, after some weeks and months, when the meditation or chanting should have taken me to a higher level of awareness, I always fell back to the old, familiar, inchoate faith. I knew Bhagwanji was not far, but very near. I preferred to apply myself to real emotional and material crises in my personal life (and there were plenty of those!) rather than spend hours trying to meditate or chant. In Vipassana and Soka Gakkai Buddhism moreover, I missed having a personal God to communicate to directly. After weeks of Vipassana, I felt as if a protective outer skin, which helped me withstand the coarseness and ugliness of the world around me, had fallen away, leaving me unbearably moved by the smallest of daily tragedies. Although I could attest to the power of the Nam-myo-ho-renge-kyo chant through several important breakthroughs in my own life, my dialogue with the Gohonzon (object of devotion) never approached the no-holds-barred communication I had with Rama or Hanuman, Shiva or Devi, the Mother-goddess, on any occasion. Finally, after many years of such spiritual sorties, I was ready to admit that I was an incurable Hindu — at least when it came to a deep and abiding attachment to the forms and names we worship as the *Sagun Brahm*.

So there I was, shame-faced but steadfast.

If I had stubbornly clung to Hindu beliefs in spite of the difficulties of countering varied levels of sophistication and political correctness among my peers, post-modern interpretations of reality brought their own challenges. The discovery of the Higgs boson seemed to suggest that another giant mystery of the universe had been unlocked. Faith in an unseen Creator, already an idea that seemed to have outlived its 'best by' date in the West, came up for mention once again. But any form of sustained or regular affiliation to a traditional faith, or any overt displays of worship, have long been absent from the global media led by the West. Not a lot is written about faith-related issues in the mainstream media, unless it's about Tom Cruise's interest in Scientology, or the selection of hymns for William and Kate's wedding. On the last day of 2012, Noam Chomsky offered this as his daily tweet: 'I don't think there's any reason to suspect that there's any validity to any such notions (as the existence of God)'. Of course, the large-scale violence between people owing allegiance to rival faiths provides a gory backdrop all over the world, further underlining questions like — is a belief in God or an afterlife sufficient reason to want to kill one's fellow humans? The world today seems to present many more reasons for non-belief, than for sustained belief in a just and benevolent God.

In fact, if all the challenges I have outlined above are to be given fair weightage, the difficulties of being a believing Hindu seem so formidable that one may be tempted to put aside the whole question of faith forever! Truly, if one believes, what does one believe in and where does one find the encouragement for that belief to continue?

If I had even been willing to take such a step, to throw out the whole caboodle of faith in Bhagwanji simply in order to escape the many difficulties of being a believer, I would still be confronted by the *other* problem of faith in a country like India.

The difficulties of being an atheist are profound in a country like ours, where being a non-believer means maintaining a disconnect with millions of manifest believers. Our land is so suffused with faith that there are constant reminders of God around us every moment of the day. Whether it is visual cues of calendar pictures, roadside shrines or car mobiles dangling from rearview mirrors, or audio reminders, no day passes without adequate sensory stimulation nudging us to consider the divine. Alongside my personal struggles with questions of faith, and reflecting my repeated displacement to different regions of the country, I have always had such reminders enliven my day. When I was growing up in Maharashtra, I often woke to the sound of the radio playing Bhimsen Joshi singing *abhang*s or Asha Bhosle's '*Kanhada O Vitthalu*'. The years I lived in Faizabad brought me the sound of *salaam*, *marsiya* and *nauvha* being sung at several mosques, besides, of course, *azaan* five times a day — the punctuation a more effective way to tell the time than any clock. In Chennai I recall M.S. Subbulakshmi's iconic '*Suprabhatham*' plus the sound of the *Thiruppavai* from many neighbourhood homes in the cool mornings of December.

To turn my back on such riches, to deny that any of it has any significance for me personally, is something that is beyond me. I have, instead, succumbed gratefully to each of these memories. I have concluded that, in spite of my claims to any worldliness or sophistication, I have quite a lot in common with those millions who throng all places of worship in our country — seekers of a friend greater than all other friends.

Anyone who has occasion to travel any stretch of our country by train or road will have encountered large groups of pilgrims during different seasons. It is impossible to miss the annual migrations to various destinations, unless one is completely cocooned, or simply indifferent and unobservant. Besides the large numbers of Varkari rural peasants walking to the religious site of Pandharpur in Maharashtra in the months of June–July, I have seen people walking to Shirdi to receve blessings at the Sai Baba's temple, encountered masses of Amarnath pilgrims on trains all through July and August, seen small groups of people shouldering wooden crosses and walking to the Vailankanni shrine at Nagapattinam. I have been a part of large crowds heading to Tirupati, and the biggest gathering of humans I have personally seen, at the Mahakumbh Mela in 2001. I have also been awash in a sea of saffron-clothed *kaanwariya*s at Haridwar and Deoghar, the temple of Baba Baidyanath.

These journeys, often involving physical hardship, taking people far from their homes, are one of the most visible ways in which faith is expressed amongst us. For me, the people walking, travelling, singing, resting, on their way to meet their God, have always aroused a variety of emotions, curiosity among them. What do these journeys mean to those who tread these paths? What does one find when one actually sets out to meet one's God? Is the relationship with God wrought by man or God? In 2011–2012, I decided to focus on the journeys millions undertake for Shiva — the powerful deity who represents the destruction of the universe in order to recreate it, in the Hindu trinity of Brahma, the creator of the universe, Vishnu, its preserver and Shiva himself — to find some answers.

This book is a result of these travels, and the accumulated belief that has withstood all challenges, all my life.

Chapter 1: Achaleshwara *(He Who is the Lord of the Mountains)*

Few sights in my life have evoked quite such a feeling of being a small, infinitesimal dot as the sight of the huge mountain visible from the bus in which I was travelling to Kedarnath. The bus was winding around one mountain, on a narrow snaky road so typical of Uttarakhand's Garhwal region, while across a gorge, with a silver river flowing swiftly right at the bottom, the sheer, solid, implacable face of the huge mountain was towering above it all. It was so tall and stark, so devoid of slopes, its bulk so uncompromisingly visible to our tiny human eyes inside the bus, that it seemed to be reinforcing my smallness and vulnerability by its mere presence.

'Are we dragged to these regions for a *darshan* (vision of the divine) of Shiva only to be humbled by a few million tonnes of rock?' I wondered to myself. As a pilgrim who had crossed the holy towns of Haridwar and Rishikesh, and was headed for the revered destinations of Kedarnath and Badrinath, I was entitled to muse upon the significance of this particular sight.

The peculiar mixture of awe, wonder, a frisson of fear and sometimes, a stirring inside that is a strange feeling of *oneness* with what the eyes behold — all this can be a part of an experience at a stormy beach, or just sniffing the night scents of a forest in a night bus on a highway. Small moments in the overwhelmingly ordinary nature of things, they nevertheless represent the only opportunity we have to feel part of a mysterious whole. We breathe in the night air, or stare in fascination at the breakers rising out of a vast horizon, and wordlessly acknowledge the possibility that there's an immensity around us that defies description. I consider such moments spiritual thresholds for the most practical, most disenchanted amongst us. The romance of reality has the power to cut through all forms of denial.

The sight of that rockface was similar and yet different from many other awe-inspiring moments. It is true I felt reduced to a tiny dot in a way that even the surging, stormy ocean had not made me feel. And yet, as a dot, as I kept gazing at the dark and forbidding expanse, its very stillness seemed to be offering a deep reassurance.

'I am here. I am real. I am much bigger than anything or anyone you choose to or happen to fear in this life,' it seemed to be saying to me. For a moment, I was aware of Achaleshwara, one of the many names by which Shiva is known, a name that ties him intrinsically to mountains.

It is impossible to travel in the Garhwal Himalayas without repeated mention of the mythology surrounding Shiva. These mountains have been witness to several important chapters in the story of Shiva, Parvati — his wife for eternity and an incarnation of Devi — and their family, still venerated at holy sites dotting the region.

The climb to Kedarnath begins from Gauri Kund, a hamlet in Rudraprayag district that marks the spot where Parvati did penance for hundreds of years before Shiva would agree to marry her. Moved by her extreme austerities, Shiva finally declared that he would be her groom. Thinking of it as the place where they finally locked eyes, his holding the glimmer of a smile as he willingly accepted defeat in the face of her fierce determination, hers melting in adoration and anticipation, rather than showing the slightest hint of gross conquest, made Gauri Kund very special for me. But if the guides were to be believed, the actual proposal of marriage by Shiva to Parvati happened at Guptkashi, 14 kilometres away.

The Gauri Mata temple in the village of Gauri Kund pays homage to this period of Parvati's life. But the biggest draw for pilgrims heading to and returning from Kedarnath, are the warm, sulphur springs that fill a large bathing tank called the Tapta Kund, from which the place gets its name. Parvati must have bathed in these warm, subterranean currents.

My arrival with my family at Gauri Kund one October evening coincided with a power cut, so the flickering lamps and candles in tiny homes and shops is my most enduring impression of the place. The cold was already more intense than we were accustomed to, having arrived from the distant seashore of Chennai. As we had our dinner by the light of candles, I looked at the heaps of quilts stacked at one end of a large dining hall and marvelled at their size and weight, wondering how it would be possible to sleep crushed under one of those. I needn't have worried, though. One night later, at Kedarnath, I was wishing for not one but two of those cotton heaps to cover me.

Beginning the climb to Kedarnath, however, meant first bathing in the Tapta Kund. Men have the luxury of lying submerged in the warm and gently steaming waters of this underground spring, while women have a separate enclosure to bathe in privacy. Only, the privacy comes at a price — instead of a large tank where one can stay submerged for some time, there is a single water source, a thin stream emerging from the sculpted stone mouth of a lion's head. Women have to huddle beneath this and try to get the warm water to wash over their bodies. Naturally, a queue forms around the bather, and women in varying stages of undress mill around the warm trickle, waiting for their turn.

Shivani, my daughter, and I struggled to discard our many layers of clothing, sweaters, shawls, caps and purses. While wrangling for a place under the tap wearing only underwear, we heard languages and dialects from many corners of India, from Tamil and Gujarati, Bengali and Telugu, to Bhojpuri and Konkani. Women muttered instructions and exclamations to each other, and this feminine mêlée made me wonder how it must have been in Parvati's time. Did she have to scramble in the undignified fashion we did, while the men of her town lolled luxuriously in the waters next door? Or was the pool exclusively for her use when she bathed?

My musings were disturbed by the shrill, piercing voice of a woman standing and watching the crowd at the tap from the side, fully clothed, with her saree drawn over her head in a rustic *ghunghat*. '*Kapde utaar lo, nange hona padta hai!* (Take off your clothes, you have to be naked!),' she was saying. '*Kedar Baba gussa ho jaate hain* (Kedar Baba gets angry, otherwise).' I ducked under the tap in my underwear with my daughter, hoping her comments were for several other ladies, some bathing fully clad in sarees. But no, she came a few steps forward and pointed at me with one shaking finger, '*Nange hona padta hai, Baba gussa ho jaate hain!*' she said again, in her piercing rural voice. Shivani was doing an elaborate eye roll heavenwards, and even I was thinking, 'Where has she sprung from, this authority on Kedar Baba's temper? How absurd to think that a bra and panty can come between us and God, as a bone of contention. Oh, these people and their superstitions!'

Less than half an hour later, clothed and restored to a sense of normalcy with a *kulhad* of steaming hot tea from a roadside stall, I was ready for the 14-kilometre climb to Kedarnath, and shaking my head at the wisdom the rustic woman had offered at the bathing enclosure. No pretence or artifice can be tolerated in the presence of God. Only complete, naked vulnerability marks the heart of a true devotee.

Gauri Kund is the spot at which Parvati did her penance, and Guptkashi the site of Shiva's proposal, but the actual wedding of Shiva and Parvati was conducted at Tirjuginarayan or Triyuginarayan. This village, also in Rudraprayag district, around 5 kilometres from Gauri Kund, has a Vishnu temple with four sacred bathing ponds called the Rudra Kund, Vishnu Kund, Brahma Kund and Saraswati Kund respectively. It also has an eternal flame burning in a *havan kund* in front of the temple, into which devotees make offerings of wood and ghee. This flame is said to have been burning from the time of Shiva and Parvati's wedding — it is the fire around which they took their vows, with Vishnu playing the role of Parvati's brother. Ashes from the havan kund are distributed to pilgrims to safeguard marital harmony in their homes.

The serene and beautiful temple, situated near the meeting point of the Mandakini and Songanga rivers, is in the same unostentatious style as the temple at Kedarnath. It is said to have been built by Adi Shankaracharya, the renowned eighth-century philosopher, and is always crowded with devotees who come to worship the images installed in the shrine of Vishnu, Lakshmi, the goddess of wealth, and Saraswati, the goddess of music and learning. Tirjuginarayan was the capital city of King Himavant, Parvati's father and the human manifestation of the snowcapped peaks of the Himalayas. Imagining the divine wedding, with Brahma officiating as the priest, a tearful Mena (Parvati's mother) nearly fainting away at the sight of the ghouls and ghosts accompanying Shiva, and the bride and groom themselves — radiant Parvati, a picture of demure contentment and Shiva, broad-chested and fair, with coppery locks of hair tumbling to his shoulders — imbues this quiet place with the romance it deserves.

After the wedding, Parvati must have continued to enjoy at least the occasional bath at Gauri Kund, for she was immersed in its water one day when a tired and hungry Shiva returned from one of his work trips away from home. Unfortunately, the small sentry that Parvati had breathed life into, fashioned out of the turmeric paste she had rubbed over her body, challenged Shiva and bade him not to cross the threshold beyond which his mother was bathing. Shiva, not knowing that Parvati loved this creature like a son and regarding him as a pest who had no business to prevent him from entering his own domain, promptly cut off his head. When Parvati emerged and saw this, she was so grief-stricken and incensed that Shiva had to rush out and search for the nearest available creature whose head he could place on the figure and bring it to life once again. Thus the head of an elephant came to adorn Parvati's son, and Shiva, the renunciate with a retinue of social outcasts, extended his family to include Ganesha.

The spot where the little sentry was beheaded by Shiva and then given an elephant head is quite close, about a kilometre from Gauri Kund, with the Sirkata Ganesha temple marking it for devotees.

Shiva's complete domination of the mountains of Garhwal is, however, best expressed in the story behind the Panch Kedar temples — Kedarnath, Tungnath, Rudranath, Madmaheshwar and Kalpeshwar. The temples are centuries-old, so ancient that they are supposed to have been originally constructed by the Pandavas, heroes of the *Mahabharat*. Their present structures, however, owe their existence to Adi Shankaracharya. What fascinated me was the story the guide of our Garhwal Mandal Vikas Nigam (GMVN) tour repeatedly told us in our tour coach, and which was reinforced by local pundits and vendors. In the story, Shiva comes across as exactly the kind of god I can identify with — one to whom human cruelty and cunning is distasteful.

As the story is told, after the horrific events of the Mahabharata war, the Pandavas felt burdened by their sense of guilt for having committed the sins of fratricide by killing their own Kaurava cousins and the slaying of Brahmins like Dronacharya (guru of the Kauravas and master of the martial arts). Seeking atonement, they surrendered the kingdom they had so bitterly fought for to their kin, and went to look for Shiva to get his blessings and gain a divine pardon, so to speak.

But Shiva didn't want to be propitiated by them. The deceit and aggression of the war, in which thousands had been killed, made the Pandavas his least favourite people just then.

Reams are written about the Mahabharata every year and we never tire of extolling its epic canvas of human greed and corruption alongside the healing gospel of the Bhagavadgita. However, it is the very nature of Sri Krishna's engagement with the major characters of the war that has always disturbed me. While the idea of an impersonal God favouring one or other human agency in the daily battle of life through the see-saw of circumstances is something I can be comfortable with, the idea of God in visibly human form facilitating one against the other in a battle is tough to digest. Shiva's rejection of the Pandavas is closer to how I would expect myself to feel in the Mahabharata context, and perhaps, therefore, seems easier to understand and accept. Anyway, whether or not my approval matters even a jot, Shiva chose to become inaccessible to the Pandavas.

They went in search of him at Kashi (Varanasi), the city on the banks of the Ganga where he is said to be ever present, and very happy, too. But they failed to find him there. He had, in fact, left Kashi and taken refuge in the Garhwal mountains, in the form of a large bull. The spot where he went incognito to is Guptkashi ('Gupt' being the word for 'hidden'). Still yearning for the blessings that would rid them of their sins, the Pandavas continued on their search and arrived in the mountains. It was here that the mighty Bhima, standing with a leg each on two adjoining mountains and surveying the surroundings, spotted a remarkably handsome and powerful bull peacefully grazing on the nearby slopes, and recognized this bull to be Shiva himself.

He roared and gave chase as the bull, raising his head and seeing Bhima, began to run away at a thunderous trot. Bhima caught the bull by the tail but it vanished by disappearing into the ground. Its huge, awe-inspiring body then emerged in parts at five different spots. The hump came out of the ground at Kedarnath, the forelegs at Tungnath, the navel and stomach at Madmaheshwar, the face at Rudranath, and the hair and crown of the head at Kalpeshwar. The Pandavas venerated Shiva at all these five places, and built the first temples here.

Today's devotees begin their darshan of the Panch Kedar temples with Kedarnath, also famous as one of the twelve *jyotirlinga* (literally, pillar of light, but with many connotations, such as the compelling Shakti or power these stone forms exude) temples of Shiva, as the resting place of Adi Shankaracharya, and one of the Chhota Char Dham destinations of the Himalayas, the other three being Badrinath, Gangotri and Yamunotri. Most tourists who are part of the package tours of Uttar Pradesh or Uttarakhand Tourism only visit Kedarnath, which is considered the most important of the Panch Kedar sites.

These five temples stand on an impressive range across the Upper Himalayas, and the beautiful snowcapped mountains that include the Nanda Devi, Chaukhamba, Kedarnath and Neelkanth peaks are visible from Kedarnath. The temple itself stands in the Mandakini river valley, and the approach to it from Gauri Kund is a mountain path from where the river can be seen gleaming in a gorge many feet below. The other four temples are at various altitudes between the Mandakini and Alaknanda valleys. Their remote locations make them less of a tourist draw because they are reached not by roads for vehicular traffic, but trekking paths that can be navigated best only between May and early October. In winter, snowfall affects these routes.

Walking to Kedarnath may not be the most demanding of Himalayan treks, but for us it was tough work, steep as it was in parts. The path is narrow, with a two-way traffic of pedestrians, ponies with pilgrims astride them and guides alongside, and palanquins carried by men shouldering their handles. Our family's progress was slow and steady, rather than briskly efficient. We stopped and ate paranthas and had tea at roadside stalls where the legend '*Muskuraiye, aap Garhwal mein hain!* (Smile, for you are in Garhwal)' was painted on the walls. We patted the broad heads of Himalayan mastiffs or Bhutia-type dogs at such places (if the canines allowed it) and saw others of their kind in the woods, tending to herds of sheep and goats, tin collars glinting at their necks to protect them if attacked by leopards.

When we finally reached the village of Kedarnath, late in the afternoon, a light rain had begun to fall, making the mountains misty and other-worldly. Even so, the first sight of the temple is one to remember. A modest structure built of grey stone, the Kedarnath temple faces south, a direction considered inauspicious in *vaastu shastra*, the ancient Indian study of structures and spaces. I feel immensely comforted by this fact — for how can the labels 'auspicious' and 'inauspicious' apply to the abode of God? It is cheering to note that the sage of Kaladi, Adi Shankaracharya, did not consider the direction to be a roadblock in constructing the temple, if indeed he arranged for stone and mortar to be erected at this and other Panch Kedar sites. Another local interpretation is that the temples existed in the form they are in, constructed by the Pandavas, and they were merely discovered by Adi Shankaracharya in his lifetime.

Rising above the grey stone temple is the slope of the Kedarnath mountain. To one side of the temple is a memorial marking the Samadhi spot of Adi Shankaracharya, for this is where he breathed his last, after travelling the length and breadth of the country on foot and giving a definitive shape to the many strands of worship in Sanatana Dharma or the eternal faith, as Hinduism is sometimes called, all in a physical lifetime of thirty-two years (788–820 AD). A very well-defined broad white trail rises along the surface of the mountain behind. I was gazing at it, wondering if it was ice, or *sphatika* rock — the crystal used to make the figures of Hindu divinities that so distinguishes it from the rocks alongside, when I was told that this was the Mahapanth (Great Path) or Swarg Rohini (Stairway to heaven!) that the Pandavas had used to climb up to heaven after they were done with their mortal journey. Somehow, squinting up at the sight in the Himalayan dusk, this seemed to me like a perfectly logical explanation.

Inside the temple, darshan was completely overwhelming. The triangular, pyramid-like hump of the bull that is Shiva, is larger in size than many of the other jyotirlinga forms in famous Shiva temples. We were allowed to touch its cool, wet surface, anointed with water from the Ganga. It was covered with flowers, *bilva* leaves (the distinctive three leaflets of the bael or wood apple tree which are as dear to Shiva as tulsi is to Vishnu) and even '*Om Namah Shivaya!*' written with sindoor (vermilion) paste, besides names and prayers which people had written on small scraps of cloth that briefly clung to the rock before being swept away by the next offering of water. There is an indescribable intimacy in the moments spent in the presence of this form of Shiva. All other feelings and sensations are wiped out other than the sheer happiness and gratitude of being there, feeling the texture of Achaleshwara beneath one's needy fingers, surrounded by a host of people all similarly focused and moved by their own darshan. The cry of '*Har Har Mahadev!*' was joined by a chorus of voices, interspersed with single notes that rang out from the temple bells struck by devotees entering and leaving the temple. A few moments in a place like Kedarnath seem like a slice of eternity.

Emerging from the temple with my family, I was immediately struck by how cold the evening air was, and our hot dinner at the Nigam guesthouse was sweet reparation, but only for a short while. The night we spent at Kedarnath is the coldest I have ever experienced — fully clothed in jeans, thermal wear and sweaters, with my head in a cap and my feet in warm socks, completely hidden by a mountainous quilt, I still had to wait a good while for my teeth to stop chattering and for sleep to carry me to dreams warmed by the everyday images of life in Chennai.

In the morning we woke to the awesome spectacle of the Kedarnath and Neelkanth peaks blazing golden fire from the light of the morning sun. Even an ordinary cup of hot, sweet tea seems ambrosial when one is gazing upon such beauty. The very stillness of mountains is their supreme attraction, and as I lingered over this morning landscape, being captured by dozens of cameras all around me, I mused on how my family and I had very nearly missed reaching these heights.

It was October 1998 when we went on the trip to Kedarnath, one of the last scheduled packages organized by UP Tourism before the temples closed for the winter. This was the same year when model, dancer and Nrityagram founder Protima Gauri Bedi had perished with several companions in a landslide at Malpa in Pithoragarh district, on the way to Kailash–Mansarovar in the Trans-Himalayan range in August. When they learnt that we were going to the Himalayas in October, friends with memories of the Pithoragarh tragedy fresh in their minds, invariably asked, 'Now? Why? Haven't there been major landslides?' In fact, there had been several destructive landslides, and the rains, which should have receded in September, were continuing intermittently across north India.

When we arrived in Haridwar, it rained in earnest, and we went up to the hilltop shrines of Mansa Devi and Chandi Devi in a fine drizzle. Even the evening Ganga *aarti*, the ritual of worship with *diyas* or lamps, and the dip in the river at the Har ki Pauri ghat was followed by lashing rain that continued to drum on the window panes of our hotel room in several spells during the night. When we set off for Rishikesh the next day, from where we were to board our bus for Kedarnath and Badrinath, we heard a lot of gloomy prophecies. 'The colour of the river is not encouraging,' said people at the hotel. 'It is so brown and churned up. It means that it has been raining for over a week up in the mountains. There will be landslides.'

'It's nearing the end of the season,' some said. 'If it continues like this, they will have to call off the tour. Come back and we will take you to some local spots!'

It was raining on the drive to Rishikesh, and barely stopped even after we reached. Our anxious enquiries about the fate of the tour coach at the hotel on our arrival were met with a non-committal response. No, the coach hadn't arrived yet; perhaps it would, later in the day. No, the tour manager wasn't around to tell us if we would actually leave. Then one of the men said the words we were dreading, 'Depends on the rain, maybe they will have to cancel this trip…' Cancel? My husband and I were both very disappointed at the thought. It was the morning of a day we were supposed to spend exploring Rishikesh, but it was pouring outside, and the thought of our further travels being abandoned was disheartening.

Still, we set out with umbrellas and raincoats after a while, determined to at least see the Lakshman Jhoola, the Ganga at Triveni Ghat and other spots. We did have some very happy moments (how could we not, when we were accompanied by two active and articulate children!) but the rain just did not let up. So much so, that when we reached Triveni Ghat, the road leading down to the riverbank had turned into a strongly flowing stream of rainwater from the town streets, racing down to the river. Instead of roaming about in a lively place bustling with shops that sell the paraphernalia of worship and tourist souvenirs, we were in a desolate market, its small booths shuttered against the driving rain.

A very lifelike statue of Shiva faced us at Triveni Ghat. Silhouetted against the overcast sky, there he was, with his locks flying wildly away from the crescent moon on his head, and his *trishul* (trident) held by Parvati on one side of his seated figure. This brightly coloured tableau acquired a magnificent, meaningful dimension accompanied by the sound of the rushing waters of the Ganga and the towering peaks visible in the distance. Clearly, Shiva was the lord of this tumultuous landscape, and any ordinary person gazing upon the scene is gripped by this realization.

We drank in its beauty glumly. I could feel a kind of despair gripping me. What if the rain didn't stop? It was already afternoon. Would our coach have arrived by the time we returned to the hotel? Would the trip be carried out according to the schedule, be modified, or cancelled? Had we come all the way to the mountains from faraway Chennai only to go back without a darshan of Kedarnath? Another strong gust of wind brought the rain under my umbrella, covering my face with cold, unapologetic raindrops. I was feeling very sorry for myself and my family just then.

So what does one do in such circumstances? I just stood there, silently, praying with all my heart, beseeching Him who ruled the mountains not to deprive us of our pilgrimage. In another few minutes, we turned away from the statue and the river to return to the hotel. The downpour had lightened to a drizzle by the time we reached the place, and to our great relief, there was a bus parked on the road outside the hotel compound. Our coach!

Considerably cheered by the sight, we set to work, getting out of wet clothes and into hot showers, putting things out to dry, eating hot pakoras and drinking pots of tea, in short, doing everything to recover from being caught in the incessant rain. At some point in the evening, we noticed that the sound of raindrops was completely absent. It had stopped raining. When we went out, we looked up to see thousands of stars twinkling in a perfectly cloudless night sky.

It was the clearest indication that my prayers had been heard. The next morning, in bright sunshine and great spirits, we began our trip by road to Kedarnath and Badrinath.

Drinking tea up in Kedarnath, watching the sun-gilded peaks, I was remembering all this, and giving silent thanks. After all, in any relationship, whether it is with a fellow human or the invisible presence of God, feeling that you have been heard and acknowledged brings the greatest satisfaction.

*   *   *   *   *   *

Hiccups in a planned pilgrimage represent one kind of challenge, but millions of people in our country face far greater hardships as they set off, on foot, to pay their respects to a beloved god. Years after the trip to Kedarnath, I was headed for Haridwar once more, this time alongside thousands of men and women dressed in bright orange, and carrying containers for water in decorated frames on their shoulders — the *kaanwariyas*, pilgrims who emerge in such large and visible numbers across north India in the month of Saawan.

Apart from Mahashivaratri, which usually falls in February–March in the Hindu lunar calendar year, the entire month of Saawan or Shravan, corresponding to dates in July–August, is considered the most significant month for the worship of Shiva. For it was in this time of the year that Shiva drank the poison that caused his neck to turn blue, earning him the name Neelkanth (Blue-throated One). The poison was a side-effect from the churning of the primordial ocean, which signalled the birth of life, the Creation of the universe. The *suras*, the heavenly deities, and the *asuras*, forces of the nether world, were ranged on either side of the spot where the ocean was churning, eager to sip the *amrit* or nectar that was to emerge so that their immortality was guaranteed. But when the poison — black, resinous and forbidding — rose up from the depths of the ocean instead, all those assembled recoiled in sheer fear, and refused to touch it. It was up to Shiva to drain the poison in one gulp, and save all of Creation from its murderous threat. This act of divine protection is forever commemorated, and the month of Saawan is, therefore, reserved for the worship of Shiva by symbolically soothing the fever that assailed him when the poison began to affect him. Devotees gather water from holy rivers, most notably the Ganga, and also others, like the Narmada and smaller tributaries of both. This water is poured over images of Shiva to cool his fevered brow in the form of puja referred to as *abhishek*. Mondays in Saawan are of special significance because of the intrinsic connection between Shiva and Som, the moon. The intense heat he felt on his head after drinking the poison impelled him to pluck the moon out of the sky and place it on his head for its cool rays to bring some respite. The crescent moon is forever visible in Shiva's locks and among his many names are several that refer to the moon, such as Chandrashekhar, Somashekhar and Chandramouli. On the Mondays of Saawan, devotion reaches fever pitch, with people fasting, and offering *kaanwar* water at their chosen temple. It is on these days that peak numbers are seen at Haridwar and Varanasi, Ujjain and Deoghar.

I set off to meet the kaanwariyas in Haridwar on the first day of Saawan in 2011, leaving by train from Lucknow. There were groups of pilgrims in loose, bright orange cotton half-pants and shirts at the crowded station before I boarded my train. I settled myself in, watching them as they swarmed on the platform. Their clothes looked new and fresh, their mood imbued with festivity, rather like children setting off on a school excursion. Unfettered by any cumbersome luggage, all they needed for the long journey to Haridwar and back was packed in small bags slung on their shoulders.

Inside the compartment, there were no orange-clothed pilgrims to be spotted, but my conversation with my fellow travellers took a distinctly interesting turn a couple of hours into the journey. A young woman, working for a large and well-known non-governmental organization (NGO) in the disability sector, was going on a pilgrimage, one very close to her heart. As she began talking about her passionate devotion to Devi or Durga, and her determination to visit all the 108 *Shakti Peeth*s in her lifetime, I was struck by how you only have to embark on one journey to encounter the possibility of another.

The worship of Goddess Durga as the consort of Shiva is an important thread of Hindu practice. There are many temples across the country that are worshipped as Shakti Peeths (the goddess is referred to as Shakti or primal power, and peeth refers to a holy place), which are directly connected to the story of Shiva and his first wife, Sati. The daughter of a proud and ritualistic king, Daksha Prajapati, Sati learnt of a special and elaborate *yagna*, a sacrificial ceremony that her father was going to conduct at his home, after she had married Shiva and was staying with him in the mountains of Kailash. Gladdened at the thought of a big family reunion, she wanted to be with her father and sisters on this occasion. But when she told her husband of her desire with girlish glee, he seemed unimpressed. 'He hasn't invited us,' he pointed out. 'We might be in the way if we went.'

'Do I need an invitation to go to my own parents' home?' asked Sati indignantly. But Shiva merely shrugged. When it was obvious that staying away from this momentous family occasion was going to cause her distress, Shiva let her go, but did not accompany her, sending some 60,000 of his *ganas* (attendants) instead. Sati arrived at the site of the grand sacrifice and saw portions of the ritual offerings laid out for all the heavenly deities, except the most important one, the god of all gods, her husband Shiva (or Mahadev as he is also known). Even her own arrival was acknowledged in the most casual manner by her father. Extremely agitated, Sati recognized these signs as distinct evidence of her father's wish to belittle his son-in-law.

Standing before the assembly of deities to be propitiated by Daksha's yagna, and facing him directly, Sati denounced her father. With flashing eyes and a voice that throbbed with emotion, she declared her love for Shiva, a love so profound that she would be his wife eternally, across countless lifetimes. She cursed the yagna, and declared that it could serve no purpose if it was based on the exclusion of Shiva.

The dialogue between Sati and her father Daksha, described in the Rudra Samhita of the *Shiva Purana*, brings out some vital aspects of what Shiva represents to those who worship him. Sati stood before the assembly that included Brahma and Vishnu, and addressed her father, '*Prajapate*! Why have you not invited Shiva, the most auspicious of all deities to this yagna? He who renders this whole universe of living beings pure, who is himself the yagna, the supreme offering of a yagna, all its ingredients, all its charity, as well as the one who conducts it (*yajaman*), how can you conduct a yagna without him? Just thinking of whom grants one purity, conducting a yagna without such a deity (Shiva) will make everything impure! Mantras, materials, oblations, supplications — whose very form are all these things — without the presence of that very Shiva how could you even begin your yagna? Have you made the error of considering Shiva an ordinary deity and thus show him this disrespect? Your mind has been corrupted. That is why you seem so repugnant to me today, even though you are my father!'

Daksha's reply is typical of the sophisticated supremacist, convinced that he is superior to others who may lack his learning or worldliness. He addressed his daughter as '*Bhadre!*', a cultured woman, to remind her of her roots, 'What is the point of your saying so much? You have no business being here at this time. Whether you choose to stay or leave, it is entirely up to you. Why did you come at all? All the scholars know that your husband stands for inauspiciousness. He has no pedigree, is far removed from the *Veda*s, and surrounded by demons, ghosts and other loathsome creatures, whom he rules over. He is always badly dressed and unkempt. That is why Rudra has not been invited to this yagna. Dear daughter, I know Shiva very well, know that he has no knowledge of the *shastra*s, has an anarchic and destructive personality. Unfortunately, I heeded Brahma's advice and got you married to him. Now that you have come to attend this occasion, calm yourself, sit down, and take your own (daughter's) share.'

Daksha's words had the effect of making Sati feel revulsion at the very idea of being his child. She felt a resultant loathing for her body. Enraged beyond all limits by this arrogant reply of her father's, and anguished at the thought of how she would face her husband after hearing him insulted thus, when he had expressly warned her against coming, Sati decided to destroy herself. She focused inwards, thought of her husband Shiva, and self-ignited through *yogagni* (fire produced by means of yoga). Some accounts describe her jumping into the *yagna kund*, a sacrificial cauldron.

The assembled deities were aghast and raised an uproar. The 60,000 ganas who had escorted Sati were so overwrought that thousands of them died of self-inflicted wounds along with Sati. The remaining ganas rushed to attack Daksha and his yagna companions, but were repulsed by an army of Hribhus — divine helpers who had materialized out of the yagna fire at the urgings of the sage Bhrigu. A few of the ganas managed to return to Kailash and informed Shiva of the terrible occurrence at Daksha's yagna. Shiva was extremely angry when he heard of the treatment meted out to Sati. He pulled out a lock of his hair and banged it on the ground, and out stepped the fearsome and terrible Veerbhadra, a demonic aspect of Shiva's divine powers, from one end, and the equally daunting goddess Mahakali from the other. Despatching these two to deal with Daksha and his yagna, Shiva spent just a few moments in private, grief erasing every other feeling in his heart.

Veerbhadra arrived at the site of the yagna and killed Daksha, tossing his body into the very fire that he had mustered with such pride. Veerbhadra, Mahakali and the army of ganas under their leadership spread terror and destruction, scattering the assembled deities and forcing them to return to their heavenly abodes. An interesting sidelight of this sequence is Veerbhadra's battle with Vishnu, as well as their dialogue, in which Vishnu declares that he is not distinct from Shiva. The *Shiva Purana* uses this episode to clarify many aspects of the nature of Shiva and Vishnu, and concludes the story in a peaceful fashion, with Shiva forgiving Daksha and bringing him back to life. Daksha then surrenders to him completely.

But the story of Sati's sacrifice has other, more far-reaching consequences, described in the *Kalika Purana* and the *Devi Bhagavata*. They continue describing what transpired when Shiva himself appeared at the scene of Daksha's pride and his fall, and had eyes only for the half-charred body of his wife. Overcome by grief and rage, Shiva picked up Sati's corpse and carried it on his shoulders. He mourned the death of his wife as he carried her body and moved about, gradually beginning to dance the *tandava* dance of destruction, which threatened the very existence of the universe and all its living creatures. Alarmed by this turn of events, Indra, Brahma and other gods urged Vishnu to exert himself to save creation from the terrible effects of the tandava. Realizing that Sati's corpse was exerting a powerful influence on Shiva, Vishnu used his *sudarshan chakra* (discus) to cut the body into pieces, which then fell to the ground. Sati's body was cut into fifty-one pieces by the sudarshan chakra, according to the *Kalika Purana*, but the *Devi Bhagavata* describes these as 108 pieces falling in as many locations. These became holy sites or Shakti Peeths at various places across India, Nepal, Bangladesh and even Sri Lanka.

My companion on the train was on her way to the Purnagiri temple in Tanakpur, a town in the Champawat district of Uttarakhand, bordering Nepal. She was talking to another young man, employed in a bank, about how many of the 108 Shakti Peeths she had been to, while he murmured in appreciation, and spoke of how he had only been to Vaishno Devi. 'Naina Devi, Jwala Devi, Sarkundi…' the names tripped off my female companion's tongue and I just watched her face, avid with enthusiasm, unable to make too much of these confidences. For all my travels, age and experience, many of these were names I was hearing for the first time. Pilgrims and devotees have their chosen flavours, just like any other form of human endeavour or interest. In another train, another compartment, two south Indian devotees may have similarly discussed how many of the 108 *divya desam*s (Vishnu temples venerated in the Sri Vaishnavism established by Hindu theologian and philosopher, Ramanujacharya, 1017–1137 CE) each had prayed at. Even though I have been to a fair sprinkling of divya desams, three out of the Char Dhams, several Shakti Peeths and jyotirlinga temples, four out of eight Ashtavinayak temples dedicated to Lord Ganesha and seven out of eleven Akhara Maruti temples established in the seventeenth century for the worship of Hanuman, the young woman's account of Purnagiri and elsewhere was enough to reinforce my sense of still being an apprentice —

nowhere near an adept. If I spend every week of the rest of my life travelling by train, bus, or on foot, I will still not be able to cross the threshold of all of India's temples.

Getting off the train at Haridwar, I heard the first sounds of pilgrims shouting '*Bam Bam Bhole!*' and '*Har Har Mahadev!*'. Groups in bright orange were immediately visible on the platform, organizing themselves before they began the walk towards the Ganga. I got into an autorickshaw and headed to a hotel in the Niranjani Akhara. Here I had a rooftop room opening on to a terrace with an awesome view of the sweep of the vast river, the mountains in the distance and the ghats, where I could see kaanwariyas bathing or resting with their kaanwar pots carefully balanced on bamboo stands.

The annual Kaanwar Mela at Haridwar in the month of Saawan is the second largest gathering of pilgrims, after the Mahakumbh Mela. Estimated figures of those who came for the 2011 mela are 1.15 crore, or nearly eleven and a half million people. In 2012, this was set to increase by at least another 5 lakh or half a million devotees. Although this traffic is spread out over the course of a month, it still poses grave questions of crowd control and security arrangements for the district administration. The large numbers are made up of pilgrims from Delhi, Uttar Pradesh and Uttarakhand, Haryana and Himachal, Rajasthan and Bihar, though pilgrims from the latter are twice as likely to go to Deoghar in Jharkhand, as they are to come to Haridwar.

Such a huge influx of people in Haridwar town, when the entire Haridwar district, comprising surrounding villages in addition to the town, had a population of a little over 19 lakh in the 2011 census, affects the life of every resident. Newspaper reports speak of occasional skirmishes between kaanwariyas and the local residents, and the movement of people in such large numbers affects conditions in the National Capital Region

(NCR) as well. Leaving my hotel room, I was surprised to find order prevailing everywhere, with all shops and businesses calmly serving ordinary customers. When I asked why there were no hordes of saffron-wearing pilgrims around, I was told that they had been told to follow specified routes that skirted the town.

I soon found the saffron crowds headed for Har ki Pauri, the hub of worship and bathing in the river, where the famous Ganga aarti is held every evening. There was a festive air to these pilgrims who had just left their homes, calling out to each other, jumping into crowded tempos for a quick tour of Haridwar, or buying small trinkets and knick-knacks to gift people back home. Walking for just a short while in the charged mela atmosphere, I found myself in a clear area where the riverside had been widened into a ground holding foodstalls for the kaanwariyas. Spotting a sizeable number of policemen, I enquired about their senior officer and was fortunate to soon be in conversation with R.K. Kanaujia, the sector officer assigned to Rodi Belwala Maidan, where we were seated.

'The arrangements for the Kaanwar Mela are very elaborate and have evolved over the past few years,' sector officer Kanaujia told me. 'Earlier, kaanwariyas used to move on the highway, and also used the streets in the marketplace. Since 2009, a very clear plan has been in place that restricts their movements to specific areas. The numbers have increased so much that if this had not been done, God knows what chaos we would have been dealing with!' he said. The administrative plan for the Kaanwar Mela begins many kilometres away from Haridwar, where the Gang Nahar, a man-made canal of the Ganga, emerges at Murad Nagar in Ghaziabad district. There are pavements laid out on both sides of the canal which act as special tracks for kaanwariyas, keeping them off the highway.

The police presence for the Kaanwar Mela begins from

places like Roorkee, a neighbouring city of Haridwar, and Bahadurabad, a town in UP's Saharanpur district. From these distances, there are distinct zones identified for a strong police presence and patrols, with sector officers supervising arrangements. They complete a reconnaissance of roads every day, checking on street lighting, patrol vehicles and first-aid arrangements. It's a vast web of policing, which is quite impressive. As a pedestrian walking along the most crowded streets of the mela, I noticed a police constable every twenty feet or so.

'The first wave of kaanwariyas arrives from Rajasthan,' Kanaujia informed me. 'They spend their first two days or so sightseeing and visiting different spots, before collecting the water from the river and going back. Then wave upon wave arrives from the NCR, west UP, Haryana and Punjab. They come in mini-trucks, and for the last couple of years we have been confiscating their amplifiers, loudspeakers and loud music systems at the Haridwar border, to get the noise levels under control. On the last day of the Kaanwar Mela, around two-and-a-half to three lakh motorcycles serve as vehicles for kaanwariyas, who ride them in a procession to collect the holy water. That's quite a sight!'

This urbane police officer, the son of an army officer, went to school in Nainital and initially joined the army himself, before a trekking injury made him appear for the Provincial Civil Services (PCS) examination and become a police officer, was a mine of information about the kaanwariyas, and the picture of decency and chivalry. When I asked him if he shared the belief or religious fervour of the mela pilgrims, he looked slightly mischievous and answered in the negative. But I saw him dealing with dozens of queries from his constables and the kaanwariyas and all kinds of situations without losing his cool for an instant, or even lapsing into a single swear word! Quite a feat, in the street conditions of north India.

From him I learned another peculiar feature of the Kaan-war Mela. In the dates of the Hindu lunar calendar, some five days during the month of Saawan fall in the *panchak* period. On these five days, it is considered inauspicious to gather the kaanwar water, so a brief lull takes place in Haridwar. Pilgrims who arrive during these days, while away their time by visiting nearby temples and sight-seeing. Finally, after the panchak days have passed, they fill their kaanwar pots to take the holy Ganga water home to be poured over their own village and town Shivalingas.

The sector officer told me about the *dak kaanwariya* teams that run from villages and towns to Haridwar, and back, within a specified time limit. 'They wear uniforms, and practise running, somewhat like a relay team, for quite a few weeks before the mela,' he said. 'A vehicle from their village accompanies them. They place their kaanwar pots in the vehicle, then run after it, fill the water and go running back. The idea is to accomplish the journey within the set time of fourteen, sixteen or twenty-four hours, whatever time is set for the distance. It is like a relay in the sense that each person runs for a specified number of kilometres before being relieved by another team member.'

'Seems like a real community effort,' I said. 'Is it for the honour of the village, or something?'

Kanaujia shrugged, in half-agreement. 'It is definitely a matter of prestige,' he said. 'The dak kaanwariyas get prizes in their own villages and towns for their effort.'

'Are the kaanwariyas harassed by the police?' I asked. 'Aren't they vulnerable, walking around barefoot, with the minimum of belongings? Do some sections of the police exploit this vulnerability to extort money under false pretexts?'

Kanaujia raised his eyebrows at these questions. 'We have to be very strict with rowdy elements!' he said, in defence of the police. 'In fact, we have to keep a keen eye on potential troublemakers, and we are strict in enforcing rules. But if you are asking about police brutality, you will not find it in the Haridwar mela.'

Then, softening somewhat, he told me, 'See, I was earlier posted in Meerut. There, the Sargana tehsil was the site of many communal disturbances. First, kaanwariyas had been involved in some minor skirmishes in Muslim neighbourhoods where they were attacked by the resident gangs. Then, they started deliberately going through those neighbourhoods for retaliation strikes. We dealt with that, solved those problems. Compared to that, the situation here is quite different, it's peaceful. We are vigilant and strict, but there is no call for any excessive force.'

I walked to the nearby dhabas, where all the customers were saffron-clothed kaanwariyas. Slipping into conversation with a very large group waiting to be served their meal, I found that, just like officer Kanaujia had told me about the earliest arrivals for the mela, they were all from Bhiwadi in the Alwar district of Rajasthan. For the next half an hour, I chatted with Budh Ram, a twenty-eight-year-old farmer, who was on his third kaanwar yatra; Sonu, twenty-six, who worked in a school, making the trip for the second time; Ajay, twenty-five, a carpenter, on his maiden kaanwar journey; teenagers Rahul, Sandeep and Ajit, Rajesh, twenty-two, and Sanjay, twenty-four, carpenters and odd-job men. Aside from a single Brahmin and the three carpenters who belonged to the Vishwakarma caste, these were all Valmiki or Dalit young men, who were taking a long break from work. They had left home on 15 July, and hoped to be back on the 28th because the panchak break fell in the middle of their yatra.

'What inspired you to begin coming to Haridwar?' I asked. 'How did you become such dedicated devotees of Shiva that you had to come miles away from home to bring him water from the Ganga?'

Their source of inspiration was a local temple, they said. '*Hum vahin par jal chadhaayenge* (We will offer this water in that same temple).' For the last several years, they had been seeing music videos being played at the temples they passed during the kaanwar yatra, showing millions of people coming to Haridwar to the accompaniment of folk-pop songs and a general air of festivity. Seeing such large numbers of people make their merry way to the banks of the Ganga got their attention, they admitted. '*Haan, humko bhi laga iss mein bahut mazaa bhi aata hai, aur Bhole Baba mannat bhi poori karte hain* (Yes, we too felt that this is such fun, plus Bhole Baba rewards us by making our prayers and wishes come true).'

This year, for the first time, a woman from their village, Vimla Devi, had accompanied them. I turned to where she was quietly sitting and eating at the next table with two elderly men, and asked her why she had come. She revealed that it was because her husband had been ill for the last three years and been able to work only intermittently. She hoped that her sacrifice in walking to Haridwar and carrying the water back for Bhole Baba would help cure him.

'But water is heavy,' I said. 'And you have to walk such a long way. How will you carry your pot?'

She was unperturbed by my question. Nodding her head as she raised a mouthful of dal-roti to her mouth, she said, simply, '*Woh taakat dete hain. Woh poora karwayenge* (He gives me the strength. He will help me complete my yatra).'

Such calm certainty in the matter of Bhole Baba! In the next few days I met pilgrim after pilgrim, only to encounter the same absolute declarations of faith.

Turning back to Budh Ram and his group, I asked about whether the dak kaanwariyas also came from their village. 'Not from our village itself, but from nearby, a team does come,' they said.

'So if someone gets tired, or can't carry the kaanwar, then can you put your pot in the vehicle and go back home in the vehicle?' I asked. They stared at me, probably thinking that it was a strange question.

Then they shook their heads vehemently and one of them said, '*Nahin! Aisa nahin hota. Dono alag alag yatra hain. Hum apna kaanwar kisi aur ko nahin de sakte, na neeche rakh sakte hain. Jal lene ke baadisse bas Shankar ji tak le jana hai* (No! It's not like that. Both are separate journeys. We can't give our kaanwar to anyone else, nor can we even place it on the ground. After collecting the water, we just have to carry it to Shankarji).'

They had spent enough time talking to me and eating their meal. It was time to get up and resume their yatra, and I got up along with them to resume my own wandering. As we were settling our bills with the dhaba owner, I asked them if they had a system of keeping accounts, or whether each person bore his own expenses. The answer was, 'We note the accounts in a notebook. One person pays for everything, till he or she can, then it is time for the next person to pay, and the next and so on. At the end of the yatra we add up the amount and give equal shares of what has been spent.'

Tying their orange *gamchha*s (towels) around their heads or waists and picking up their few belongings, they addressed each other as '*Bhole*' and I realized that during the yatra, all other names had fallen away, just as their caste identity had disappeared, leaving Brahmins, Valmikis and Vishwakarmas to travel, stay, eat and pray together. In their journey to and back home from Haridwar, they are all 'Bhole'.

Haridwar is spelt as both Hardwar and Haridwar. 'Har' refers to Shiva and 'Hari' to Vishnu, and Dwar means a gate, for, of course, Haridwar is the gateway for both the Kedarnath and Badrinath shrines, as well as the gateway to that part of the Himalayas where saints and sages venerated in the Hindu faith have traditionally practised *tapasya*, years of meditation and austerities. It is one of the four holy places where, according to the Hindu mythology of Creation, the pot of nectar, churned up from the primordial ocean, and containing the seeds of immortality, spilt a few drops when it was being carried across the heavens. The other three places where these drops fell are Ujjain, Prayag (Allahabad) and Nashik. This qualifies Haridwar to be the site of the Kumbh Mela every twelve years and the Ardh Kumbh every six years. The last Kumbh Mela held here was in 2010. This is the first point of the plains where the Ganga flows, with its fresh, cold water giving a clear message about its journey through the mountains after its emergence from its source at Gangotri in the Himalayas. The evening aarti at the Har ki Pauri ghat is spectacular, with the additional attraction of hundreds of lamps fashioned out of flour, placed in leaf-bowls containing flowers left to float on the waters by devotees. At one place where there is a fork in the stream of the Ganga, a huge statue of Shiva stands upright, holding the trishul, and with a hand raised in blessing. The strong mythological connection between the Ganga and Shiva finds expression in cries of 'Har Har Gange!' and 'Har Har Mahadev!' that resonate there.

I wandered the streets of Haridwar, finding a town abuzz with languages from every part of India. Just walking through the streets of Niranjani Akhara brings one face to face with Bengali and Marwari dharamshalas, restaurants advertising every kind of regional cuisine, from dosas to chhole bhatura to Gujarati thalis and Jain preparations with their promise of extra purity, cooked as they are without onions and garlic. There was a happy bustle in the narrow bylanes. Even the crowds of poor people waiting to eat a free meal at one of the temples did not look as destitute as the poor in some of the bigger cities. Of course, the fastidious tourist could have found many points for improvement in terms of hygiene and civic amenities. But I still found it a more cheerful place compared to the depressing scenes of poverty in many urban areas of India.

The shops selling beads and *rudrakshas* (necklaces made from the seeds of the rudraksha tree called the eyes of Shiva), semi-precious stones and pearls, were fascinating. They still had beautiful wooden prayer beads in several colours for only Rs 10! I was completely charmed and intrigued, too. How could anything with some lasting value be produced in 2011, pass through a series of middlemen, and still be sold for this price? I could imagine those beads, strung with some other miscellaneous ones, being sold in an upmarket city boutique for several hundred rupees. In fact, the shops had examples of such trendy assemblies as well. But the most attractive for their price were the Rs 10 prayer beads.

When I entered the small tea shop next to my hotel the next morning, there was only a sadhu sitting on a bench outside the shop, and the moustachioed proprietor, Prem Vallabh Pokhriyal, standing behind a counter with large glass jars of toffees and peppermints, ladoos and peanut brittle. Drinking in the peace of the morning street scene, shops slowly opening their shutters, a cow or two ambling past, some pilgrims returning from a Ganga *snaan* (bath), I asked Prem Vallabhji about the growing numbers of people that participated in the kaanwar yatra every year. Had he noticed any change from his time to the present? What was making people more devout and what made them take up such an arduous task every year for Shiva?

He was silent for a few moments, focusing on his tea-making, with slow, deliberate movements. Then he began speaking. 'This form of the kaanwar yatra is a recent phenomenon,' he said. '*Hamare samay mein Shivaratri mein zyaada shraddhalu aate the, Saawan mein kam* (In our time, more pilgrims arrived for Shivaratri and less during Saawan).' Then he paused, and served me a large glassful of tea. Finally, exchanging a glance with the old sadhu sitting in the morning sun on the bench outside, he said, 'Only twenty out of every hundred people who come for the kaanwar yatra are truly devout. Why, this test of the people who throng the holy places and melas, has been conducted by Shiva himself!'

I pricked up my ears. 'How?' I asked.

'You know how much people praise the Mahakumbh Mela, and how much is talked about the value of going there and giving charity during the mela?' he asked, and I nodded. 'Well, one day when Shiva and Parvati were watching the crowds going towards the Mahakumbh, Parvati exclaimed, "How devout all these people are! Surely they are all deserving of *moksha* (freedom from birth and death)!" Shiva, also watching, disagreed with her. "But how can they not be granted moksha?" questioned Parvati. "Isn't every step taken in the Mahakumbh Mela and doing charity there equal to an Ashwamedh yagna?" Her husband remained unimpressed. "Lets test these millions of people ourselves," he proposed.'

'So what was the test?' I asked Prem Vallabh. He took his time to speak, obviously enjoying the effects of his story on me. I was halfway through my glass of tea. He offered me some freshly baked *nankhatai* with great courtesy, and I waved them away, impatient to hear the rest.

'Shankarji took the form of a leper,' he said. 'And Parvati took the form of his very beautiful young wife. They arranged themselves at the mela *sthal* (ground) so that pilgrims going and coming from their holy baths in the Sangam could see them. Then Parvatiji began entreating the crowds going for their snaan, "Please, O please! Somebody help me get my husband to the river for his bath!" The sight of an ugly leper was enough to repel most people. Moreover, this leper had a very beautiful wife!' Vallabhji smiled under his long, droopy moustache.

'Some of the passers-by looked at her with pity, some made suggestive comments, or volunteered to be her husband instead of the *kodhi* (leper), some hurried on and shunned both the leper and his wife, but no one came to her aid. Finally, a young man stopped, and without any comment, just a simple greeting, lifted the leper who was really Shiva, bathed him gently in the water of the Ganga, brought him back to the bank, bowed to Devi Parvati, and left.'

'So who was he? What did it mean?' I asked.

'That is exactly what Parvati asked Shiva!'he said triumphantly. 'And the truth was — this man did not need to be granted enlightenment as a special gift — *uss ko to yahin moksha mil gaya tha* (he was already enlightened). If a leper and an ordinary man was one and the same to him, if another man's beautiful wife was like his own mother or sister, and deserving of the same respect, then he was enlightened, wasn't he?'

'Yes,' I nodded, 'So...?'

'So coming back to what you were talking about, the vast majority of these kaanwariyas of today are not really *bhakts* (devotees). Purity of heart and unshakable faith is important for anyone who undertakes any such yatras. Do you really think these boys are pure of heart?' Before I could volunteer an answer he muttered, 'Just wear a vest and tie an orange gamchha around their middle; take money from their homes and arrive for some fun, that's what they do!'

An hour later, this tart assessment of the kaanwariyas was still ringing in my ears as I took up a vantage position on the bridge where they were making their way past the crowded areas of the town. I saw a plethora of very ornately decorated kaanwars — elaborate constructions of bamboo, cloth and tinsel, with holders for one or sometimes two pots of water. It would have been tough for me to balance such a contraption for even ten feet without banging into something, or overbalancing and tilting it, I considered, watching kaanwariyas walk calmly past me, the picture of concentration and poise. I saw happy young boys, epitomizing kaanwariya style — sunglasses and colourful wristbands, trendy hairdos and an unmistakable swagger. Instead of the latest film songs, however, they were raising their voices to chant 'Bam Bam Bhole!' or 'Har Har Mahadev!'

Among the bright orange clothes, I caught a glimpse of two men carrying thick bamboo poles on their shoulders with a brass pot tied at each end. Neither the stick nor the pots were decorated in any manner, though they gleamed a shiny yellow. The men wore white vests and the dhotis of ordinary peasants, which they wore tied up to their knees, like a farmer might wear while tending his fields. Serious and intent, they seemed different from the other kaanwariyas, even as their pots of Ganga water marked them as pilgrims with the same objective. They were Kanwar Singh, sixty-two, and Inderjit Singh, twenty-eight, from Bhiwani, Haryana. I greeted them when they paused to have tea, and the older man looked at me enquiringly, a reassuring twinkle in his brown eyes giving me the courage to talk to him. His weathered face was dominated by an impressive moustache that curved over his upper lip. Kanwar Singh had stopped keeping track of how many times he had undertaken the kaanwar yatra. His companion was a fellow villager who was on his first one. When I remarked that they seemed to be carrying a lot more water than the others, he gravely agreed with me, without comment. When I continued talking to them, he finally said a few well-chosen words. 'I do this yatra the way my elders have always done. No *taam-jhaam* (ostentation), no *nasha* (use of intoxicating substances). Just plain walking, and remembering Bhole.'

A large, mixed group of men and women from Hodal village of Palwal district, Haryana, were all aged between twenty-two and forty and on their first or second yatra. They told me they were all labourers, yet each one spent Rs 10 to Rs 12,000 on these two weeks of the kaanwar yatra.

'Isn't that very expensive?' I asked. 'How do you manage?'

'*Itna kharcha to karna hi padta hai* (Spending at least this much is necessary),' they told me, then one among them clarified, 'When we return, we will have a *bhandara* or feast for *panch kanya* (five young girls) besides other village guests. That is why we spend this money. But on the tour, we share all expenses. There is no *tera-mera* (yours-mine) here.'

From this group of relative newcomers to the yatra, I got the first murmurs of protest, that arrangements should be a lot better than they are. 'Facilities are non-existent for us kaanwariyas in Haridwar,' one of the women told me. 'Even Rishikesh is better. Here, at Har ki Pauri and anywhere else on our route, there are no toilets or shelters. The police and administration are very strict with us.'

It seemed obvious to me that these people are perceived as potential offenders, rather than as citizens entitled to conveniences and facilities. Is this because the vast majority of kaanwariyas are not people who are from privileged or empowered sections? It is a tragic feature of life in twenty-first-century India that simple questions of the rights of ordinary citizens and the duty of the state to provide a better quality of service at public places get mired in emotive and exacerbative issues. Right-wing politicians and intellectuals immediately convert any discussion about facilities for pilgrims at Hindu sites into a slanging match about facilities extended to Haj pilgrims. As if cancelling out one will mean greater satisfaction and comfort for the other! If public discourse remains dominated by those who foam at the mouth about imagined slights while refusing to give voice to genuine needs and aspirations of citizens, we are still many decades away from improved times for kaanwariyas and, quite simply, ourselves.

My headiest moments with the Haridwar kaanwariyas were those I spent with an all-woman group from Bhati-Mais Sanjay colony, near Mehrauli. They were wives of labourers who often worked alongside their husbands digging roads and on construction projects. I met Dadli, fifty-five, on her seventh yatra, while Ram Pyari, sixty-three, was emerging for her first one. Najo and Pallo, in their thirties, had come once before, while Shano, forty-five, Reshma, sixty and Krishna, fifty, were seasoned yatris of several years. They were teasing each other, resting their tired feet and backs with mock-moans and much laughter when I went up to them. Dadli told me that her husband had been confined to bed for eight months, and she had to take care of him. After going on six kaanwar yatras, she had been unsure of whether she would be able to go for the seventh. 'Three days after I declared that I would still be going this year, no matter what, he began sitting up, and seemed much better. I could leave with a lighter heart.' When I asked her why she comes back year after year, she was very clear about her motive, 'Why do I come back? To give thanks, of course! Last year's wish has been granted. I am saying thanks and asking for the next one!'

Her twinkling eyes and the way all the others greeted this with laughter left no doubt that this was partly a witticism and partly the truth of their lives — the wish-fulfilling nature of Shiva provides a continuity of hope when kindness from more powerful and privileged people is very hard to find.

Even these women leading the hard lives of casual labourers had one important resource — their mobile phones. But this did not mean they craved for connectivity with home at all times. As Krishna, on her sixth yatra, told me, 'I never call home once I am on this journey. After we have left home for the kaanwar yatra, our connection is only with Bhole. Who wants to know if the children have eaten, if the daughters-in-law are fighting? I only call when I have reached Mehrauli, a stone's throw away from home!'

I entered the serene premises of the Panchayati Akhara Shri Niranjani through its small but welcoming Hanuman temple and asked to meet the Mahantji. After a short wait, I was ushered in to meet Lalita Giri Guru Niranjan Dev, the secretary of this big Haridwar *akhara* of sadhus. Unlike other sadhu heavy-weights whom I had met in Ayodhya, this powerful sadhu did not have a visible security detail of gun-toting guards. He was also very soft-spoken and hospitable, giving me uninterrupted attention while we spoke about several matters, including the kaanwar yatra.

I asked him how the yatra had developed into such a big annual event. Was the Saawan yatra always celebrated on such a large scale in Haridwar? 'The water of the Ganga and the month of Saawan, both are forever linked to Shiva,' he began. 'Earlier, the faithful in villages used to make vows that they would fulfil if a wish was granted. Going to Haridwar to bring back Gangajal for their village Shiva seemed a big sacrifice in those days. Also, it was something even the poorest could attempt, unlike some very elaborate or expensive rituals. That is the most attractive aspect of worshipping Shiva. *Shankar ji niyambaddha nahin hote. Ve anaadi kaal se shraddheyahain* (He is not bound by rules, he is worshipped in the simplest form, from time immemorial).'

Lalita Giriji considered the growing commercialization of religion as one of the prime reasons for the yatra growing into such a big event. 'Look at the role of television channels,' he told me. 'The roadside astrologer plying his humble trade has been replaced by the oracle on television spouting all kinds of advice about planets and rituals. Haridwar has not escaped commercialization, either. Even dharamshalas today have turned into air-conditioned ones!' he said with a smile.

Although a crore of kaanwariyas visited Haridwar in the last two years, Lalita Giriji said the practice has grown at other centres as well. 'In Muzaffarnagar, Khatauli and Ghaziabad, the followers of Dayanand Saraswati, the social reformer and spiritual leader, have also begun to take up the kaanwar yatra, though he himself was not even an idol worshipper. Their kaanwars are offered to the Pura Mahadev Shivalinga at Meerut, which receives ten to fifteen lakh kaanwars every year. It is growing everywhere.'

'Didn't the movement for a Rama temple in the 1990s have something to do with such an outpouring of people?' I asked.

Lalita Giriji agreed. '*Haan, kuch had tak aaj ki kaanwar yatra Ram mandir ke andolan kiupaj hai* (Yes, to some extent today's kaanwar yatra is born out of the movement for the Rama temple). But the character of the kaanwariyas is very different from the militant crowds that used to be seen in those days. For instance, there is absolutely no caste discrimination. *Sabhi Bhagwan Shankar ke priyahain* (All castes are dear to Bhagwan Shankar). Then, the Muslims also play a big role during the kaanwar yatra. They earn a lot by making kaanwar frames and decorations. It is almost exclusively their craft. And even otherwise, Muslims feel less threatened by Shiva whom they consider akin to their prophet, Baba Aadam. The atmosphere is not hostile and confrontational like the Rama mandir days.'

The rivalry between various sadhu sects for the order of bathing during the Mahakumbh Mela has grabbed a lot of headlines in Haridwar in the past. In fact, the Kumbh Mela in 1998 had seen bloody battles that left many sadhus seriously wounded and sullied the image of Haridwar and Hinduism. Perhaps sensing that I might go into such matters (although I did not) Lalita Giriji took the trouble to tell me about the various sects of sadhus, and how the *shahi snaan* (royal bath) processions took place during the Kumbh Mela.

There are seven sadhu akharas in Haridwar. An akhara is a venue or fighting ring where sadhus, especially those who follow Sanatana Dharma, are trained in wrestling and martial arts, besides preparing them for more spiritual pursuits. This was because the sadhus were guardians of the Hindu faith, and their trishuls were meant to underline this fact. The Juna, Niranjani, Anand, Avahan, Nirvani, Atal and Agni akharas have a strong presence in Haridwar. Apart from this, there are five other Hindu akharas, making twelve in all for deciding on their bathing order during the mela. 'The British had shown wisdom in drawing up a time-table for the various akharas,' said Lalita Giriji. 'Then it became a "might is right" situation. The Nirmal Akhara is a Sikh akhara and its members also arrive for bathing. Not only were there fights between the twelve Hindu akharas, but with the Sikhs too, and this led to many sadhus getting slaughtered — till a hierarchy was drawn up. Now the Nirmal Akhara comes at number thirteen, after the Hindu akharas have bathed and retreated, and the timings for the various akharas are set and announced by the administration.'

Prem Vallabh Pokhriyal's poor opinion of the kaanwariyas may have been an individual one. Did all tradespeople and locals have such views on the saffron deluge in Saawan? I set out to meet Vikas Tiwari, co-ordinator of the Haridwar and Roorkee Bharatiya Janata Yuva Morcha (the youth wing of the BJP), a representative of traders and an office-bearer of the Dharamshala Association in Haridwar. We met in a small travel agency belonging to his brother, and spoke about the kaanwar yatra's close association with Haridwar.

I asked him, 'Has the quality of the yatra changed over the years?'

'Yes, the quality of the yatra has changed,' he said. 'Since we began seeing it in my childhood in Haridwar, there is a definite shift, even what one can call a generation gap. Earlier it took place on foot, or on bicycles. People lacked so many facilities then. These days, the motorbike riders who come towards the end of the yatra are truly spectacular. Three, and sometimes four riders to a bike, the chain of their vehicles remains unbroken for miles and miles. At the peak of the yatra season, at Shankaracharya Chauraha, one can see women, children, even babes in arms, just watching the kaanwariyas. *Kaanwar dekhna aas pass ke gaon mein bhi ek pastime ho gayahai* (Kaanwar watching has become a pastime even in nearby villages).'

'Are there any simmering tensions with locals, any communal disturbances or confrontations like those seen around kar sevaks in the 1990s?' I asked.

'No, the yatra remains largely peaceful,' he asserted. Fishing around in a drawer, he produced his identity card, which proclaimed him as a special civilian police officer for the period of 15 to 29 July 2011. 'Our association has meetings with the administration before the yatra to discuss ways to prevent any possible trouble. I am authorized to help the police in their work during the Kaanwar Mela. We don't have any outbreaks of violence; maybe minor fights break out between kaanwariyas and individual shop-owners, that's all.'

'But no communal disturbances?' I insisted.

'See, communal disturbances arise out of the smallest things even when there is no Kaanwar Mela,' he said. 'The Muslims once created a big ruckus because of a pig crossing the ground where they were to say their namaz. Can anyone stop them? But there is no communal colour to the kaanwar yatra or Kaanwar Mela.'

As a young Bharatiya Janata Party leader (he was twenty-eight at the time of our conversation) I found Vikas Tiwari admitting with rare candour that the Rama mandir issue was dead. 'The leaders of that time are now in their fifties, more concerned that their children should study, their families make progress. My generation also thinks differently. See, whatever my political career is, it has to be secondary to the time I spend with my family, my small child. This is quality time that cannot be compensated for in later years. In fact, although you might want to make a simple connection between the Rama mandir movement and the kaanwar yatra, it is not just because a residue of that religious outpouring (*uss dharmik bhavana ka avshesh*) impels people to carry kaanwars today. It is difficult to pinpoint any one cause, but religiosity is growing at every level.'

Tiwari was upset about the scarcity of funds for the mela. 'For such a large gathering, growing larger every year, there should definitely be more funds available. When the Kumbh Mela happens, the administration sits up and funds arrive, but for this annual mela, there are far less resources than needed.'

The Kaanwar Mela budget in 2011 was Rs 25 lakhs. This covered generators, hand-pumps, toilets and policing at every 10 feet. Even on paper, this amount looks inadequate. The volume of pedestrian arrivals was such that for seven to eight days, a 150-kilometre stretch of highway had to be closed to vehicular traffic. How can so little money provide any decent level of service and amenities to so many people?

Since the lives of those who live in Haridwar are so inextricably bound with the Ganga river, I asked Vikas Tiwari what he feels about reports that forecast the melting of glaciers and the Ganga drying up in some decades. Isn't the future of belief in some ways tied up to the sustainability of the environment? What will we have to believe in after we have soiled all the rivers, encroached all the forests, replaced every natural wonder with a man-made monstrosity? The young trader/politician/special police officer grimaced with deep regret evident on his face. 'What can one say? When I went up to Gomukh, where the Bhagirathi river originates from the Gangotri glacier, I followed the discarded gutkha sachets and bottles of Bisleri all the way up a deserted path to Gomukh itself. Thousands are visiting where only dozens ventured earlier. If you cook and bathe, and light fires in the mountains, of course the glaciers will melt before our very eyes.'

I was deep inside an annual phenomenon that most Indians in urban centres in the north only know about vaguely as a nuisance factor to be borne in the months of July and August. Who are the kaanwariyas? Where do they come from and where do they go? What do they hope to achieve? These are not questions that seem particularly important if one is sitting impatiently drumming one's fingers on the steering wheel of a car stuck in a traffic jam in the NCR region, waiting for thousands of orange-clothed pedestrians to pass. I had come in search of the answers to these questions, but I was receiving them only in oblique terms.

Hoping for more direct clues, I met Kaushal Shikhaula, senior correspondent, at the Haridwar office of *Amar Ujala*, a leading Hindi daily. He had also been a kaanwariya for some years, and knows the yatra inside out. His perspective was different from Tiwari's in some aspects. 'The Kaanwar Mela is a residue of the 1991 *junoon* (obsession) of the Rama mandir movement,' he said. 'There is no great religious or ancient sanction for this yatra. Following the enthusiasm of that period of the '90s, people began collecting Gangajal for Shiva, and it quickly established itself as a tradition.'

'Yes, but the growing numbers are not connected only to the 1990s, 'I said. 'People taking up the kaanwar today are mostly young people.'

He nodded in acknowledgement, then offered an explanation, 'The numbers have been fed by the growing prosperity of farmers in western UP, the improved means of *prachar-prasar* (communication, transmission and propaganda) and the *dekha-dekhi* (seeing and imitating) among people. Those who have gone on the yatra a couple of times and had their wishes fulfilled speak of their journey to others, who then want to go. Anyway, people's wish lists are also growing very long and ambitious, necessitating help from God!'

Shikhala reinforced the views expressed by many others of the qualitative difference between today's kaanwariyas and the crowds of kar sevaks in 1991 and 1992 during the Babri Masjid demolition. 'There is no evidence of any militancy on the part of the kaanwariyas, such as that displayed by the slogan-shouting mobs of that time. Kaanwariyas are focused on 'Bam Bhole' and stay within those parameters. The fights and brawls that led to the present crackdown by the police were nearly all about disputes with shopkeepers in the matter of rates. *Kuch dukaandaar bhi bahut badtameez hote hain, khaas kar Bhimgoda mohallemein* (Some shopkeepers are also very rude, particularly in the Bhimgoda area).'

Further stressing the lack of any disruptive communal element in the kaanwar yatra, Kaushal Shikhala said, 'Nearly ninety-five per cent of the kaanwar-makers are Muslim craftsmen. They earn enough in this season to be able to sit idle for some months thereafter. While Muslim organizations and individuals do not offer any sustained or organized help to the yatra, there are, of course, public relations initiatives like putting up small refreshment stalls at places along the yatra route. It is a cordial atmosphere.'

I later also spoke to the bureau chief of *Amar Ujala*, Ajay Chauhan, on the phone, and found him more forthcoming about the motivation and mood of the kaanwariyas. 'This yatra is growing every year, and is not likely to lessen any time soon,' he told me. 'In earlier years, more people used to come in the month of Phagun, for Mahashivaratri, but now the Saawan crowds beat all records. This is due to their wishes being granted – the chain forms like that. You go for one, make a wish, come back to say thanks when that wish is fulfilled. A friend who has seen you gets inspired, and wants to come too, so you return with him, and so on. Faith reinforces and attracts more faith. *Yeh sab yatra ke dauraan Bhole mein rehte hain* (All of these people stay immersed in Bhole during the yatra). So much so that even criminals take up kaanwar, and abstain from crime not only during the yatra, but for some time beyond! It is true that crime rates come down in the town during this period.'

That evening, my last one in Haridwar, I sat on the terrace of my hotel room, gazing at the broad, gently flowing expanse of the Ganga, the mountains, and the human flow of saffron-clothed figures clearly visible across a distant bridge. My mind was a jumble of thoughts. The river below had a soothing, hyp-notic effect as I watched the lights come on and their reflection began twinkling in the water. I felt immensely sad and deeply comforted at the same time — a peculiar feeling that I did not try to analyse then — it was simply beyond me. I was thinking of Dadli and Budh Ram, and the thousands I had seen over just a few days. Did they really meet their Shiva at Haridwar, or was he present in the entire yatra, in their friends and companions, the food and laughter they shared? I thought of the leper's test and how many of the present kaanwariyas may have failed to pass it. But did that mean that he loved them less? The heart of Achaleshwara was big enough to have place in it for the shallow ones, the vain and silly ones, just as it did for the good and the learned devotees – of that I was certain.

I may not have carried kaanwar water on my shoulders in the Saawan yatra and taken it to be poured on him. But my journey was drawing me inexorably, unmistakably closer to Shiva.

Chapter 2: Unmattavesha
(He Who is in the Guise of a Mad One)

The lights went out a minute after I had finished checking the locks on my bags and hauling my luggage to the verandah of Surya Kunj, a bungalow for guests and visitors in the sprawling campus of the Theosophical Society at Kamachha, Varanasi. I left the dark heap of bags and cautiously made my way to a bench near the verandah steps. As my eyes slowly got accustomed to the darkness, I realized that a storm, the dust-raising, windy *aandhi* of the northern plains, was just beginning to push around the leaves, papers and twigs in the Society compound.

Little Jageshwar, the nephew of the Society's caretaker, Ramadhar, had gone to fetch me an autorickshaw for a ride to the station. As my wait on the bench in the darkness lengthened, I began to wonder if he would find one in the storm, or whether he was too small to be taken seriously and the autorickshaw drivers were ignoring him. I then recalled that I had a torch nestled somewhere in a large green canvas bag that held my footwear and toiletries, camera, tape recorder and odd bits of shopping. I was groping in the dark among all these assorted objects when the autorickshaw arrived and tiny, agile Jageshwar jumped out, immediately coming to my side and beginning to assist me with the luggage. *'Rehne, do, Jageshwar* (Leave it),' I said, feeling guilty that a child should have to lug a suitcase. I was carrying more luggage than a single passenger should carry, but since I had spent ten days on my own in Varanasi, I needed plenty of clothes and other necessities. I was now taking back an equal amount of memories in concrete form.

Finally, I was in the autorickshaw with all three of my bags, and we had completed our farewell formalities — I patted Jageshwar on the head and gave him a hug, while he leapt to touch my feet in a more feudal gesture. The autorickshaw driver, who had kept his vehicle running and had taken no part in any of our luggage hauling, drove out of the Society gates into city roads that were in the grip of a terrific dust storm. Polythene packets, paper, small bits of cloth from tailor shops and dried leaves chased each other in ghostly swirls, while cyclists and pedestrians loomed briefly in our headlights, their eyes and faces tightly screwed up against the wind and the dust, before being lost again in the all-enveloping darkness. It was a total blackout, with only intermittent slices of light coming from emergency lights in shops or homes. In April 2000, inverters were not in such common use across the country as they have become in 2012.

I had to draw my dupatta across my mouth to prevent the dust from entering it. Trying to suppress the nervousness that came out of being driven in the dark by a driver whom I had seen only as a shape in the front of the autorickshaw, I engaged him in conversation. From his responses, and the occasional bits of light that slanted on him, it became clear that he was a man in his late thirties or so, a type who could be classified as a 'family man'. I felt some of my tension lessen, even as we exchanged talk about the storm, and when the lights were likely to come back on.

A few more turns later he had elicited from me the reason I had come to Varanasi — to meet and write about toymakers who sold their rattles, trumpets, windmills and other handmade toys on city streets. He seemed amazed that anyone should want to focus on such itinerant souls, specks in the seething humanscape of a town like Varanasi. In fact, he became a lot more animated and enthusiastic after this revelation. From the increasing density of luggage-carrying humans and traffic, and the cluster of shops, hotels and restaurants, I sensed that we were nearing the railway station. My driver asked me one final question. 'Now that you are going away from here, what is the one thing you liked most in Varanasi?' he asked me. I smiled in the darkness. Was there ever a doubt? '*Yahan ke log* (Its people),' I said, and heard him express instant approval.

The darkness was nearly impenetrable in the railway station. The driver parked his autorickshaw, touching one in front and another at the back, and left me sitting inside surrounded by the voices of drivers and struggling passengers as he went off to look for a coolie to help me with my luggage. The train, in the helpful way that happens in such circumstances, was not leaving from the most accessible Platform 1, but one that had to be reached by climbing an overbridge, Platform 4. I began groping for the torch for the second time that evening, trying to quell my panic by reminding myself that there was plenty of time for departure.

I had still not found the torch by the time the driver returned with a coolie, and he now began taking out my bags and loading them on the coolie's head. I got out of the autorickshaw with my hand still inside the bag and began following the two men towards the entrance. My eyes were now quite adjusted to the dark, and people lit matches, and yes, shone torches, plus an emergency light lit up the station entrance. But what was this? The coolie was wandering off at right angles to the entrance, and the driver had to run after him, saying '*Ae! Kahan ja rahe ho?* (Where are you going?),' then he was in front of the coolie in a leap and saying in frustration, '*Un-hun! Tum bhi! Yeh gamchha sahi karo* (Oh you! Tie this towel properly).' I then realized that the man carrying my luggage on his head in nearly complete darkness had one end of the towel he had placed under the bags hanging over his forehead and eyes, completely obscuring his view. Feeling the urge to giggle hysterically at this further addition to absolute chaos, I waited till the driver had tucked in the offending bit of gamchha under one of the bags. I could only see the back of the man carrying my luggage, and saw now that he was not a red-shirted official coolie, just a casual labourer. The driver, saying a respectful goodbye at the station entrance, said to me apologetically, 'There were no coolies to be found, that's why I brought him.' I nodded, with one eye trying to keep track of the man lumbering away with my bags, and a hand still groping for the damned, confounded torch!

And then, miraculously, a few minutes later, I was on Platform 4, and there was an empty bench before which the labourer had stopped with my luggage. I helped him bring the bags down in the dark, then flopped down on the bench in relief, with my hand once more rummaging in the bag. The man now made a strange sound, like a growl, that sounded like this, 'MrrreaAAAH-PAAss'. 'What?' I said, wondering what the sound was meant to convey, and he repeated it, something in its guttural urgency making me sense that it must be about the money I owed him. As my hands finally closed around the smooth shape of the torch in the bag, I drew it out, and shone it on the face of the man standing before me.

What I saw made me nearly drop the torch back again. A cry rose from deep inside me. 'O Kashi Vishwanath! What manner of creatures and men find shelter in your domain!' But my mouth remained silent and dry.

The face of that casual labourer was a face that must have been bashed in by a rock when he was a child. That was the only explanation for a forehead split in two, eyes staring in opposite directions, teeth that looked like the snarl of a gargoyle. No wonder he had found it so difficult to articulate the words, '*Mere paise!* (my money)'. My hands were shaking as I counted out a generous amount from my purse for this special coolie, and the torch lay on the bench, its beam uselessly playing on the grey of the platform floor.

Minutes later, as the lights came on to reveal my train arriving over the horizon of the tracks, I was still feeling completely shaken by the sight of that face. How sentient was the man behind the mask, and what kind of life was he eking out in the twenty-first century? I was ashamed of the sudden fear that had gripped me when I saw his face; then I tried to remind myself that it had finally given way to compassion.

Some of the most unfortunate human beings, who possess none of the required qualities to survive in a Darwinian survival-of-the-fittest sense, still manage to make a life and living in Varanasi. And what perhaps contributes to their being sustained by their environment is the nature of belief. Pilgrims and local residents in Varanasi are both familiar with the concept that if you are a devout seeker, you had better not show any insensitivity/cruelty/neglect to such people as that labourer 'found' in the darkness of Varanasi station. Because, as anyone who prays to Shiva quite understands, who knows? The creature or person you are cruel to or neglectful of could be Shiva himself.

In the realm of rationality and logic I had just had the living daylights frightened out of me by a very poor and deformed man. But in the realm of belief, perhaps what had just blessed me was a visitation — a farewell salute from Vishwanath of Kashi. Which seems the much more attractive idea of the two?

*   *   *   *   *   *   *

Varanasi is the place where Shiva decided to settle after his marriage to Parvati. From being a mountain-dwelling ascetic with matted hair, he now chose a spot on the plains, between the ancient Varuna and Assi rivers, where the mighty Ganga, flowing out of his locks, would become the focal point for people to craft a complex web of culture and civilization. It is often referred to as the city of light, because its ancient name was

'Kashi' or the shining city, where Shiva was believed to have emerged from the column of light that conclusively established his place on top of the Hindu holy trinity of Brahma, Vishnu and Mahesh (another name for Shiva).

Brahma, the creator, and Vishnu, the preserver, were arguing about who was the greater between them when a huge column of light, without beginning and end, dazzled them with its brilliance, forcing Brahma to take to the skies on his white goose, searching for one end, while Vishnu took on the shape of a wild boar and began digging deep within the earth, searching for the other. Neither managed to find the limits of this brilliance, and returned, exhausted. Then Shiva walked out of the column of light, revealing that he is the very essence of *jyoti*, the light that banishes the darkness of ignorance. The place that marks this divine emergence for all eternity is Varanasi.

Unlike the rugged mountains that provide Achaleshwara with a vast canvas of primordial sights, washed by colours that change in tune with the seasons, Varanasi represents the bustling, man-made canvas of worship and mourning, commerce and creativity. Here Shiva has chosen to live as a domesticated Vishwanath, the ruler of the world married to Parvati as Annapurna, the goddess who feeds the world with the abundance of her creative powers. But in case one is getting carried away with this tamer, safer image of Shiva as a force fettered by the rules and requirements that spell civilization (and which are reinforced by every incarnation of Vishnu), Varanasi is also the place where Shiva can be seen in the guise of the mad one. In fact, if there is a single factor that makes me love this place with great passion, it is the city's all-pervading ambience of amused tolerance, its ability to destroy pretension and make room for dissent and difference.

By some strange combination of circumstances, all my three visits to Varanasi in the past twelve years have coincided with the nine days of homage to Devi, or Durga, known as Navaratri. In April 2000, I arrived on the first day of the Chait Navadurga, or nine-day period of worshipping the goddess that falls in the month of Chait (March–April). So, along with abundant reminders and references to Shiva, I was made aware of the many practices associated with Devi worship. I found that there was a specific temple in Varanasi for every name of Devi during Navaratri. Beginning with Shailputri, worshipped on day one on the outskirts of the city, where a huge mela is held, the goddess is worshipped in a different form each day. She is revered in a small temple on the ghats as Brahmacharini on day two, and on every subsequent day in different temples in the established order – Chandrakanta on day three, Kushmanda on day four, Skandamata on day five, Katyayani on day six, Kaalratri on day seven, Maha Gauri on day eight and finally as Siddhidatri on day nine. Women carried *thalis* or steel plates with flowers, lamps and other items of devotion, and walked around in small processions, singing devotional songs, their colourful sarees drawn over their heads. I saw them at many places in the town, and also went to the temples of two major Devi deities – Shitala Devi at Agalpura on the banks of the Ganga in rural Varanasi and Vindhya Vasini Devi at the carpet-weaving town of Mirzapur, about 64 kilometres from Varanasi. At both these places, huge crowds thronged the melas that had sprung up for the Navadurga festival, giving me ample scope to observe the toymakers I had come to meet, and the families that were their customers.

Bhojpuri songs in praise of Devi, known as *pachra* were playing from many shops and small temples, and I grew specially attached to one or two of them: '*Nimbiya ki daari maiya dale li asanva, ki jhoomi jhuli na. Maiya jhule lin jhulanwa ki jhoomi jhuli na* (Mother chose a bough of the neem tree as her seat and began swinging from it. Mother swings happily from her perch on the neem tree).' Even today, hearing these lines evokes the sights, sounds and smells of Varanasi for me.

My second visit to Varanasi happened in September and October 2008, when Durga Puja pandals punctuated the streets in the week before Dussehra. The next time I went, in March and April 2012, it was again during Chait Navadurga! During the first visit, I stayed enough days to develop a rhythm of sorts for myself, wandering and exploring the town. Following a particular toymaker, I went to the neighbourhood inhabited by weavers, where each home had men and women bent over silk looms, and saw the abject poverty that produces some of the most enduring and beautiful images of India's artistic tradition. I wandered over the steps of several of the over eighty ghats along the Ganga that came up in the seventeenth and eighteenth centuries and provide the definitive image of Varanasi. On some of these steps, I conducted interviews, and savoured the delights of feeding the fish at Lalita Ghat, or watching urchins jump into the water around the leaning Shiva temple at Scindia Ghat, or hitching rides by holding on to the boats ferrying tourists, laughing and calling to each other.

I took to spending the still, summer afternoons in the Sankat Mochan temple at Lanka, where a large langur was usually perched on one of the low branches of a tree in the courtyard. He was such a large and impressive monkey that his presence succeeded in keeping away the more boisterous crowds of red-faced rhesus macaques. But when I expressed admiration for the langur, and how his sweeping gaze held the power to banish the other *bandar*s, the owner of a sweetshop in the temple courtyard said, 'Yes, he is a good langur, but not a patch on our Raja. He ruled over our temple for more than a decade.'

My ears pricked up immediately. 'How?' I asked.

'Raja was also a big langur, maybe even bigger than this one,' said the shopkeeper. 'But more than his size, it was his *dimaag* (intelligence) that was so powerful. He would sit on these same branches, then suddenly get off and go to the rickshaw men waiting outside the temple. He would ask one of them for a beedi, by signalling with his fingers and mouth, as if he was smoking. Then after he got his beedi, he would sit in the rickshaw, and make a gesture with his hands, which meant, "Come on, let's go!"'

'And he got his ride? The rickshaw wallah listened to him?' I asked.

'Of course! No one dared disobey Raja,' said the man. 'He would be taken for a round, and brought back safely. Then he would get off and go back to his branch. This one doesn't have the brains to do stuff like that.'

I nodded. Of course, it was not unusual for a monkey to earn the affectionate epithet 'Raja' in a place like Varanasi, which is so laid back and languid, that ordinary people greet each other with a *'Ka, Raja?'* or *'Ka, Guru?* (What's new, Prince/ King? or What's new, Guru?).' No one has less than princely status in this charmed city.

It was because of my habit of spending afternoons at the temple that I had the most memorable encounter of that entire stay one evening at Tulsi Ghat, a meeting of great luminosity.

The Mahant, the head priest of the Sankat Mochan temple at Varanasi, Veer Bhadra Mishra, is a descendant of Goswami Tulsidas, who first built the temple at this spot after he saw a vision of Hanuman. Later, the temple was given its present structure by Madan Mohan Malviya, the founder of Benares Hindu University. Mahantji, as he is known, lives at Tulsi Ghat, a short distance from the temple, and I was keen to meet him. Just the previous year, in 1999, he had been named the Hero of the Planet by *Time* magazine for his work in the cleaning and conservation of the Ganga.

One evening, after my customary afternoon hours spent at the temple, I went to Tulsi Ghat, to Mahantji's home, and found he was resting and had still not emerged to receive his evening visitors. Preparations were on for the wedding of his son, I was told, and that is why he had retired for his afternoon rest a little later than usual. 'Should I wait here, or return in an hour's time?' I asked the polite man who was volunteering the information. He hesitated, not wanting to appear rude. 'It might be better if you came back after a while,' he finally said. I nodded acceptance, and headed towards the river.

A few twists in the narrow street, and there before me was the familiar, glorious vista of the Ganga, a slight curve showing me the kilometres of terraced steps of the various ghats. The horizon to the right and left of me was dominated by an expanse of gently flowing water gilded by the evening rays of the sun, and dotted with the occasional boat. As a way to spend an evening, it could hardly be bettered, I thought to myself, settling down to face the river.

But it appeared there was more in store for me than just the luxury of being alone with my thoughts in that golden hour. A man was singing behind me, in one of the verandahs of carved stone where the steps of a ghat ended. A very subtle drum accompaniment was all that could be heard apart from his voice, a voice that clearly carried across the space that separated us.

> *'Saaj samaj piya le aaye*
> *Auri kaharwa chaari*
> *Babhna bedardi dard na boojhe*
> *Jorat gaanth hamari re*
> *Aayee gawanwa ki saree.*
> *Abahin umar mori baari re, aayee gawanwa ki saree…'*

I felt the stirring of powerful emotions when I heard these lines. They describe how a young man has arrived to take away his young bride to her married home and she, faced with the paraphernalia of her *bidaai* (sending off), which includes four bearers for her palanquin, is lamenting that she is still too young, that the saree sent for her by her parents-in-law, has come much too soon!

Mesmerized by the voice, I got up and began walking towards the verandah where it came from, and soon reached the spot. A blind man was singing, playing a large single drum that he held in one hand and gently stroked with the other. He was so thin that all his ribs showed, and his deeply sunken eye sockets showed he had been blind from birth. A motley group of men around him, all looking slightly disreputable, sat quietly and listened. They made a place for me to sit when I arrived.

> '… *Tootal gaanv nagar se naata*
> *Chhootal mahal ataari*
> *Bidhi gat baam kachhu samajh pade na*
> *Bairan bhai mahataari re, aayee gawanwa ki saree.*'

The blind man continued to sing the young girl's lament. Now she spoke of the bonds that were breaking, with her home and village, the structures and buildings getting left behind. She regretted the cruel twist of fate — her marriage — that was making even her mother seem alien. As I got deeper into the song, I finally recognized the form, and what it was actually describing. The married home was another world, the world one entered after death, and the beloved groom was death itself, waiting to claim one before one was ready. The saree had arrived too soon.

> '…*Nadiya kinaare balam mora rasiya*
> *Deenh ghunghat pat daari*
> *Chaar jana mil doli uthawat*
> *Gharwa se det nikaari re, aayee gawanwa ki saree.*'

'By the side of the river did my beloved cover my head with a ghunghat,' went the song. 'Four persons carried my palanquin and finally took me away from my home.'

How fitting these lines were when one was sitting in the vicinity of those very ghats where people came to be cremated. I felt goosepimples ripple across my arms, and my eyes prickle with tears of recognition and joy as I thought of Shiva being the waiting one beside the mighty river, waiting to tenderly carry me across when I died. That song and voice were so incredibly moving, that if it (death) had happened just then, I would have waltzed across to the other world without a backward glance.

> '…*Kahat Kabir suno bhai sadho*
> *Kshamiyo chook hamaari*
> *Ab hin ka gauna, bahuri nahin auna*
> *Mil leu bhent ek baari re, aayee gawanwa ki saree.*'

Kabir! Of course, it had to be him, the great poet speaking of the threshold that strikes others with dread. In the final stanza, the young girl asks forgiveness for any wrongs she has committed. 'When I leave now, who knows if I will ever return? Let's therefore meet just once,' she tells her village friends, because of course, the saree from her married home has already arrived. As the song was drawing to a close, I was thinking to myself that if I had stayed for any length of time in Varanasi and remained untouched by the particular voice of the mystic weaver from Benares (another name for Varanasi) I could have considered my time wasted. So the words of Kabir were sent to me in this unmistakable form with great clarity.

A minute of silence followed the end of the song. The blind man placed his *dafli* (drum) on the ground and wiped his face. The men around him, seeing me as the only outsider in their little group, turned expectantly towards me, as if seeking an explanation.

'Namaste!' I said. '*Aap ka gaana hamein yahan kheench laaya* (Your song drew me to this place).'

The blind man turned in the direction of my voice. '*Arre, mataji* (Oh, mother!),' he said, using the respectful form of address that is common in Varanasi for mature women. '*Aap aayee hain? Bahut khushi hui, baithe rahiye. Mera naam Mithai Lal hai. Main Hanuman bhakt hoon. Gharwala, pariwarwala hoon. Shaam ko yahan baith jaata hoon, kuch log milne bolne aa jaate hain, to mujhe achha lagta hai, kyonki main sagun aur nirgun, dono ka upaasak hoon* (You have arrived? I am very happy, do keep sitting. My name is Mithai Lal. I am a Hanuman devotee. I am a family man. In the evenings, I sit here, and some people gather to meet and talk, which makes me happy, because I worship both the forms of God — the one with form, and the formless one).'

These words resonated inside me with a sense akin to deep shock. I felt completely humbled in the face of what was surely miraculous. Why did he begin to describe himself first and foremost as a Hanuman devotee? Surely he could not have known that I spent the better part of the afternoon every day at the Sankat Mochan, and that my guru, Neeb Karori Baba, had been considered an incarnation of Hanuman. Why did he greet me as if he had always expected me to come to him? How many single middle-aged women from the upper middle class, unaccompanied by guides or escorts, landed up to sit among his friends? And the most remarkable of all was his final, signature statement about his approach to life — something that so tallied with my own that I felt like it was a direct personal message to me. '…I worship both the forms of God — the one with form, and the formless one.'

That sums up why I have such a difficult time speaking about my faith or spirituality to any of my peers. My educated, articulate, secular friends would be completely comfortable with a discussion of the song Mithai Lal had sung, a fine example of Kabir's *nirgun*. But they find it tough to understand why I am so attached to shrines and temples, or to the people who throng them! My tradition-bound Hindu neighbours in a very ordinary area of Lucknow find it odd that I do not join them in endless fasts and rituals. They consider my attachment to God to be altogether too abstract and 'modern' for them.

I made what replies I could to Mithai Lal, and stayed on to sing a bhajan or two myself, to which he courteously played the dafli. At one point, he was greeted by a man walking across the ghat steps, a man who wore a tiny loin-cloth and whose lower body was completely caked in mud, obviously one of the labourers engaged in desilting work along the riverbank. '*Arre* Mithai Lal!' he called out, and they spoke to each other with easy familiarity. Then the man came up the steps to the verandah, and took out a dirty pink two-rupee note from his waistband — the humble note was still then in circulation. He offered it with great reverence to Mithai Lal, who took it with equal humility, both bowing their heads. When the man was walking back down the steps after a final namaste, Mithai Lal felt the note in his hands and exclaimed with delight to his seated friends, 'It's two rupees!' It was a heart-wrenching display of both — their poverty and their innocence. I felt blessed to see both the giver and the receiver.

Another few minutes and some of the men around me became restless. '*Bhog kab chadhe?* (When will we start our offerings?)' one of them asked and I heard another reply, *'Arre nahin, abahin mataji baith rahin* (Not yet, mataji is still sitting here).' I realized that they were all ready to smoke their chillum filled with ganja, as cannabis is known in most parts of India. Not wanting them to be further inhibited by my presence, I got up hurriedly, made an offering of a folded note to Mithai Lal, and left. My matronly persona did not permit me to ask to share in their smoke, and I had received my 'high' anyway. The events of that evening made me feel like I was walking on air as I left.

Treating the consumers of cannabis with the same respect, giving them the same space as you would for any ordinary person is more likely in Varanasi than other pilgrim or tourist towns. How can one frown on the chillum smokers when Shiva himself is adorned with a green paste of the leaves of bhang or hemp in temples across north India? Besides, even the men around Mithai Lal were referring to their smokes as 'bhog' or the offering one makes to God to later consume as prasad. And ganja is generally consumed with a cry of 'Bam Bhole!' at many places, whether behind the Mahalaxmi temple in Mumbai, or in the artsy tourist destinations of Himachal Pradesh.

What is the connection between a divine construct like Shiva and a mild intoxicant struggling to acquire a legal status in most parts of the world? How is one to reconcile Shiva with structures of social and moral codes? The answer is fairly simple, one doesn't. Because in permitting people to remember him as they lift marijuana to their lips, in being himself depicted at various times as a beggar, a vagabond, a leper (remember the Kumbh Mela story?), Shiva is only showing his true form as that infinite space within which all of creation lives, breathes, works and dies. Shiva is the space that holds us all, all kinds, all types. Believing in him as the space within which all of life is lived challenges us to refrain from complaining that there are people around us who are different from us, who think, act, or behave differently. We can bring such people to book, should they commit acts against the common good through the laws we have made. But we cannot deny their existence, nor can we force them to be like us, as a condition for co-existence.

My second visit to Varanasi was in October 2008 with my son Shishir, then studying law at Kolkata, and spending ten days of his Puja holidays with me at Faizabad (UP), where I then lived. I was divorced from Shishir's father, and when he came to stay with me at my second husband's home, he was always struck by how people stared at him on the street in Faizabad. For one, he is six feet tall, in a town where men are usually between five and five feet five inches tall. For another, he wore shorts and sandals, or T-shirts and jeans, when everyone was much more formally dressed in long-sleeved shirts and shoes, or kurta-pyjamas. Even going out to buy bread or fruit would make him come back muttering, 'What's with this staring, Ma? Don't people have anything better to do?'

I soothed him with some maternal noises. 'Don't worry, I'm taking you to a place where nobody stares, no matter what you wear, or how you walk,' I told him.

'Where?' he asked, startled.

'Varanasi,' I said, and he nodded, not looking too convinced.

It did not take him even ten minutes after our arrival at Varanasi station to concede that I had been speaking the truth. In front of us, was a rickshaw with a tall, thin foreign woman, her hair piled on top of her head, and an immense stretch of back showing from her halter top, talking animatedly to her bearded male companion. Men in skull caps and lungis manned several food carts and tea stalls to one side of the road, sadhus in dhotis and rudraksha beads could be spotted every now and then in the crowd, and learned, professorial individuals passed us on their cycles when we were stuck in traffic. This was no provincial hamlet looking goggle-eyed at newcomers. It was, literally and figuratively, the world. What delighted my son even more were the healthy-looking animals on the street. In Faizabad, the roadside dogs look whipped and sickly. In fact, they are a barely tolerated lot. Very few cats are seen, and the stray bulls and cows present a sad picture, trying to eat paper and cardboard in front of one's eyes, in a desperate attempt to survive.

In stark contrast, on the second morning of our visit as we made our way out of the modest hotel we were staying in, we passed a wonderful sight. A very large bull was lowering his head to drink from a hand pump, while a man worked the lever for the water to flow for him. 'Do you think I have nothing to do all day except give you your drink?' he was good-naturedly asking the bull in Bhojpuri. The huge bull paused for a breath or two, before lowering his head again. It seemed like a long-standing relationship.

Later in the day, we were in a cycle rickshaw, moving slowly through the crowded market area around Godowlia, when we saw a bull sitting in the middle of a brightly lit clothes shop. Startled enough to crane our necks at the sight, we noticed that a picture of the bull found pride of place in the signboard above the shop, too. 'Do you think it's a pet?' asked Shishir wonderingly. We had not yet read the story of the shop where a bull wandered in and became the business's mascot. The mystery was unravelled in the 2 January 2010 issue of *OPEN* magazine:

'Holy Bull'

by Haima Deshpande

Twenty-five years ago, a bull walked into the Lucknow Chikan Shop, a cloth store tucked away in the dusty folds of Varanasi. It stayed on for half a day. Paramanand Chhugani, the shop owner, rubbed his eyes and scratched his head.

The next day, the bull returned and stayed put till the lights went out at 9 p.m. Chhugani's surprise took on the form of devotion. A devotee of Lord Shiva, the supreme deity of Varanasi, Chhugani decided that the bull's visit was a sign from the Lord. By the third day, the bull had a name —

Nandi Baba. 'Outside every Shiva temple there sits Nandi (bull). I am a bhakt of Shivji so it was natural to name him Nandi Baba,' Chhugani told *OPEN*. 'I am overwhelmed by his presence in my shop.'

The first Nandi Baba died. But other bulls followed, all named Nandi Baba by Chhugani. The current incumbent is Nandi Baba the Fourth. Chhugani's business has expanded since his first bovine visitor. In 2003, he opened a second shop, Lucknow Chikan Centre. It is mandatory for employees of both shops to pay obeisance to Nandi Baba IV.

Chhugani saw a divine hand even in the inauguration of his second shop. He spotted a Nandi in the vicinity and realized he had found his chief guest. 'I kept the door open and waited,' Chhugani said. 'Sure enough, Nandi walked into the shop. What's more, it went straight to Shivji's idol inside the shop. It looked at the idol for some time, then licked it. Afterwards it sat down at the foot of the idol. We couldn't believe our eyes. Since then, Nandi Baba visits my shop every day.'

Nandi Baba is organized. It arrives at the shop at 9.30 a.m, except in the summer, when it waddles in half an hour later. The shutters are opened only after the bull reaches the shop. It walks in first and everyone else follows. Then, it walks up to the idol of Lord Shiva, licks it and sits down at its feet. The shop is cleaned even as Nandi Baba sits there. The area around the idol is cleaned only after it leaves the shop in the afternoon to stroll around the market. Chhugani ensures that it gets a sumptuous lunch. Post-lunch, it returns and sits till closing time. Fearing that the bull will be inconvenienced if the shop is closed, Chhugani keeps it open every day of the year.

Shoppers in Varanasi are used to Nandi Baba's presence. In fact, the shop has become a tourist attraction. People in Varanasi have anointed Nandi's visits to the shop as a miracle. Sometimes, they flock there only to worship it. The Chhuganis do not turn back anyone who is keen to worship their Nandi Baba.

'We are blessed by Nandi Baba's presence. How can we deprive other devotees of the pleasure of worshipping him?' Chhugani asks.

Returning to Varanasi with Shishir gave me the opportunity to revisit some of the places I had wandered in on my own eight years earlier. What brought us the most pleasure was being able to connect with the people I had befriended in that period. Elderly boatman Raghunath Majhi from Dashashwamedh Ghat was one of them. This gentle, bearded old-timer has been described in my book *The Toymakers: Light from India's Urban Poor*. When we tracked him down and he came down the ghat steps to meet us, I could see Shishir quite overcome with the meeting. Raghunath was older, more frail, and therefore doubly precious. My son tried to make conversation in his halting Hindi, then gave up and we just stayed with each other for a few minutes, happy to have met again.

It was while in search of another place I had liked very much on my first visit – the Dwarka Lassi shop at Chowk –that we saw another sight that defined Varanasi for Shishir, and reinforced for me the unique, Shiva-imbued nature of this ancient city. We had gone for a boat ride on the Ganga, and when we told our boatman that we wanted to go to Chowk, he touched shore at Manikarnika, one of the two main burning ghats at Varanasi. We got off on steps blackened with the soot and grime of countless cremations, and walked past piles of logs. An obviously rich family, in the ritual attire of silk dhotis, was speaking to the cremation crew about the ceremony for their relative.

We observed them quietly, overhearing scraps of conversation, apparently about money for different arrangements.

Much has been written about the mysterious network of the Doms at Varanasi, the clan that has a hereditary right to conduct cremations at Varanasi's burning ghats much before the time of the thirty-sixth Suryavanshi king, Harishchandra. This king, wedded to the cause of truth and justice, gave away his entire kingdom to the sage Vishwamitra, and had then no place to go – except Kashi (Varanasi). Here he apprenticed himself to Kalu Dom, the Chandala who was in charge of cremating bodies. Harishchandra had become separated from his wife and son when he had sold them to a Brahmin householder, unable to provide for them. The travails of Harishchandra were intense enough to create an indelible impression on the mind of the boy Mohandas Karamchand Gandhi when he saw the film *Raja Harishchandra* (1913). This was the example that inspired him to be forever aligned with truth. As the story goes, when Harishchandra's son died of snakebite, his wife was utterly without resources for his cremation. In an unbearably moving twist of the story, the wife arrives for their son's cremation, and her appearance is so altered by poverty that Harishchandra is unable to recognize her or his dead son. It is only when she attempts to pay for the cremation with her *mangalsutra* that he recognizes it as the one he had placed around his wife's neck at their wedding. In spite of these cruel blows of fate, Harishchandra never wavered from his duty, or the path of truth, thereby earning the blessings of all the gods, including Yama, the god of death, who was revealed to be none other than Kalu Dom! The blessings resulted in his son being brought back to life, and subsequently going on to further the dynasty. But the time that Harishchandra spent as a lowly assistant to the Dom, has meant that the Dom began to be regarded as the actual Raja who ruled over his royal subject, thus bringing about the term

'Dom Raja' – the main head of the Dom family is still called 'Dom Raja' in modern Varanasi. When one goes for a boat ride on the Ganga, along the ghats, the tall house of the Dom Raja, with the figures of tigers on its roof distinctly marking it out from neighbouring buildings, is always pointed out by guides and *pandas* (priests).

The Doms are so astute about assessing the financial worth of prospective customers that they quote cremation prices based on your name, the place you have come from, your caste and appearance, in a way that closely matches your actual ability to pay. It is said that they have a vast network of informers across the country who help them nail lies if a family is pretending to be poorer than they are! Thus one of the bigger Marwari merchant families from Kolkata can shell out a few lakhs for a cremation, and a teacher from rural Gujarat can get away with paying a few thousands.

That afternoon, as we passed the family speaking with the Doms, we entered the narrow streets that lead out of Manikarnika into the crowded market of Chowk. A corpse, covered in green brocade, was being brought down to the ghats by bearers carrying it at a trot, and we had to stand aside to let them pass. We began walking again, and another narrow side street opened to one side of us, from which an old man, carrying his grandchild perched on his shoulders, came out and began walking just ahead of us. The child, with a few coins clutched in one fist, and swinging his head with every step his granddad took, was obviously headed to a sweet shop we could see ahead, and seemed to be singing a song. It was with a shock that I came closer and recognized his childish cry was '*Naam naam chhat hai!*' replicating the '*Ram nam satya hai*' that funeral carriers intoned as they carried bodies to Manikarnika daily. For the world, this reminder of God's name being the only truth, is a grim symbol of death. For a child growing up in Manikarnika, it is a jolly chant to accompany a ride on Grandpa's shoulders. Varanasi never fails to reinforce an impression of the eternal continuum of life and death. It flows.

When we came out into the teeming chaos of Chowk and located Dwarka Lassi, my son and I lingered over our big earthen kulhads full of sweet lassi topped with cream and pistachio flakes. The young man churning the lassi in a huge pot with capable, be-ringed hands, had shoulder-length hair and a red tilak on his forehead, the picture of Benarasi chic. I remembered him even younger, from eight years ago, and told him so when we paid for our drink. 'It's as delicious as I remember it from the time I came here with toymakers, several years ago,' I told the young man about the lassi. He smiled in acknowledgement, my words making him steal a shy glance at my face, as if to try and remember. 'I was writing a book,' I prompted. 'About *khilonewallas*.'

That detail was enough to make his smile turn big and warm, though he still continued to look downwards at the change he was counting out. When we left the shop in the next instant, he was touching his hand to his heart in that peculiar evolution of the folded-hands namaste that is prevalent in UP. A hand to the heart accompanied by a head ducked in your direction represents the telegraphic form of respect being bestowed on you. I responded in similar fashion; then we were away from the lassi, and the labyrinthine lanes of Manikarnika, the childish voice saying, *'Naam naam chhat hai,'* still echoing inside me.

*   *   *   *   *   *   *

In late March 2012, summer had already set in when I reached Varanasi for my third visit. This time, the friend accompanying me took me to Assi, where his friend was working on a memorial marking the birth spot of Rani Lakshmi Bai of Jhansi, the legendary warrior-queen who fought British forces during India's

First War of Independence. Something in the twists and turns around the place made me recognize the office of the Sankat Mochan Foundation, the NGO working to protect the Ganga, headed by Mahant Veer Bhadra Mishra.

Since we had some time to kill, I continued walking in the direction of the river, finally reaching it via a slope where a board identified the place as Assi Ghat. I wondered to myself, 'Can this be? Is it the place I had come to all those years ago?' We stopped to have tea at a shop on the steps of the ghat, and I decided to find out if I was indeed close to the spot I had visited that evening in the summer of 2000. I walked up to two men lounging nearby and inquired, 'Tell me, does a blind man sit here and sing somewhere nearby in the evenings? A man called Mithai Lal?'

Both immediately turned to look at me with interest. One was fair, with white hair standing up at the oddest angles on his head, and the other was darker, with bloodshot eyes. 'Yes, he does,' said the fair man. 'Do you know him?'

'I have met him,' I said. 'Several years ago. I would like to meet him again, if its possible.'

'Of course, its possible,' said the darker man, who later identified himself as a boatman called Hanuman. 'Shall we bring him here, or will you come up to see him?'

I was so happy at the thought that I might see Mithai Lal soon that I immediately said, 'Oh, I will come with you!'

The friend I had accompanied and his architect friend working on the Rani Lakshmibai Memorial were startled to find me suddenly walking away with the two men after a few seconds of conversation. I tried reassuring them with a wave, saying, 'I'll be back soon.' Then I was following Hanuman as he began climbing the steps next to the tea shop.

Hauling myself with some difficulty over steps that were much steeper than ordinary ones, I finally reached a door on the second flight that opened into the courtyard of Rewa Kothi. Several young boys, who looked like students, were sitting or standing in the stone verandah that enclosed the courtyard, and men who looked like police personnel off duty were washing clothes at a tap. I learnt that this place had been donated by the rulers of Rewa, a small kingdom in the erstwhile Central Provinces (now in Madhya Pradesh), to the university, so that students who wished to learn classical music would have a place to stay.

I stood close to the door that led to the ghats, just inside the courtyard, feeling a little awkward in the all-male ambience, while the boatman and his fairer companion set up a cry for 'Mithai La-aal!'. A few minutes later, a small, very thin Mithai Lal, wearing a checked shirt and trousers and using a thick stick, came out from somewhere inside the rooms of Rewa Kothi accompanied by Hanuman, the boatman. He came towards where I was standing, and I greeted him, introducing myself while he washed his face and hands at the tap. Hanuman said that he had been taking a nap.

Mithai Lal listened intently to my babbled introduction as he wiped his face. 'You had sung a nirgun of Kabir's,' I said. 'I had come from Chennai and sat with your friends for a while. And I also sang a few songs,' I said, feeling suddenly shy and ashamed of my enthusiasm.

Mithai Lal thought a little, then said, 'I greeted you as "Mataji" and when you left you gave me money,' he said, recalling the exact offering. I was so relieved that he had remembered that my awkwardness of a few minutes ago changed into happy gushing.

'Do you have time to talk now?' I asked him. 'Shall we go and sit somewhere?'

'Of course,' said Mithai Lal, leading the way down the steps to the river with his thick stick, Hanuman watchfully walking behind him, with a hand just below Mithai Lal's elbow. I kept exclaiming over how happy I was that he had remembered me after all these years. As we walked along the ghat steps, I saw that he was leading me to the exact spot where I had sat twelve years ago.

We took our seats inside the stone verandah, and I continued to babble, till he said, 'But why should I forget? You haven't forgotten, have you? It's a common mistake made by people who see. Actually, they see a lot less than they think, and we know.'

I finally calmed down — such was the effect of those salutary words.

He sang the Kabir song again, and this time I could record it and note down the words. 'This song was much liked by Dr Kashinath Singh, too,' he told me. 'The writer who has written the film being made by Dr Chandraprakash Dwivedi, called *Assi ka Kashi*.'

'You mean the one starring Sunny Deol and Sakshi Tanwar?' I asked, dimly recollecting some mention in the Lucknow papers. 'The same,' said Mithai Lal.

Later, I was sitting at the famous Pappu Chaiwalla's shop with the regulars who come to Assi every day, sometimes even twice a day, to have tea and talk for hours about everything from local gossip to philosophy and literature, politics and personal angst. During the conversation I had with men like Ashok Pande, who quoted political leader Ram Manohar Lohia, Vashishth, who sat in a corner and made plenty of comments, a gentle professor from BHU and a young freelance journalist, I learnt that Mithai Lal had been featured in the film too.

Mithai Lal was born on 10 July 1956 in a village near Varanasi, bordering Bihar. He was an only child, and much loved by his maternal grandmother, who left him a small shop. He got married to a blind woman and they have one son, who has normal eyesight. 'My wife lives in the village and is cared for by a Yadav family since the roof of my house fell down. I do want to repair it, but where is the money? I also have to see that my son gets admitted to a decent college,' he told me. In 1978–79, Mithai Lal joined the Music Department of Benares Hindu University, and was allotted a room at Rewa Kothi. He has been in the premises ever since, not lucky enough to get a room, but managing to sleep in the verandah or wherever there was place, even though every now and then he faces the threat of eviction from some new and zealous administrator.

Since I found him again twelve years after our first meeting, I have met Mithai Lal several times in Varanasi and in Lucknow, where he stays in a small Shiva temple near a large police campus. This temple seems to be exclusively a hangout for men who smoke chillums, at least it appeared so to me whenever I went there. But it is well protected from any resulting complications by the fact that a large percentage of the chillum-smokers are police personnel.

I once asked Mithai Lal about ganja. 'Perhaps you wouldn't be so thin if you ate as much food as the ganja you smoke,' I said jokingly. He shook one hand in the air in denial, his long bony fingers only inches from my face. 'I am blessed,' he said. 'Bholenath forgives me. The amount of ganja I have smoked, what can I say? Another man would have got cancer or TB by now. But thankfully, I am still upright. I have sat at the cremation ground for twenty-four hours and more, without food, on ganja alone.'

His music is intrinsically tied up to the cremation ghats. 'We sing and have *satsangs* in the evenings. On Saturday evenings, the music is at Harishchandra Ghat, and on Mondays it is at Manikarnika. It is lovely that on Saturdays we rejoice and sing the name of God at the spot where bodies have been cremated, although *rudhivaadi* (orthodox) belief has it that temples should not be visited after one has participated in a cremation. On Saturday mornings, there is feeding of the poor at Harishchandra Ghat.'

We skirted around the topic of his poverty, though eventually he did come out and say, 'I am a very poor man. The hardships I have undergone — may God never give them to anyone else! I miss good home-cooked food. The food at roadside carts and dhabas can never be the same. I wander around, and people give me something to eat or drink now and then.'

'So people in your neighbourhood must be familiar with and fond of you,' I said, building a rosy picture of him sustained by the kindness of his neighbours.

'Oh yes, people are familiar with me all right,' said Mithai Lal. After a moment, he added, 'For my *gaalis* (abuse). I am very well-known for the stream of gaalis that I can effortlessly direct towards someone who has upset me. Women make their sons deliberately address me to listen to my gaalis, so that they can laugh behind their pallus,' he said, dispelling my idyllic mental picture. 'Somebody will call me, "Mama! (maternal uncle) Come and have some tea!" and I reply, "A***ole! Do I look like your uncle? Or in need of your miserable tea?" Then I hear the women laughing, and one of them will apologetically say, "We are all waiting to hear these words from you, that's why we told him to call you!" It gives them pleasure to tease me like this.'

Mithai Lal's song repertoire covers the classical and the ordinary, the folk and the familiar, commercial bhajan. Most often celebrating Shiva as the patron deity of ganja smokers and bhang consumers, he sang several songs to me on this theme. Here's one in Bhojpuri where Shiva is affectionately referred to as *hamaar jogiya* or 'our renunciate':

'Dim dim damru bajavailen hamaar jogiya.
Gale sohe mund mala, ang latke naag kala,
Ang mein bhabhuti ramavailen hamaar jogiya.

Naache bhoot prait sang, sada rahe adbang
Bhang dhatura chavavailen hamaar jogiya.
Boodha baila par savaar, chanda sohe laali laar,
Chhala ser ke bichhavailen hamaar jogiya.
Aisan daani na koi jaisan Bhola hamre hoi
Jaune maangi taune lutaavailen hamaar jogiya.
Dhaara Ganga ke bahavailen, hamaar jogiya.'

(Dim-dim goes the damroo [drum] our renunciate plays. He wears a garland of severed heads, and a black snake hangs down his body, his body covered with ashes looks beautiful! He dances with ghosts and remains forever ungainly, awkward and clumsy, chewing bhang and the poisonous dhatura whenever he wishes. He rides a wise old bull, wears a crimson slice of moon in his hair, and spreads a tigerskin to sit on, our renunciate. Our Bhola is a giver like no other. Whatever people ask of him he gives generously and freely, just as he makes the Ganga flow!).

I draw strength in my faith from Mithai Lal and his relationship with the Shiva of the cremation ghats and the ganja-smoking fraternity. This is not because of some aberrant gene or some regrettable voyeuristic instinct that resides in me. Why I hold Mithai Lal and his Varanasi close to my heart is intrinsically tied up to how I have come to grips with the faith into which I was born.

Hinduism is, for a lot of its confessed practitioners, not the easiest to preach or translate for those unfamiliar with its labyrinthine maze of stories and symbols, its multiplicity of forms and the contradictions inevitably thrown up in discussing its various aspects. While at some level it is highly structured and codified with the *Vedas*, *Puranas* and *Upanishads* providing moral injunctions and pointers to its practice, at another level it is completely unfettered, leaving the believer free to be ignorant of all the texts and mythology if he or she wishes, and content with the occasional acknowledgement of one or the other deities of Rama or Krishna, Shiva, Devi or Ganesha. In fact, for many young people caught up in studying or working in the big cities, being a Hindu means occasionally praying at a temple, or during festivals which are primarily family occasions. When, or if, such people decide to take their faith or spirituality a little more seriously, they find a wealth of material to reinforce their faith. But should they never feel the need to do so, they can still call themselves 'Hindu' their whole lives and risk no punishment for lying.

Adi Shankaracharya, in his infinite wisdom, brought together all the different strands of worship in Sanatana Dharma, or the eternal faith that is Hinduism. This signal service made it possible to label the faith of millions of people spread across diverse geographic regions, who evolved their relationship with the divine in myriad ways as broadly one belief system. That this was done without robbing these different approaches of their validity and identity, is remarkable in itself. Thus worshippers of Shiva and Vishnu, Devi or Shakti, the sun, Ganesha and Kartikeya (Shiva and Parvati's second son) can all co-exist under the umbrella of Hinduism, as can the worshippers of countless village deities that roughly correspond to any of the above. This is very comforting in its inclusiveness. On the flip side, this inclusiveness is translated as a kind of religious imperialism by those who seek to project Hinduism as a super-religion. They then begin to claim Buddhism, Jainism and Sikhism as offshoots of the Hindu faith, giving these beliefs a derivative status, rather than accepting that they are founded on differing world views, and have come into existence after rejecting the dominant practices of the Sanatana Dharmis of the period corresponding to the lives of Gautama Buddha, Mahavir and Guru Nanak.

Undoubtedly, the factor that caused the emergence of parallel faiths in the same terrain as the reach of Hindu belief and practice is still the biggest headache for anyone wanting to stay true to Hinduism. In the twenty-first century, this huge obstacle is the continued reference to caste, at every stage of ritual and prayer. All other religions of the world also face challenges from sceptics and non-believers in the modern era, but no one can be accused of reinforcing injustice and inequality down the ages by those same sceptics and non-believers in the way Hinduism can.

Twenty-first-century India is indeed a time for penance and introspection for the Hindu faith – penance for the way in which our forefathers used religion as a means to justify the oppression of their fellow humans, and introspection about how this can be overcome if we are to keep our faith alive for the future. Today, what is crucial is how we each view the institution of caste, and have it play out in our individual lives, the choices and decisions we make, to either disregard it completely, or silently submit to it. These choices we make as Hindus (and as citizens of a democratic India) will determine whether caste remains a threat to social justice and equality for future generations, or gets relegated to the realm of anachronistic, relatively harmless beliefs that remain as vestiges of our ancestors' identity.

If we take from Shankaracharya just the outline of the scope of Hinduism, without going into the philosophical merits or otherwise of his doctrine of advaita, or non-duality — which holds out the possibility of the human soul or 'atma' being one with the absolute reality of God or Brahma — it is immediately apparent that within the larger faith, it is possible to have distinctly different world views and conceptions of a nurturing God. The six-fold path of worship means different ways of connecting to their own personal God for different sects, with all ways being supported by ample scriptural references, festive occasions in the lunar calendar, and particular ways of worshipping. For instance, a person living in Maharashtra may celebrate Diwali like all other Hindus, but may have Ganesh Chaturthi as his or her main annual focus, pilgrimages to Ganesha temples as family recreational outings, and Ganesha images as the installed deity at home. A person living in Guwahati may consider Kamakhya Devi to be the beginning and end of all his or her religious invocation and prayer. Even daily practices of eating, drinking, housekeeping and child-rearing can be completely different across different communities within the Hindu spectrum, but these do not give cause for grievance or hostility. A Tamilian who worships Shiva and Parvati's son as Murugan happily enjoys Durga Puja celebrations at a Bengali Association pandal without feeling that he or she has abandoned their faith. A Vaishnav family from Gujarat takes the yatra trail to Amarnath or Kedarnath convinced they are only strengthening their faith, not showing dissent with Vishnu. This intermingling of devotion and celebration is actually an accommodation of many different ways of looking at the world. It is what keeps the faith resilient and resistant to a single, totalitarian dogma.

In the 1980s and 1990s, the political right-wing groups in India attempted to replace the multiplicity of Hindu belief and practice with a single-point agenda — a temple for Sri Rama, an incarnation of Vishnu. In the final month of 2012, when the twentieth anniversary of the demolition of the Babri Masjid at Ayodhya came around, it was possible to turn on the television and hear Congress leader Mani Shankar Aiyar challenge Jai Bhagwan Goyal of the Rashtrawadi Shiv Sena about the right-wing claim to being representative of the vast majority of Hindus. But in the months leading up to the events at Ayodhya, or even the riots in Gujarat, the speakers and intellectuals who were coming out to challenge the aims and intentions of the Vishwa Hindu Parishad (VHP), stopped short of speaking as practising Hindus. They were too focused on proving their credentials as secularists, and seemed to subscribe to the regrettable but all-pervading belief among Indian thinkers and intellectuals, that to support secular governance and the rule of law one cannot be seen to have any religion. In this sanitized view of secularism, all who desire justice for all and discrimination against none should ideally be atheists. So lyricist Javed Akhtar speaks out against the divisive politicians of the Kashmir Valley, but emphasizes his atheism. Govind Nihalani makes a film about the Gujarat riots showing two Hindu policemen, one anguished by the communal violence and another complicit with it, but he makes the anguished one (Amitabh Bachchan) express his feelings in the name of the Constitution. He stops short of having the character mention God.

This secular discomfort with the idea of God, and secularism's refusal to engage with the issue of identity in any manner other than outright condemnation created millions of scarred and confused citizens. India, unfortunately or fortunately, continues to be a place where even professed atheists send silent prayers to temples they pass, on the way to their examination halls. It is also a place where people remain attached to the cultural symbols that proclaim they are of one kind or another. Thus issues of faith and identity continue to pose a dilemma to those who grapple daily with what means more to them, being Indian, or being of a certain caste, creed, or region, or, as the Salman-Khan-created brand in films suggest, being human.

And yet, examining how our faith was used to subvert the very values we hold dear, is very important not just for us as individuals, but for the larger social fabric that includes millions of people of very different social and economic status under a religious denomination. How were our own deities used to justify the aggression and violence of mobs? When did Hanuman turn bloodthirsty, or Rama change into an orphaned and homeless entity searching for a home? Can we be comfortable with the politics of grievance?

If there were voices using scriptures and sermons to ask these questions, and pointing out the absurdity of the key propositions of the VHP-sponsored Rama mandir movement for the public in the 1990s, they were insufficient in number, volume and depth to have much impact. Since then, it has mostly been the people themselves, Hindus and Muslims, Christians and Sikhs, who have muddled along with their expressions of faith, sometimes celebrating peace and brotherhood, at other times erupting in murderous clashes. India survived, and faith survived too, in its many different forms, but no credit can be handed out anywhere for this, least of all to those who claim to be above faith, or, in other words, secular.

In an ideal world, the values and morals preached by religion help people to distinguish right from wrong and those actions that bring benefit to all from those that do the opposite. When religious symbols and practices are used to create and justify a culture of grievance, the symbiotic relationship between religion and the social order breaks down, resulting in a travesty of values and ideas we have held dear for centuries.

A lot of us have grown up thinking that Hinduism is an open, tolerant, non-proselytizing faith. For us, 'Hindutva' arrived as a rude wake-up call that we were unable to counter, largely because the very open-ended nature of Hinduism, and the casual nature of our own observance of it, had left none of us feeling confident enough to be authorities on the subject. Politicians had no such reservations or subjective hesitation. They focused on a narrow bandwidth of history and mythology, which gave them room to ascribe present problems to past wrongs and stir the emotional cauldron, so to speak. Unfortunately, with the emergence of Hindutva, some of that tolerance within the larger faith got rubbed off forever. We entered an age of 'hurt sentiments', of some community or other always having cause to complain that perfectly ordinary events and developments were giving it collective heartburn.

When religion turns away from being a support system for social harmony and order into a trigger for social ruptures and chaos, it seems a vindication of those who argue against faith itself, against the tyranny of belief, the U.G Krishnamurtis of the world. But for the vast majority, iconoclastic prose can never replace the sheer poetry of their relationship with God. To me, often returning in my mind to the slogans and symbols of the fanatics of the 1990s, and contrasting them with the ideas of Bhagwanji I had imbibed from my childhood, some things became gradually apparent. I saw the breakdown of the social order to be, ironically, enabled by those very people who most worshipped social order, or at least, held it up as a desired attribute of the deity they worshipped.

The preservation of the status quo, the maintenance of life, the restoring of order and calm is ascribed to Vishnu in the Hindu holy trinity of Brahma, Vishnu and Shiva. An incarnation of Vishnu, Sri Rama, is hailed as Maryada Purushottam, signifying the pinnacle of being human and devoted to maintaining social and moral values. The nature of Vaishavism as it has been practised down the centuries, reinforces a craving for order in its followers. Order and predictability in the real world can best be brought about through the conformity of the majority to a moral code. Thus, Krishna emerged as the incarnation of Vishnu best suited to a pastoral society that needed to care for its cows. Further, elaborate injunctions against the eating of cow meat prevented the pastoral society from losing its much-prized assets.

Definitions of morality, what is 'good' and what is not, what is prescribed and what is proscribed do not reveal themselves in the practice of any of the forms of worship in Shankaracharya's outline, to the extent that they do in the worship of Vishnu. Nor do ideas of hierarchy and supremacy, the concepts of 'lower' and 'higher', and the overarching ideal of *shuchita* or purity.

Through its sheer definition, any idea of purity is put severely to the test, not just in today's world of all-pervading pollution, but by the random nature of life, relentlessly turning out hybrids and alloys through continuous processes of accommodation and assimilation. Because purity is essentially unreal, trying to hold on to it can mean a lifelong struggle for the sturdiest soul. In fact, holding on to purity in one's personal circumstances can mean great hardship and inconvenience for others. Gandhiji's life, otherwise such a fine example of service to suffering humanity, became an example of Vaishnav cruelty when it came to the question of having his ailing wife treated by medicines that had non-vegetarian ingredients — he chose to remain pure, rather than have her cured.

Even the philosophical tenets of Vaishnavism, including the concept of *saranagati* that emphasizes the value of complete surrender to a recognizable God (Vishnu) who is special, are placed on a much higher pedestal than oneself. Typically, those regions where Vaishnavism has more of a hold are also places with well-defined rituals for daily practice and the dos and don'ts around them. They also have a plethora of superstitions that have grown around the main faith, thriving in the minds of people who are used to practising conformity to rules and surrender to a higher power as part of their daily routine.

Gujarat, like Mathura–Brindavan in UP, is a region where Vaishnav practice has included 'guru' figures for families and communities. These travelling personalities, who are hosted by their followers in their homes, have served as counsellors, guides and mentors for people plagued by business worries or emotional discontent for many generations. Sometimes, they have been used to deliver powerful messages for the common good, like Shyamji Antala's ideas of creating small watersheds for irrigation in parched Saurashtra during the late 1980s, which were endorsed by many such guru figures. At other times, they still represent an outside authority from which followers receive an interpretation of religious truths. In societies where such practices become well established, adherence to the edicts of an outside guru and conformity with the rituals of belief becomes the parameter for deciding who is 'good' and 'moral'.

A culture where individual takes on God and spirituality are considered inferior to, or deviant, from the prevailing norms, lends itself more easily to ideas that require a collective falling in line. Ideas of regional pride, or moral and religious supremacy find willing followers in such a culture that seeks an endorsement of its dominant beliefs and practices by its members. *Asmita* (self-respect) and *garv* (pride) in belonging to a denomination or region are such endorsements.

I digress so much on the question of Vaishnav practice, and its endorsements of concepts of purity and supremacy, because it is the one factor that prevents me from saying out aloud with any garv that I am a Hindu. Nearly all the prayers I say each day are by Goswami Tulsidas, the most beloved of all the names of God to me is Rama (even though this book is about Shiva!) and there are some passages of the *Ramcharitmanas* I can never read or hear without being deeply moved, be it several times in a day. And yet, I cannot accept religious sanctions for any hierarchy among humans, or submit to the authority of those who have appointed themselves as interpreters of religious texts, and even acquired acceptance as gurus. A first-hand encounter with a couple of them in the dying months of 2012 reinforced for me all my deep distrust of Vaishnav preachers and preaching.

I met these interpreters at a friend's home in 2012. She holds a senior position in government service. Her personal acquaintance with tragedy and loss made my friend seek spiritual answers from the Bhagavadgita, through the guidance of a lady she deeply admired, and a gentleman who holds a weekly Gita class not far from her home. In the manner of friends, I discussed the ups and downs of life with her and what attempts I was making to deal with any emotional or material crisis I was facing. At such times, she often said, 'Scharada, I think you should forget all this and turn to spirituality. Become more spiritual.' I always felt disturbed by these urgings, because in my own mind and heart, I have been living a life enriched by spirituality for twenty years and more! 'Something is wrong if she is unable to see how much you derive from your connection with God,' I would say to myself. 'Am I really a bad person who seems mired in materialism, or has she been exposed to completely different definitions of spirituality?' I asked myself at other times.

I understood what my friend meant when I found out that *sadhana* or the effort for spiritual advancement had been defined for her as doing numerical rounds on the *tulsi mala* of the *mahamantra* '*Hare Krishna, Hare Krishna, Krishna Krishna, Hare Hare. Hare Ram, Hare Ram, Ram Ram, Hare Hare*' every day. This is what she was being taught by the lady she looked up to, that her spiritual bank balance was growing in direct proportion to the rounds of beads she had completed. I did not find this in itself a unique or outlandish concept. Many sects encourage such daily targets. Even a new age faith like Nichiren Daishonin's Buddhism encourages *daimoku*, the chanting of 'Nam-myo-ho-renge-kyo' in abundance if one is to improve life's quality. I accepted my friend's attachment to prayer beads and her Gita classes as perfectly legitimate endeavours in a larger spiritual quest. However, all such efforts, for me, have always come with a rider. If the chanting and praying is accompanied by more mundane efforts of maintaining a positive outlook, acceptance of people and circumstances rather than always seeking to apportion blame, it invariably results in great good. When people confine themselves to the textbook sadhana, and don't make any other attempt to address their ideas or emotions, there is a definite danger of becoming self-righteous and judgemental.

When I attended a few of the Gita classes, I had a chance to observe the messages emanating from them myself. I found the teacher's exaggerated claims on behalf of Hinduism embarrassing. According to this person, every form of faith in the whole world was nothing but a distortion of the one, the true belief, that of Sanatana Dharma. In my growing-up years, some of the most moving and enjoyable reading I had done was of the beliefs and mythologies of different civilizations, through seminal works like James George Frazer's *The Golden Bough*, or Joseph Campbell's *Hero With a Thousand Faces*. The ways in which God has been depicted by people at different times and places weave a rich tapestry of the human heart and imagination. Why would anyone want to reduce it to a blueprint of Sanatana Dharma one-upmanship? And suppose it were to be asserted, and even proved that all belief in a Higher Power for all of humanity, did emanate from the Indian subcontinent alone, what is the value of such an assertion, except to make us smug in an imagined superiority while the rest of the world races ahead to fresh realizations and understanding?

The profound poetry of how God has been perceived across cultures and peoples of the world can be seen in all of Joseph Campbell's work, and here's an example:

'...a great divinity of prehistoric Peru, named Viracocha. His tiara is the sun; he grasps a thunderbolt in either hand; and from his eyes descend, in the form of tears, the rains that refresh the life of the valleys of the world. Viracocha is the Universal God, the creator of all things; and yet, in the legends of his appearances upon the earth, he is shown wandering as a beggar, in rags and reviled…

…But the most extraordinary and profoundly moving of the traits of Viracocha, this nobly conceived Peruvian rendition of the universal god, is the detail that is peculiarly his own, namely that of the tears. The living waters are the tears of God. Herewith the world-discrediting insight of the monk, "All life is sorrowful", is combined with the life-begetting affirmative of the father, "Life must be!" in full awareness of the life anguish of the creatures of his hand, in full consciousness of the roaring wilderness of pains, the brain-splitting fires of the deluded, self-ravaging, lustful, angry universe of his creation, this divinity acquiesces in the deed of supplying life to life.' (Joseph Campbell, *Hero With a Thousand Faces*, New World Library, 2008)

Is there any dividend to be gained by a modern-day Hindu from proclaiming that Viracocha is actually a form of Shiva, or Vishnu, or even Indra (from the thunderbolts he carries)? I did not see the least advantage from the claims of the Gita class teacher for my own Hinduness.

But this was still bearable, when compared with his extreme inferiority complex at not having been born a Brahmin, and his cringe-worthy comments on the innate superiority of Brahmins. I truly cringed, not because I felt guilty to have been born a Brahmin in such circumstances, but because the Bhagavadgita was being used, chapter and verse, to reinforce ideas of hierarchy and supremacy. It was only out of a sense of loyalty to a dear friend that I did not create any disturbance in the Gita class before other middle-aged, educated, upper-middle-class listeners.

The final assault on my equanimity came at an exclusive session with the lady whom my friend looked up to as her guru. The lady had turned to the Bhagavadgita while she was still in service as an officer of the Indian Administrative Service, and she had completely immersed herself in studying and writing about it after her retirement and widowhood. Her husband was also an IAS officer. The gentleman who conducted the weekly Gita class was present at this session, as were two young girls and their widowed mother, and my friend's sister, who is herself a senior officer in government service.

It was many years ago that I read Dr S Radhakrishnan's translation of the Bhagavadgita. Although it left a powerful impression on me at the time, I can neither claim to have developed a special attraction for it, nor do I feel I am missing something only because I do not read it daily or weekly, or even yearly. My most enduring impression of the Bhagavadgita is still in trying to decipher the difficult Sanskrit slokas, sitting with my brother and cousins in a row, after my bath, at my paternal grandfather's house in Jabalpur. I, therefore, listened to the lady expounding on the importance of yagna with a fair bit of detachment.

What shattered my calm, however, was the lady saying something about the true role of women, which was as protectors of 'dharma'. 'What is this? Does this absolve men of responsibility towards dharma, then?' I was mentally asking myself when the weekly class gentleman jumped in. 'How brave you are to be saying this!' he applauded the retired bureaucrat. 'When I say such things, people disagree with me, including, I am sorry to say, my own wife! It takes a Brahmin to understand the fineness of such things.' (The lady is a Brahmin by marriage and a Kshatriya by birth.) She accepted his homage as her due, but felt honour-bound to clarify her acquired Brahmin status. He conceded that this was perfectly acceptable, and bestowed her with the qualifications for possessing *gyan* (knowledge).

I was, naturally, not only uncomfortable even revolted, by this exchange. There was more. The lady, warming to his appreciation, finally revealed that she had only two regrets in life — one, giving too much importance to Western culture, and two, leaving the home to go out and work. After taking up the Gita, she had realized that she should have fulfilled her true role at home.

I was dumbstruck by these revelations. The widow, mother of the young girls, who was seeking husbands for both her young daughters, began to laugh in an embarrassed manner. She has always been very proud of her younger daughter working with a well-known IT firm in the US. That girl, home for the holidays, and listening to this, looked stunned too. Her mother said, ruefully, as if explaining herself to the Gita expert, and taking responsibility for sending her daughter out of the home, 'I was the one who told her it was a good job…' All the other women present, senior bureaucrats themselves, said nothing, and I didn't either, although I was seething with a most unholy rage.

The previous evening, I had addressed a group of semi-urban and rural women, many of them Dalits, who bring out the award-winning newspaper *Khabar Leheriya* in the Bundelkhand region of UP, and have launched editions in Faizabad and Ambedkarnagar. Leaving the confines of the home to articulate the concerns of their people, and being able to take on the role of journalists who are looked up to with respect by their peers, is precious for these women. In the short interaction I had with them, I had tried to use incidents from my own life as examples to show them that they need never feel alone or afraid. Their overwhelming and affectionate response was still very fresh in my mind.

In complete contrast to their transparent pride in their empowerment, I was now faced with the self-confessed regret of a woman with an empowered status. A woman who had been born into privilege, who had spent over two decades in government service that provided her with money and prestige and the power to affect lives far beyond her own family, was saying that she should have been content guarding dharma from the confines of her home instead. Her regret about not having fulfilled her 'dharma-protecting' role seem very fake to me. In terms which are very understandable to the man or woman on the street, this seemed a clear example of the adage '*Sau sau choohe kha kar billi Haj ko chali*' (After killing and eating hundreds of mice, the cat went piously to Mecca).

Such are the interpreters of religion who find acceptance among many in the upper middle classes, seeking to reconnect with their roots and find the spiritual path. I had found this encounter so upsetting because it was very difficult to reconcile with my own understanding of human potential and the true yagna we perform for God with our own lives. I thought of the large-scale operations of similar preachers from all faiths worldwide, and was momentarily frightened by the harm they can do. In this little gathering, the *gyani* lady had pushed the girls and their mother into a defensive mode about their own aspirations. How much more troubling could be the sermons and injunctions of the gurus classifying all meat-eaters as *adharmi* (opposed to the path of faith), inter-caste marriages as being opposed to our *Vedas*, *Puranas* and other such hypocrisies. When religion is used to invalidate what we have ourselves understood about life, from our observations and our experience of fellow humans, it becomes suspect. Fortunately, God often intervenes to thwart the designs of these preachers, through a device known throughout the world as 'common sense'.

This is the reason why I place such a premium on the insights of Mithai Lal, and the image of Shiva as the mad one who roams the streets of Varanasi and any other place he fancies (not unlike the Peruvian Viracocha). The deadbeat, the dropout, the devout and the domestic – all have a place in Varanasi and all feel validated by Vishwanath himself, the ruler of the universe. The so-called morality and the self-serving piousness of the preachers of the Gita I've described vanish into nothingness when you consider that Unmattavesha, with his russet locks and pink-tinged eyes, his broad chest and his half-smile does not ask for even the price of saranagati when he says to the lowliest, the poorest, the crooked and the virtuous alike:

'Live! And do not fear Death. For when you die, you come to Me.'

Chapter 3: Vyaghrakomala
(*He Who is Tender to the Tiger*)

It was only a 16-kilometre ride to the temple of Jageshwarnath from the town of Damoh, but the poor condition of the roads made it seem much longer. What made the bumps and dips seem none too important, however, was the glorious view of the full moon rising. There it was, a large, luminescent orb, the bottom half pale orange and the upper half lightening to a creamy yellow. It was impossible to ignore, absolutely straight ahead of us as it was and quite low on the horizon, so that it appeared as if the car would drive straight up to it at some point. Even the scarred and pitted road was redeemed by its rays, appearing like a silvery path in patches. On both sides of the road, the flat, empty fields shimmered, reflecting the light of the moon.

I visited my paternal aunt and her large family in Damoh, 100 kilometres away from Jabalpur (Madhya Pradesh) in the summer of 2000, on my way back from Varanasi to Chennai. No visit to Damoh is complete without going to the temple of Jageshwarnath in Bandakpur, a Shiva temple dating back to the seventeenth century when it was built by one of the Maratha rulers in this region. Witty repartee was being exchanged among my cousins in the car about the state of the roads, and my nephews and niece were being teased by all of us — we were a happy bunch, enjoying even the dust and cowdung-scented air.

Arriving at the temple, I saw it was a modest but pretty whitewashed structure set inside a courtyard. Outside the temple bustled a typical village marketplace offering puja paraphernalia, refreshments, plastic toys and other attractions for travelling familes. The people milling around were all unmistakably rustic, men dressed in long white shirts and white dhotis, women wearing bright sarees drawn over their heads in ghunghats, children with dusty brown hair that glowed golden in the bright light of the shops. It was the kind of place where I can be completely, effortlessly happy.

The Shivalinga at Bandakpur is a large, smooth stone encircled by sculpted snake coils that reach up to form a large cobra hood. It was almost my height when I went to touch its cool surface, and I came away with an enduring impression of its size. It was after I emerged from the temple's sanctum, a white-washed room, that I heard the story of the temple from my cousin, Alok, the eldest son of my aunt. Apparently, the Shivalinga was considered 'live' for a couple of centuries because it kept growing every year. After being installed as a small stone, it was found that every year, during the annual festival when the priests went to dress the Shivalinga in a dhoti and garlands made to the measurements of the previous year, they always fell short! Also, old-timers who visited the temple after a gap of several years always seemed surprised to find the Shivalinga bigger than they remembered it. The legend of the temple grew and spread.

In order to contain the ever-growing Jageshwar Shivalinga, concerned elders and priests got together to consider what could be done. Finally, a long silver nail was hammered into the stone to the accompaniment of special prayers and mantras. Jageshwarnath has since remained the same size, but is still big enough to strike wonder in a newcomer to the temple with its size, just as it had done for me.

On the white-washed walls of the sanctum, the practice of giving thanks for hopes and prayers that have been answered finds a visual form. When people arrive, to ask for a wish to be granted, they dip their hands in red sindoor water or the oily *alta* (a liquid used to decorate hands and feet on festive occasions) and make an impression of both their palms pointing downwards on the white wall. After their prayers have been answered, they return to repeat the process, this time with palms pointing upwards. I stood and mused for a while in front of the wall with rows and rows of red palm imprints. Sometimes, in considering the idea of God in an abstract sense, one misses completely the sheer intimacy that millions share with their own, personal god. The Bandakpur wall, the threads tied to the filigree walls of the dargah of Salim Chishti at Fatehpur Sikri, the rows and rows of candles at the Mahim church, all these are visible evidence of the fact that for so many, someone, somewhere, seems to be listening, even if His existence is a matter of discussion, debate and outright denial for others.

Outside, the campus of the temple holds another shrine of Shiva's consort, Durga. This is separated from the main shrine by several yards, but not too far away, either. Both the room that houses Jageshwarnath, and the temple of Devi, have beautiful *shikharas*, spires bearing long poles topped with saffron and red pennants that reach up towards the sky. Similar pennants can be seen fluttering from temples all across the country. At some, like the Jagannath temple at Puri, the long strands of the gold and saffron pennants waving in the sea breeze are gathered by devotees after they are taken down. Here at Bandakpur, the pennants offer a reminder that the true miracle of this place is not confined to the ever-growing nature of Jageshwarnath. In fact, the miracle relates to the devotion of pilgrims to the wonder of their faith.

Every year, during the festive period of Mahashivaratri in February or March, lakhs of pilgrims arrive at Bandakpur from rural areas in Damoh as well as neighbouring districts like Jabalpur, Chhatarpur, Sagar, Katni and Tikamgarh. These devotees carry water from the Narmada, and smaller rivers like the Byarma, Sunar, Kopra and Gourayia to pour over their beloved Jageshwar in the manner of their kaanwariya brothers from elsewhere in India. Old-timers relate that when ten lakh devotees have completed their kaanwar offerings, the flags atop the two temple domes bend forward and meet across the corridor that separates them.

As I squinted up at the pennants that summer evening, they looked rather aloof on their spires. It is only the collective devotion of so many lakhs of people that makes them bend. It is unlikely that I will ever see this spectacle — but just hearing about it was reassuring, in a strange sort of way. We spent about an hour in the temple. A crowd of several families, with children running about at top speed, chattering women with their heads covered and men huddled together, listened to a group of singers accompanied by the harmonium, dholak, manjira, chimta and other folk instruments. I listened to them for some time, enjoying the energy of the constantly moving scene. We washed our faces, hands and feet at a well with whitewashed sides, from where I saw a long shed which was dark, except for a part of its floor, which was glowing with embers.

'What is this?' I asked Alok.

'The place where the sadhus sit and meditate. That is their *dhuni* or ritual of penance,' said Alok. It was April, and the evening air was dry and hot. Sitting near a fire in that temperature was indeed a form of penance for the sadhus, I thought.

I could have spent a lot more time at Bandakpur, but my aunt was getting worried about her grandchildren needing to eat and sleep. When I was turning back to look longingly at the temple from the marketplace outside, she gave me her crinkly-eyed smile, and said, 'Don't worry, Scharada. We have more attractions chalked out for you later tonight.'

'Really, Bua?' I asked, wondering what had been planned in the night life of quiet Damoh.

While the children were given their dinner and put to sleep, I sat on a swing in the verandah and spent a quiet hour with my cousin Alok. He is a gentle farmer whom people often recognize and greet on the streets of Damoh town. 'I wish I could come here one time during Shivaratri,' I said to him. 'If it weren't so far from Chennai, I would come much more often.'

'What would you like to do, carry kaanwar like the village women?' asked Alok, only half teasing.

'Why not?' I said. 'I would love it. It wouldn't be a lonely practice either, would it? There would be thousands of people for company!'

He smiled and agreed. 'The village women travel in groups from their villages,' he said. 'And as they walk, they sing two-line poems for Shankarji, known locally as *bambuliyan*. They sound very sweet-voiced, and seem to be happy carrying their kaanwar water.'

'Hmmm…' I pondered. 'Seems like I have narrowly escaped being a bambuliyan singer or poet in this lifetime. Why don't you give me some lessons for my next one?'

And that is how Alok began to sing the kaanwar women's songs to Shiva. In his strong, untutored, but surprisingly musical voice, he sang,

'Mahadeo babba aise to mile, Mahadeo babba aise to mile
Aise to mile re, jaise mil gayin mahtaari aur baap ho!
Mahadeo babba, ho.'

(Mahadev baba, oh, how he met us! He met us as if we were meeting our own mother and father!)

'Ittar ki do do shishiyan, Ittar ki do do shishiyan
Do do shishiyan re ek sandhya chadhayen ek bhor ho!
Ittar ki do, ho.'

(Two bottles of perfume do I have. One to offer in the evening, and one in the morning.)

'Narbada ji ki murkan mein, Narbada ji ki murkan mein
Murkan mein re jaise Gaura phairaaye kaare kes, ho!
Narbada maiya, ho.'

(In the twists and pools of the river Narmada, it is as if Parvati is spreading her long black hair.)
And finally, the lines with the most telling social comment,
> '*Daras ki to bera bhayi, daras ki to bera bhayi*
> *Bera bhayi re, pat khole nahin panda beimaan, ho!*
> *Daras ki to, ho.*'

(It's time for darshan, oh, it's time! But though it's time, the mean priest still keeps the door locked!)

These are the songs of people who live their entire lives far removed from the city lights and facilities that spell home to us. Mud walls strengthened by cowdung, the seasonal rhythms of summer, winter, rain, crops and animals to be tended, this is the canvas against which these singers live their lives. I listened to Alok singing and saw the groups of women in my mind's eye, balancing their kaanwar pots, and sharing the pain and joys of their existence between the singing of bambuliyan and laughter. For surely, when you journey together with your peers, there must be much to be happy about.

What else brings joy to our villages and those who live in them? In 2012, after hearing about farmer suicides in various regions of the country for nearly a decade, and after a series of exposés had revealed the completely corrupt and cynical way in which natural resources that belonged to the people had been sold to vested interests in the country and abroad, it was natural to wonder — have sixty-five-plus years of democracy left God as the only refuge for our deprived rural population?

I was in a mellow mood after my introduction to the kaanwar songs, but the evening was far from over. My aunt finally appeared in the verandah where we were sitting, ready to accompany us to the next part of our evening – the treat she had hinted at in the marketplace at Bandakpur. 'Come now, get ready to leave,' she told me. And I wondered where we could be going in Damoh at the ripe hour of 10 p.m.

The promised attraction truly lived up to its billing. It was a *rut-jugaa* of a *satsang* and *naam-jap* (a whole night of community prayer songs and chanting) at the home of Rajiv Nayan Dikshit, a local advocate who hosted such events every month, on the night of the full moon. We arrived to be greeted with respectful namastes and were taken inside, from where we could see a hall in which a large altar had been set up with pictures of Sri Rama, Shiva, Devi, Krishna and other deities. Bhajans were being sung, and senior Congressman and former Union Minister, the late Vidya Charan Shukla, was eagerly awaited. Knowing that he often passed through Damoh on the way to his guru's ashram, Dikshit had invited him to his monthly rut-jugaa.

Dispassionately, I watched the spectacle of Shukla's arrival, how he was greeted with deference, then given the privilege of leading the aarti and finally, was seen off with equal ceremony. The whole episode gave me the opportunity to speculate on the political aspirations of the young advocate who was our host. In this, I was assisted by some pithy comments from Asha, Alok's sister, which almost made me break out in a hysterical fit of giggles. Luckily, the bhajans and the aarti were completed without me disgracing myself with such mirth. Then I went into the kitchen to find women at work rolling out *puris* and making huge amounts of *sabji* and *halwa*. They looked up at me from where they were working, shyly refusing my offers of help, looking a little bemused that I had asked at all. 'Good for the men to be getting spiritual with the satsang,' I thought to myself. 'After all, it's the women who do all the work and enable them to aspire to a higher plane!'

Such were my thoughts as I took in the rut-jugaa scene.

I returned to sit next to my aunt and Asha, this time outside in the hall. It was then that a person arrived – the man who would puncture my superior, urban, sneering way of thinking with effortless ease.

The first impression I had was that he was a hardworking man from a local government office. A thin, grey-haired man of indeterminate age, dressed in a shirt and pants, with a handkerchief tucked into the back of his collar to prevent the sweat from ruining it, he could have been somebody who just wandered out of the Damoh municipality office. He held a small cloth bag too, reinforcing the completely ordinary image. He sat down for a few minutes in the hall, close to where we were all sitting on the dhurrie-covered floor.

The aarti had represented the culmination of the song cycle of the rut-jugaa. After that, the crowd began singing the mahamantra 'Hare Ram, Hare Ram, Ram Ram, Hare Hare, Hare Krishna, Hare Krishna, Krishna Krishna, Hare Hare' and would do so till morning. Men took turns to take the lead, beginning with a slow tempo, then gathering momentum to chant faster and faster, till, after reaching a crescendo, someone else took up the chant, and began once more with a slow rhythm. A harmonium, several pairs of brass manjiras, even a dholak player, all kept time to the *mantra-jaap* (chanting of the mantra). The man who had arrived a few minutes ago, put his hands in his bag and took out a cloth bundle, placing it on the floor next to him. Then he stood up and took off his shirt.

I looked at Asha, surprised. What was he up to? She also noticed him taking off his shirt and turned to whisper to her mother. 'Is this him?' My aunt nodded, as if to say, 'Yes, he is.' I was intrigued. Folding his shirt with great care, the man then tied a white dhoti round his waist, calmly removed his pants under the cover of the dhoti, folded it and placed it near the shirt. He then sat down in his vest and dhoti, and opened the white cloth bundle — it contained long strings of *ghungroos*, the metal bells that are tied to the feet of dancers. Slowly, intently, he began tying the ghungroo strings on one ankle, till the small bells covered it right up to his shin. He closed his eyes, and folded his hands, listening to the 'Hare Ram' chant for a minute.

Then he got up, and began swaying to the chant, sometimes tapping the foot covered with ghungroos to give it an added rhythm, sometimes quietening his movements to keep up with the slow and deliberate chant. 'Who is he, Bua?' I asked my aunt. My curiosity was completely aroused by this man's calm, self-possessed antics.

'He is someone who comes here every month,' said my aunt. 'He stands up like this after wearing his ghungroos, and then sits down again only when it is morning, and the rut-jugaa has ended. He doesn't take a single break for the whole duration.'

I looked with renewed interest at the man. Was he going to be dancing all night to the mahamantra? It certainly seemed so. He had a definite method in his dancing. For 'Hare Krishna' he would begin to balance on one leg and make a gesture with his hands as if he was holding a flute to his lips. For 'Hare Rama' he would make a sweeping, vertical gesture with his right hand, as if he was holding a bow on his shoulder and running his hand along its string. At other times, he would keep his eyes closed, swaying to some memory or image in his mind, his ghungroo-covered foot tapping a constant reminder of his presence. When the beat became faster, the pace of his movements turned much quicker too, matching the beat. With the chanting crescendo came the quickened movement of his feet, just like a Kathak dancer's.

Completely fascinated, I continued gazing at this man, whose name was never told to me, as no one around me knew what it was. I felt completely humbled. Far away from anyone who could sing paeans of praise about his bhakt, this devotee just flowed along with the waves of his single-minded passion for God, not caring about who saw him or what they thought.

The outside world just melted away for him, leaving only the sheer delight of hearing the divine name. Recalling my value judgements of the rural satsang earlier in the evening, I felt ashamed. How was one to judge this affirmation of faith? It was a madness — the madness of a supremely self-sufficient individual who was one with his God. There was not a single citified, superior evaluation I could think of for this madness, which was mesmerizing for an onlooker.

This then, was my glimpse of the nightlife of the small town of Damoh, in the state of Madhya Pradesh, in April 2000.

*   *   *   *   *   *   *

Some passages in Goswami Tulsidas' *Ramcharitmanas* describe how after the day's battle, Sri Rama cast a compassionate look on the army of monkeys and bears that had set out to assist him in his mission to reclaim Sita from Ravana, the king of Lanka. It was by the grace of this look alone that the animals felt refreshed and regained their energy to fight another day. I like these passages because for me the idea of God is tied up to all His creatures, not just to the species proved most murderous time and again — *homo sapiens.*

All living beings, it is said, have a spark of the divine and the presence of this divinity is celebrated across religions. Consider the poet Gerard Manley Hopkins (1844–89), who contrasted the sullied world that man has created with the regenerative one that is God's.

God's Grandeur

The world is charged with the grandeur of God.
It will flame out, like shining from shook foil;
It gathers to a greatness, like the ooze of oil
Crushed. Why do men then now not reck his rod?
Generations have trod, have trod, have trod;

> *And all is seared with trade; bleared, smeared with toil;*
> *And wears man's smudge and shares man's smell: the soil*
> *Is bare now, nor can foot feel, being shod.*
> *And for all this, nature is never spent;*
> *There lives the dearest freshness deep down things;*
> *And though the last lights off the black West went*
> *Oh, morning, at the brown brink eastward, springs –*
> *Because the Holy Ghost over the bent*
> *World broods with warm breast and with ah! bright wings.*

— *Gerard Manley Hopkins*

Belief in the regenerative power of nature and the environment is not confined to those who believe in God, but substantiated by the findings of science. What causes so much anxiety for us in times far removed from Hopkins' is the evidence piling up to show that we have done irreparable harm to our planet, and the natural processes that have helped to sustain us. For us, a large part of our existential angst is undoubtedly the distance we feel from our own roots, the missing connection with the earth. Many individuals and groups across the world seek meaning in their lives through trying to change the definition of 'development' — not as an inevitable process of raping natural resources, but adapting lifestyles and products to keep it sustainable.

In our country and society, those who have the least share of the fruits of development often have to pay the highest price for the environmental degradation it results in. This is not to be wondered at, because disrespect for any form of life will ultimately lead to disrespect for human dignity and rights too, as has proved to be true in the case of many development projects backed by both government and private corporate interests. Opposition to the exploitation of natural resources has spread across the spectrum from Maoists to NGOs and civil rights groups, campus protests and columnists in magazines. But this has not prevented the complete marginalization of millions of rural Indians, who do not reap the benefits of development, from the very sensibility of our nation.

In my childhood, mainstream Hindi cinema often depicted the lives of villagers and farmers of our then newly independent India. Moneylenders were easily identifiable villains, the greed of contractors and their avaricious eyes on natural resources, were themes we were familiar with. Today's children and young adults are growing up in the grey area that we have become accustomed to for a long time now — where success is respected, however it has been achieved, and 'competition' is the bogey with which parents scare their children into submission. For nearly three decades after the early 1970s, urban characters and stories have dominated the big screen, and for a few years, it seemed as if London and Switzerland would become a lot more familiar to children growing up in the cities than districts they had never visited, nor would visit, such as Surguja or Koraput, Banda or Srikakulam.

To the millions of people who have literally fallen off the map for their urban cousins, Shiva is an elemental deity worshipped in the simplest and most basic of ways. His wild, untamed manifestation resonates strongly with their own closeness to the features and forces of nature, and his abundant compassion extends not just to them, but to their occasional nemesis, the tiger as well. Shiva as Vyaghrakomala is not a selective conservationist who seeks to protect animals within a reserve where wood-gathering villagers are not welcome. Neither is he the development deity who seeks to flatten forest and field alike for gleaming new factories.

*   *   *   *   *   *   *

Vyaghrakomala — he who is tender to the tiger — can be worshipped in any village, as a simple stone under a tree.

In the weeks before Mahashivaratri on 23 February 2009, I had been following the story of a tiger that had strayed away from the forests around Pilibhit, in the state of UP, on 11 November 2008 and entered inhabited areas where it somehow evaded officials of the Forest Department for over three months. Making a kill of a domestic animal every few days or so, it covered an immense distance, coming very close to Lucknow, then retreating via neighbouring Barabanki to a forest patch near Faizabad, at Kumarganj.

I then lived in Faizabad, the twin town of Ayodhya on the banks of the Sarayu river, and every morning, the first thing I did was to check the papers to see whether the tiger had lived another day — for the UP Forest Department was following it only to shoot it down. They apparently lacked the skills to capture it alive, and it showed remarkable intuition in the way it evaded them. Unable to kill the tiger themselves, the Forest Department had enlisted the services of a Hyderabadi Nawab, someone who was fond of the sport of shikar and had a personal arsenal of several licensed rifles.

Waking up on Mahashivaratri morning in an exceptionally good mood, I was humming 'Jai Ho' from A.R. Rahman's track for *Slumdog Millionnaire* as I drove my mother-in-law, quiet brother-in-law Raju (whose functions have been impaired by a brain tumour in adolescence), a friend and his wife and child to the Shiv Baba Mandir at Akbarpur, now Ambedkarnagar, around 70 kilometres away from Faizabad. The air was crisp, with just that hint of approaching spring and summer.

Akbarpur town is close to the village where my guru Neeb Karori Baba was born, which was why I was keen to go there, although we were not headed for the temple built in his memory in 2001, but the Shiv Baba temple. It is a little distance from the town itself, around 5 or 6 kilometres closer to Faizabad. Small groups of brightly dressed pedestrians, perhaps headed for a rural fair, walked on the side of the highway, several kilometres before we reached the place.

The large, open field around the Shiv Baba temple was laid out with the tents of hundreds of little shops. I parked the car and we plunged into a typical mela. Shiv Baba here refers to the ascetic Brahm Shiromani Shiv Baba Maharajji who is said to have sat at the very same spot during his prayers and meditation. I had no idea if this holy person had lived here, because no one knew. Everyone was intent on making their offerings, shopping, eating a little, or resting after their darshan.

A large banyan tree was the focus of all the devotees. In front of the tree was a long bamboo railing with hundreds of brass bells of all sizes hanging from it, interspersed with the small ribbons of red cloth trimmed with gold threads that are typically offered at Devi temples in north India. I found the ones being sold here inscribed with the salutation 'Jai Shiv Baba' along their length. The air was heavy with the smoke of incense.

Negotiating the crowd carefully with my elderly mother-in-law and slightly disabled brother-in-law, I climbed the raised platform around the base of the ancient banyan tree. People were walking around in a *parikrama* around the tree, with a massive heap of flowers, leaves and the round fruit of *babool*, sporting green porcupine spines, around the base. I began walking, thinking we would also complete a parikrama, and then enter the temple. But there was no temple – and no priests either. Somewhere, under those heaps of flowers and bilva leaves, the sweet, bubbled rounds of *batasha* (a form of sugar dried in round shapes after being liquefied) offered for prasad, the incense sticks and the hundreds of red-and-gold ribbon tributes were the stone *saligrams* meant to denote Shiva – smooth spherical rocks gathered from riverbeds and worshipped in homes and temples as Shivalingas – visible during ordinary days. On that festival day, even these were completely submerged under the sheer weight of the devotees' offerings.

I paused and took in the completely crowded scene, trying to adjust to the fact that this tree was the Shiv Baba temple; there was no structure or building beyond it. I watched people praying at the sides, some tying bells, some ritually pouring water over the heap of flowers and leaves in the centre, just as they would over a Shivalinga, some lighting incense, others gingerly stepping onto the slushy, slippery floor of the raised platform around the base of the banyan tree. 'Surrender,' an inner voice told me, 'Why does it have to be a temple with four walls just because you drove over 50 kilometres to come here? Surely you should know by now that faith is not about the form, but the content. Stop struggling to accept a place of worship that is contrary to what you are used to and stop trying to measure whether it is up to standards you are accustomed to! Think whether you are up to the standard of these people's devotion instead.'

After five minutes of such contemplation, I began to feel completely comfortable — and comforted — in the open-air shrine, where no priest was intoning mantras or regulating worship — there were just hundreds and hundreds of fellow devotees to join in with.

On our way back from this rustic shrine we stopped at a cane-crusher's small wayside unit and watched the dark cane juice cascade down into waiting vats. We also bought fresh *gur* (cane sugar). It seemed the perfect ending to our day.

The next morning, the newspapers reported that the tiger at Kumarganj had been shot by the Hyderabadi Nawab. As I read the news, tears welling up in my eyes, I read the most horrifying detail — the 'tiger' had actually been a tigress. The UP Forest Department, on her trail for months, could not establish even such an elementary fact.

I was so completely devastated by this tigress' death that my own emotions shocked me. I cried inconsolably, feeling that I had been so happy that day — on Mahashivaratri — when the tigress was being killed. I was anguished for weeks, and temporarily distanced from Vyaghrakomala too. What was the point of a God who could not or would not save his creatures? I felt engulfed in an ocean of ignorance, stupidity and cruelty and it appeared that no divine wand would be waved to counter these human failings — at least, not in my lifetime. Accounts of the Hyderabadi Nawab in the local papers, including the awe he felt for the magnificent beast as he pulled the trigger, seemed to make things worse. I was bawling, bereft in a way it was hard to believe a fifty-year-old woman could be, from something not immediately affecting her.

Or so it seemed. As the months of 2009 wore on, it became gradually clear to me that my tears had been as much for the consequences of my own displacement, from the gentle and predictable surroundings of a southern city, to the bleak and brutal landscape of small-town UP. My divorce after twenty-two years of marriage had meant leaving a safe and stable world, and with my remarriage in a vastly different setting, I seemed to have entered a starkly new world without the comforting presence of my friends. That same year, I contracted a virulent attack of typhoid, then had to stop teaching a class of rag-picker children I had begun at my home, because I was diagnosed with pleurisy, the beginning stage of tuberculosis. For a time, in November 2009, I used to stare at the ceiling from my bed and feel sure I was going to die soon.

It took me nearly a year to understand how my tears for the tigress had actually been about my own mortality. In a sense, I might have understood sooner if I had gone back once more to the words of Hopkins, a devout Jesuit and an unfailingly honest poet. This poem, written to a young child crying over falling leaves, may as well have been addressed to me when I was grieving over the tigress:

Spring and Fall

To a Young Child

Margaret, are you grieving
Over Goldengrove unleaving?
Leaves, like the things of man, you
With your fresh thoughts care for, can you?
Ah! as the heart grows older
It will come to such sights colder
By and by, nor spare a sigh
Though worlds of wanwood leafmeal lie;
And yet you will weep and know why.
Now no matter, child, the name:
Sorrow's springs are the same.
Nor mouth had, no nor mind, expressed
What heart heard of, ghost guessed:
It is the blight man was born for,
It is Margaret you mourn for.

—Gerard Manley Hopkins

There are a billion reasons why people pray to a Higher Power. But sometimes, one prays to God only to make it easier to guard one's own innocence. As the world repeatedly shows increasingly ugly and dangerous evidence of cruelty and neglect, leading to a loss of hope, it is to God that people turn with a kind of desperation, asking, 'Make something happen for me to believe in kindness, the power of nature to overcome assault and renew itself. Like the happiness and exuberance of children — give me some reason to hope!' In that dark period of 2009, I was praying exactly like that, and my tears for the tiger were actually a manifestation of anxiety that Vyaghrakomala himself had been wounded, that I would never find inspiration from him to regain hope.

I did receive my answers, as always, not immediately and dramatically, but through slow but unmistakable changes that led to me recovering strength, hope and courage. Along the way, I learnt that a certain loss of innocence is inevitable in the onward march of life. But if you stay committed to guard it fiercely, there are definite dividends. Slowly, surely, the lost innocence is replaced by something even more precious – the dawning of wisdom.

*   *   *   *   *   *   *

Mahashivaratri in 2012, which fell on 20 February, saw me driving again to a Shiva temple, the Lodheshwar Mahadev temple at the village of Mahadeva in the Ram Nagar tehsil of Barabanki, Lucknow's neighbouring district. This time I was accompanied by my friend and his family, and Kapil, the boy who had come to live with me as my household help, an irrepressible thirteen-year-old from a village in Sitapur district. He had been working for nearly two years in Lucknow before he entered my home. As we drove the 40 kilometres or so from the city, we were going through the same territory that the Faizabad tigress must have covered when she roamed through Barabanki.

I had seen groups of kaanwariyas dressed in bright orange, and carrying elaborately decorated kaanwars on the Lucknow–Faizabad highway every year since I had come to live in Uttar Pradesh. The temple in Mahadeva village is a big draw, with lakhs of kaanwar-carrying pilgrims arriving every year from places in UP and Bihar. In Lucknow city, several days before Mahashivaratri, ordinary local people wearing festive party caps with silver foil sprouting out of them, cycle busily in the direction of Barabanki. It is an ancient shrine, said to have been built by Yudhishthir, the eldest of the Pandava brothers, when the five brothers had performed a *mahayajna* (great sacrifice) here to prepare for the war depicted in the *Mahabharata*.

Another story about its origin, which has more basis, does not contradict its antiquity, ascribing it to the same pre-Mahabharata period, but connects it to a farmer who lived here. Lodheram Awasthi was an ordinary farmer who saw Shiva in a dream one night. The next day, as he laboured to water his field, he found the water disappearing inside a mysterious pit that had appeared in the middle of his land. He tried to plug the leak with mud, but failed. The next day, he was trying to dig in the pit once more when his spade struck an object. When he dug it out, he was astounded to find it was a Shivalinga. As the story is told, the stone was bleeding where he had struck it with the spade. Overcome with remorse, he fell at the feet of this Shivalinga, to hear Shiva whisper in his ear: 'Don't move me from this place. This is where I would like to stay.'

The farmer thus built a temple at the spot, using the first half of his name and the name 'Ishwar' for Shiva to complete the name 'Lodheshwar' for this particular deity. Although he had been childless before finding the Shivalinga and building the temple, he went on to have four sons, after whom villages have been named — Mahadeva, Lodhaura, Gobarha and Rajnapur. The installed deity in this temple still has a nick in the smooth stone surface where the farmer's spade is said to have landed.

As we began nearing Mahadeva village that Mahashivaratri day, we saw small shamianas (tents) had come up on the side of the road, where water, sharbat and prasad in the form of small leaf bowls of sweet *boondi* was being distributed by local philanthropists. Stopping to get our share of the boondi, we met Jankiprasad, a twenty-three-year-old farm labourer from Unnao who regularly visited Mahadeva — this time was his sixth straight Mahashivaratri.

'Do you walk all the way?' I asked him.

'No, I come with my friends and we take a bus or a train part of the way, then walk some distance on the last part of the journey,' he said, grinning happily. It was obvious that this annual trip was something he looked forward to.

He confirmed it when I asked him, 'Why do you come here every year?'

'*Achha lagta hai* (It feels good),' he said to me. Then he added, '*Aur mannat bhi poori karte hai* (And he fulfils our wishes too).' His companions had already begun to call out to him as he spoke to me, and he left with a cheery namaste.

We drove on and found the traffic arrangements in place for the Mahashivaratri fair prevented us from taking the car right up to the village. Around 3 or 4 kilometres before the village, there was a large arch representing the turn for the village from the main road from which point people were walking to Mahadeva. Buses, jeeps, cars and tractors were parked for miles and miles along the main road, and I had to find a small space to fit my car in somehow. Then we were free to walk up to the village across the fields. Kapil was delighted. It gave him a chance to show his knowledge of the plants and weeds that dotted the land, and the best way to negotiate the *med*s, hardened mud ridges that divided the fields. Literally dancing his way across, he led us as we rocked unsteadily over the uneven ground, till we reached the road on which a steady stream of pilgrim traffic was moving both towards the village and away from it.

The groups that were coming away were men and boys with their belongings in cloth bags slung across their shoulders, or as bundles on their heads. Many of them were swinging carved wooden sticks, thicker than the usual walking stick, and patterned with simple designs carved into them and filled with black ink. I wondered at these, since we were on flat land, not the kind of alpine surroundings where one would need a stick for support. The general air of gaiety, and the mela ambience, was unmistakable. Youths sported paper party caps made of glittering silver, gold and copper-coloured foil, with 'Bol Bam!' written boldly across the front, along with a picture of Shiva and Parvati.

Unlike Ram Navami or Janmashtami, Mahashivaratri is not celebrated for the birth of Shiva who is without any known beginning, but as his wedding day. I noticed that the kaanwariyas at Mahadeva were almost exclusively male, and considered themselves Shiva's *baraatis* or those who accompanied him as part of his wedding procession. In the manner of ordinary baraatis, it is customary for the men to joke about the bride — she is, after all, taking away one of their buddies into a territory far different from the free and easy days of their bachelorhood. Some village groups arrive equipped for song and dance performances on this theme on their way to Mahadeva.

As we walked with all the others approaching the village, we could see the temple in the distance. There it was, across a green and yellow vista of flat fields of mustard, a single-storey whitewashed temple topped by red pennants that made a splash on the horizon. It was, truly, the only structure of note in the little village, where all the other mud-brown or brick-red dwellings were modest in the extreme.

Covering a little more distance, and continuing to gaze at the view of the village, I suddenly became aware of another intriguing sight. Towering heaps of what appeared to be coloured plastic and tin foil were winking in the sunlight, and I began to wonder if they were the waste products of some unknown industrial unit in the village, perhaps one which made the ubiquitous, awful gutkha sold in plastic sachets for one rupee. It was either that, or perhaps the villagers of Mahadeva were great recyclers — they had gathered plastic from all of Lucknow and Barabanki to make into some new, wonder product of Indian

Kaanwariyas from Bhiwadi at Haridwar.

Kaanwariyas at Haridwar.

A particularly elaborate 'kaanwar'.

Shivaratri devotees at the Mahadeo temple village, Barabanki.

Glittering heaps of kaanwars at Mahadeo, Barabanki.

Kapil and a young friend at the Mahadeo Barabanki mela.

Preparations for the 'kaanwar yatra' in Madhya Pradesh, July 2012.

The Somnath temple, Gujarat.

Jatashankar cave, Pachmarhi.

Kaanwariyas raising the slogan of Bol Bam at Deoghar, Jharkhand.

Villagers travelling by tractor to Deoghar. Kaanwar pots are slung from the sides.

The group of singers who sang 'Mere Shankar Baba' with me in Mahadeo, Barabanki.

Packed courtyard of the Baba Baidyanath temple, Deoghar, Jharkhand.

Stacked kaanwar frames after their pots have been emptied at Deoghar.

An old and nearly blind drummer at the Baba Baidyanath temple.

The somber final stage of 'kaanwar' – complete focus.

Tired devotees returning home on packed trains, at the Jasidih station, Jharkhand.

jugaad (ingenuity). I squinted hard at the shiny heaps, wondering what they meant.

Another few steps, and I had my answer. The simple explanation clicked in my head, bypassing all my convoluted conjecture of gutkha-manufacturing units and recycling geniuses from Mahadeva. Those shiny heaps were the remains of the lakhs of decorated kaanwar frames carried by devotees who had offered water at the Lodheshwar Mahadev temple. As we finally reached the village, these giant, glittering heaps could be seen clearly for what they were. The mystery of the canes carried by returnees was also solved. After leaving behind the bulk of the kaanwar frame, the kaanwariyas took home only a single cane from the frame as evidence of their journey to meet Shiva.

I took pictures of the kaanwars piled on the rooftops of village homes, and the fair around the temple. There was no question of going in for darshan that day — the queue of men standing for darshan snaked several times through and around the village. I took pictures of the devotees — patient, unmistakably rural men standing shirtless in the February sun, holding simple utensils of water with bilva leaves and grass stalks sticking out of them. For some, it was a steel tumbler, for others it was a small round *lota* (vessel). Dusty, dishevelled and determined, these men would wait for as long as it took to meet Lodheshwar Mahadev. I was unable to do the same.

Instead, I met Khushiram Pasi from Malihabad and Shiv Gopal Shukla from Chowk, Lucknow, who had their picture taken with their arms around each others' shoulders. They were friends because both worked as chowkidars or watchmen in the city. Khushiram had arrived in Mahadeva for the first time, while it was the third or fourth time for Shiv Gopal.

'Is it rewarding, coming here to Mahadeva?' I asked. 'It is so crowded today, it looks like you will have to wait a long time to get darshan.'

'Oh, we may not stay to get darshan,' said Shiv Gopal. 'For us, coming here today is enough.'

'How is that?' I asked, hoping for some reassurance for missing darshan because I couldn't stand in the long queue.

'Because we have walked up to this temple, we have reached here on this important day, we have prayed here — that is enough,' said Khushiram, and his friend agreed.

'Do you often go on pilgrimages?' I asked, and they looked at each other.

'Some,' said Khushiram. 'I have been to Gola, Neemsar and Delhi with my family.' He was referring to the Gola Gokaran Nath temple in Lakhimpur Kheri district, and Neemsar or Naimisharanya in Sitapur district, besides the national capital.

'Have you also gone to these places?' I asked Shiv Gopal. Gola Gokaran Nath is a famous Shiva temple, while Neemsar is mentioned in various *Puranas*, the ancient Sanskrit texts, notably the *Skand Purana* as the place where the *Satyanarayan vrat katha* (instructions for observing the fast and rituals for worship of Satyanarayan – the form of Vishnu prayed to most often for domestic harmony and prosperity) was first recited, among other occurrences.

'Yes, I have been to Gola and Neemsar,' said Shiv Gopal. 'There is too much *panda-giri* in Gola,' he said, referring to the aggressive soliciting for pujas and rituals by temple touts that happens in many famous temples. I smiled at his words. He was a Brahmin by name, but showed his disapproval of the way in which many Brahmins hustled to make money at religious places. He was also travelling with a companion from a Scheduled Caste.

'And you don't believe in panda-giri?' I asked.

'I believe in every way to make an honest living,' said he with dignity. 'Not by making people believe that they can buy their way to God for a few hundred or thousand rupees.' It was a simple, but convincing answer. I decided to persist.

'So does this mean that you are also against the caste system in general?'

Again, they looked at each other — one fair, with oiled and combed-back hair, the other dark, with a grey stubble. *'Ab jaativaad ke khilaf to hum hain hi* (Of course, we are against casteism),' said Shiv Gopal finally using the word by which the caste system is politically opposed today — as casteism. *'Aap hi bataiye, aap to padhi likhi hain. Aaj ke din mein jaativaad ka kya auchitya reh gaya hai?* (You tell us, after all you are educated. What relevance or standing can casteism have today?).'

'*Bilkul nahin reh gaya* (Absolutely none),' I said, promptly agreeing.

'Do you both go together to other temples too? Or do you go on a pilgrimage just for Shankarji?' I asked, trying a different tack.

'We don't go for pilgrimages regularly or anything,' said Khushiram. *'Lekin Shankarji ki baat kuch aur hai. Ve sirf ek lota jal aur bel patra se santusht hone wale dev hain. Unke yahan aana bahut achha lagta hai* (But Shiva is something else entirely. He is someone who can be pleased with a lota of water and a few leaves. Coming to his place feels very good).'

All three of us quietly looked out for a few minutes at the men waiting patiently in queue for darshan on the other side of the road from where we were sitting under the awning of a tea shop. They were from some of the poorest and most disadvantaged sections of our society and each one seemed reasonably confident that he was going to get a response from Lodheshwar Mahadev, not the implacable indifference meted out routinely by the worldly powers that be.

It was time to walk back with my friends through the fair, and along the pilgrim path back to the main road. Kapil was delighted with a set of false moustaches and a beard he bought for five rupees and a plastic trumpet for a similar amount, as was my friend's son. They walked jauntily ahead of us, wearing 'Bol Bam' caps and blowing occasional blasts on the toy trumpets. I felt great love for the two of them as I did for the lakhs gathered around me just then. They represented the ranks of the easily satisfied, those devotees of Shiva.

As we progressed back towards the main road, we met a merry group of men from Unnao district, well-equipped with a harmonium, dholak and other instruments for *kirtan* (community singing). I paused and spoke to one of them, a young man called Raju Pal. 'Have you been singing and dancing all the way here?' I asked him.

'Yes, we have,' he said, wondering at my curiosity.

'Do you want to sing some more, for your safe return?' I continued, teasingly. He looked questioningly at his friends, who sat nearby. 'Bring the dholak!' one of them said, and this was the cue for several of them to bring their instruments and stand next to me. 'So come on, give us some songs,' I urged, while they looked at each other, playing a few notes and drumbeats, uncertain what to sing. I waited another moment, then something struck me.

'Okay, I will sing,' I offered. 'Will you join me?'

They brightened immediately. 'Of course!' said Raju Pal. '*Aap bas shuru ho jaiye* (You just get started).'

And that is how I was given the chance to make up for my lack of darshan at Mahadeva. I was delighted to sing a song with Raju and his friends, a song they recognized from the first two lines, and joined in with gusto. A couple of them began to dance, while the harmonium, dholak, manjira and chimta were wielded to great effect. It was a heady experience for us all. The song? It was one of my favourites, a traditional one that warns against taking the greatness of Shiva lightly, or misinterpreting the symbols that surround him.

'Mere Shankar Baba ko anadi mat samjho!
Mere Bhole Baba ko anadi mat samjho!'
(Don't make the mistake of thinking my Shankar Baba is foolish or clumsy. Don't think that of my Bhole Baba.)
'Mere Shankar Baba ke haath mein trishul hai,
Trishul ko dekh ke, shikaari mat samjho!'
(My Shankar Baba carries a trident in his hand, it's true. But don't think from this that he is merely a hunter.)
'Mere Shankar Baba ki bail hai sawaari,
Nandi ji ko dekh ke vyapaari mat samjho!'
(My Shankar Baba goes about astride a bull. But don't let the presence of Nandi the bull fool you into thinking he's a trader.)
'Mere Shankar Baba ke haath mein kamandal hai,
Kamandal ko dekh ke, bhikhari mat samjho!'
(My Shankar Baba has a vessel with a handle in his hands, like the ascetics carry. But don't look at this and think he's a beggar.)
'Mere Shankar Baba ki aankh hain gulaabi,
Aankhon ko dekh ke sharaabi mat samjho!'
(My Shankar Baba has pink-tinged eyes. But don't look at those eyes and think he's drunk.)
'Mere Shankar Baba ke saath mein hain Gauraji,
Gauraji ko dekh ke sansaari mat samjho!'
(My Shankar Baba is accompanied by Parvati, his companion. But don't make the mistake of looking at her and thinking he's a worldly householder.)

*　　　*　　　*　　　*　　　*　　　*　　　*

Shankar was waiting for me as I alighted from the bus that had brought me from Bhopal to Pachmarhi, the hill station in the Satpura range of mountains in Madhya Pradesh. This tourist guide-cum-driver, owner of a completely ramshackle but trusty and serviceable Gypsy, was to be my local escort as I set out to explore some more Vyaghrakomala territory — the caves and forests where Shiva had once hidden himself, and which still attract lakhs of sadhus and adivasis during Mahashivaratri.

I reached Pachmarhi in late June 2012, not during the all important festival, but closer to the month of Saawan when Shiva devotees set off to collect water from the major rivers and their tributaries and carry it to their favourite destination — Ujjain or Haridwar, Nasik or Deoghar. Because the place is such a small and concentrated town, it took hardly fifteen minutes for me to be comfortably ensconced in my hotel room at the Taj (a tiny little place near the bus stop, not the well-known luxury hotel chain!). Shankar had left me to have a short nap after my bus ride, and be ready to go later to the Jatashankar Mahadeo cave and other places.

An hour later, we set off for the cave shrine. It was a very pleasant afternoon. As my bus had entered Pachmarhi, I had noticed a large maidan filling up with the stalls of a typical weekly village bazaar, and when I asked Shankar, I was not proved wrong. 'It is the weekly market day,' he told me. 'Most of us like to buy provisions for the house here. Tribals come with fruits, vegetables, herbs and medicines. You can find some really good bargains. Do you want to try it?'

I murmured noncommittedly. What I sensed was his own desire to go to the market later that day for his family's shopping. I made a mental note, hoping our expedition would not take us too long or too far. I needn't have worried. All of Pachmarhi is easily covered if one has a vehicle, including the clean and scenic cantonment area, which forms the dominant half.

Jatashankar Mahadeo was a five-minute drive from where I was staying. The path to the cave was lined by shops selling black ceramic and stone Shivalingas and other artefacts. I began walking towards the cave, with rocks towering on both sides of the path, and was stopped in my tracks by the most powerful rendition of the *panchakshar*, the chant of '*Na-Mah-Shi-Va-Ya*' I have heard across so many destinations. The voice intoning the holy syllables that sing of Shiva's glory vibrated with such intensity, was so hypnotic, and ricocheted off the surrounding rocks with such an impact that I was very curious to see who it belonged to.

A few more steps and a bend in the path revealed a woman, whose hair had formed into matted brown braids at the ends. She was simply dressed in a saree, with a short sweater drawn over her blouse, and the dry sticks of native medicine she was gathering up, the piece of cloth she was folding, showed that she was a tribal shopkeeper winding up for the day.

'Was that you?' I asked. 'Chanting "*Namah Shivaya*"?'

She looked up at me, pausing in her gathering, 'Yes it was,' she said. 'I say "*Om Namah Shivaya*" as long as I sit here, and also,' she added, her face creasing into a big smile that showed her still strong teeth, 'any other time, I always say "*Namah Shivaya*".'

'Seems like you are done for the day,' I remarked, looking down at the bundles she was making of her wares.

'Yes. I have to hurry today, because I am going to the market. Otherwise, I sit longer,' she said. She was a Gond, originally from Chandrapur, Maharashtra, whose family had come to the forests around Pachmarhi a couple of generations ago. Now she stood before me, all packed up and ready to go, and I was at a loss for how to hold on to her so she wouldn't disappear immediately. She folded her hands in a farewell namaste and I folded mine too, then requested, 'Will you say it for me again?'

Without any hesitation, or artful self-consciousness, she took a deep breath and chanted '*Om Na-Ma-Shi-Va-Ya*' three times in a way that reverberated in the rocky corridor and made other visitors stop and look on, too. Then she said goodbye and I went on towards the cave temple.

The rock formations leading to the cave of Jatashankar Mahadeo show, at different points, the iconic images of

Ganesha, Hanuman, and in the overhanging rock entrance to
the cave itself, the outspread hood of Sheshnag, the serpent on
whom the world rests, according to Hindu mythology. I climbed
down into a ravine to reach the dark, moist cave, and was struck
by what I saw — the narrow crevice between two rockfaces just
at the entrance seems like the cave is being guarded by a dark,
discerning entity. Inside, the Shivalinga is a natural formation,
like one of many stalagmites on the floor of the cave, which
seem to form the ridge seen on the back of a crocodile. In fact,
it appears as if the hide of a submerged reptile is lurking in one
part of the interior. This is the cave where Shiva hid from the
dreaded demon, Bhasmasura, and it has an appropriate bowels-
of-the-earth ambience.

Shiva is the primeval deity appeased by both the dark and
the light forces of the universe. Easily pleased, as denoted by
one of his names, Ashutosh, he was accessible to several very
fearsome personalities in mythology, including Ravana, the
ten-headed king of Lanka. Shiva hid himself in this particular
cave because he had granted a boon to Bhasmasura, by which
the demon could reduce anyone to ashes, by merely placing his
hand above that unfortunate person's head. The demonic Bhasmasura, who had acquired this power after praying to Shiva
for eons, went about conquering the world, and finally homed
in on Shiva himself. For surely, if he was able to destroy Shiva,
then who could prevent him from ruling the universe? And
thus, Shiva had to hide to prevent Bhasmasura from holding
that dreaded hand over his head! Shiva took refuge in the cave
at Pachmarhi, where he gave up his trademark *jata* (locks of
hair) to alter his appearance.

But, of course, the evil Bhasmasura tracked him down to
this spot in the Satpura mountains, too.

It was finally up to Vishnu, who took on the alluring form
of Mohini, to destroy Bhasmasura through the clever stratagem

of a dance. As Bhasmasura tried to woo the bewitching Mohini who was, in fact, Vishnu, she said she would accept him as a suitor only if he could dance along with her. Besotted, Bhasmasura promised to follow all her movements, and the dance began. With his attention riveted on Mohini, anticipating that she would soon succumb to his charms, Bhasmasura did not realize that a movement of the dance required him to hold his destructive palm horizontally over his own head. The moment arrived, and suddenly, there was a heap of ash where the fearsome ex-devotee of Shiva had danced.

The destruction of Bhasmasura is said to have occurred at the Bada Mahadeo cave, another of Pachmarhi's attractions. It is a drive of 10 to 12 kilometres away from the town, so I was reluctant to attempt it that evening. I was tired by weeks of travel and in need of the soothing sensation of being in a beautiful place without any agenda. We drove in a leisurely fashion around Pachmarhi town and its cantonment. I had the opportunity to admire a beautiful church in the evening light, see how an old cinema theatre had been restored from its near ruined state and made into a school, drive past a lake which had been reclaimed from becoming a dirty little pond by the strenuous efforts of the military administration. Then it was time to let Shankar go shopping at the weekly market and retire to my room at the Taj for a short while before going out to explore dinner options in the town.

That night, as I lay drifting off to sleep in the curtained half-light of my room, one distinct memory from the day came up clearly — a smiling face that told me, 'I always say "*Namah Shivaya*"!'

I woke early, and found to my delight that tea was already available at Tiwari's tea shop right outside the Taj. Pachmarhi town was awake and active at 6.30 am. I sat on a bench and gazed at three splendid calendar images of Shiva on the wall behind the stove where Tiwariji was making tea. In one, Shiva stood straight, holding his trishul upright, looking incredibly handsome — broad-chested, half-smiling, with a leopard-skin around his waist. In another he was astride a big white bull, the very powerful-looking Nandi, Shiva's hair like a halo of flames. In the third picture he was seated in the classic posture of the meditating yogi with half-closed eyes, and his palm raised in the reassuring *abhaya* gesture designed to free his devotees from fear. I literally drank in these images as I sipped the hot, sweet tea, thinking about the all-pervasive influence of Shiva.

I also noticed how the place was small enough for people to recognize and greet each other on the road, exchanging occasional small talk. The previous evening, I had craned my neck sitting in Shankar's jeep trying to catch a last glimpse of a man cycling past with two thick tufts of bright red hennaed hair sticking up above his ears, around a bald head, just like a circus clown's. This morning, I found I needn't have strained so much for a last look – for there he was, come to have tea with a friend, and I could stare at him all I wanted. That is, when I could tear my eyes away from the three different visions of Shiva. When I went to pay for the tea, I said to Tiwariji, '*Aap ne to Shankarji ke bahut achhe poster lagaye hain!* (You have put up some really nice posters of Shankar),' and he nodded with smiling aplomb and said, '*Haan, woh hamaare hero jo hain!* (Yes, because he is my hero).' He obviously meant that he would rather have these calendar images than the likenesses of Salman or Shah Rukh Khan, Amitabh or Dharmendra. Bhole beat Bollywood, at least in Pachmarhi.

I was ready a good half hour before Shankar's arrival on the dot to take me to Bada Mahadeo and other places. While I waited, I watched television in my hotel room where a local news channel was reporting how a revered tributary of the Narmada, called the Gupt Ganga is turning stagnant and polluted at Mandla town. Apparently, the spot has a long tradition of worship and parikrama on foot among the locals. The anchor on the show cited political indifference translated into administrative neglect as the reason for this sad state of affairs. She passionately asked a most pertinent question, 'How is it that so much popular faith in a local waterbody is unable to guarantee its care and survival?'

I was watching and thinking that this is a question that can be asked about many shrines and natural sites held sacred in our country. In fact, even in Pachmarhi, the previous evening at Jatashankar, it was distressing to see polythene bags and styrofoam cups and plates floating on the sides of what is a very special pool between rocks where water emerges from hidden underground springs. However, most significantly, whenever questions are raised about the poor standards of cleanliness and hygiene at sacred spots or places of religious significance, they are always framed in the familiar 'why-doesn't-the-government-do-something or it's-the-system-that-is-rotten' terms. Even the holy men who have undertaken protest fasts about the condition of the Ganga in recent years, have done more to pressurize the government into taking decisions about stone quarrying, release of water from dams, or effluent treatment plants and so on. While these are important steps to combat pollution in most rivers in north India, it is also important to create a culture of respect for the environment. Without encouraging citizens to be accountable, to contribute with their own actions to strengthen our democracy, we are often in danger of creating a nation of cribbers and desecrators. If faith is the engine that drives a very large percentage of Indians, then why are we unable to harness that faith to take great strides for the common good?

Such questions served to temper the slightly euphoric mood I had begun my day with, so I was quite sombre on the drive to Bada Mahadeo, but the morning air, and the forested roads restored my equanimity. This was as it should be, for I was about to meet a very important and unforgettable personality — a sadhu who truly epitomizes the spirit of Vyaghrakomala.

The Bada Mahadeo cave is much larger than the Jatashankar Mahadeo one, and has a more open approach. There is a clearing in front of the cave and an ashram alongside the path that leads up to the shrine. All around, the forests of sal, which are the hallmark of the Satpura hills, encircle the place in a green embrace. Both at Jatashankar, and at Bada Mahadeo, a common sight is big and small trishuls, some plain iron, and some painted a bright orange, which have been planted in the ground as offerings by sadhus who come here for the Mahashivaratri mela. Lakhs of sadhus, local pilgrims and adivasis, carrying trishuls to offer at the 1330-metre tall Chauragarh peak, where a Shiva temple is their destination, begin trekking the approximately three-and-a-half kilometre distance to the mountaintop from the Bada Mahadeo cave.

This annual congregation is a colourful and unique spectacle. Along the way, the yatris stop at the Gupt Mahadeo cave and several other natural spots for rest or worship. The trekking path moves right along the periphery of the Satpura National Park and Tiger Reserve. While the distance from the Bada Mahadeo cave may not seem much, it is all hilly terrain, with a view of the rolling Satpura mountains all along the more level parts, and a final stretch that is an almost vertical climb of 1380 steep steps. The temple at Chauragarh is a simple structure made memorable by the thousands of trishuls that stand in colourful clusters in several parts of the temple courtyard.

I did not attempt the trek to Chauragarh on this visit. As I gazed at the peak from various points over the three days I spent in Pachmarhi, I knew it would not have been feasible for me without supportive friends or family. Instead, I comforted myself by recalling other journeys — the climb to the Mukteshwar temple in Uttarakhand, another spot where trishuls are offered, and the steep steps that had led me up to the temple atop the hill of Anjanadri, the birthplace of Hanuman near Hampi in Karnataka.

Chauragarh has always been held sacred by the adivasis who lived in the forests before the arrival of people from the outside world of the plains. When settlers from the plains arrived, it was inevitable that the tribal gods merged with Shiva, in whom the presence of all that is wild, untamed and aboriginal resonates. Thus it is that the peak still attracts adivasis as well as sadhus from the various Hindu ascetic akharas during the festivals of Mahashivaratri and Nag Panchami.

It is during such large congregations that the sadhu who runs the Virakt Ashram Siddheshwar Hanuman Mandir at Bada Mahadeo performs a continual service for many days and weeks. Shri Shri 1008 Shri Mahant Garib Das Ji Maharaj, Mahatyagi, Chauragadh, Pachmarhi as he is described, has lived here for over forty years, and is revered by the local people as a very kind and approachable sadhu who has inherited from his guru, the previous head of this ashram, the miraculous ability to be seen in more than one place at the same time. Stories abound of people meeting him in the weekly marketplace at Pachmarhi, while other visitors would have sworn that he never stirred out of his ashram during that entire time. When the sadhus and pilgrims arrive for the Chauragarh trek, he arranges food, shelter and sleeping arrangements for hundreds of people, serving them tirelessly with the other members of his staff, cleaning and cooking and serving, not keeping himself aloof like many other ashram heads.

Shankar had told me that he would take me to meet Garib Das Maharajji after I had completed my darshan at Bada

Mahadeo. I entered the shrine to find that the broad mouth of the cave forks into two and as I walked down one of the paths, I was suddenly plunged into complete darkness. Hesitantly, I moved slowly, feeling the cool, moisture-laden walls of the cave around me, rather than actually seeing their rocky surface. Then, equally suddenly, I emerged into the light of the Shivalinga adorned with flowers and leaves, a flickering lamp and a priest sitting by to offer me prasad. As I turned to go back, preparing to plunge into the darkness once more, beyond the reach of the oil lamp, a group of rural women with sarees drawn over their heads were coming out of the darkness, exclaiming to each other in the Bundelkhandi dialect, the one my paternal grandmother spoke in my childhood at Jabalpur. I smiled at them and made my way back out into the sunlight.

The area just outside the Bada Mahadeo cave is a beautiful green and rocky circle, where the sunlight filters in through the leaves of overhanging trees, and a little mountain stream flows alongside the approach path and under the cave. I spent some time next to a cluster of trishuls just sitting and watching the few devotees arrive at the shrine, hear the birds call, and feel the peace and quiet, interrupted only by the gurgle of the stream. It was a very soothing place.

Shankar came looking for me and said it was the right time to visit the ashram. Garib Das Maharaj was receiving visitors. I went to the ashram with him, and we entered a very clean courtyard, from where we could see Garib Dasji sitting on a low *takhat* (wooden plank-cot) with some dhurries spread in front of him, where a couple of gentleman visitors already sat. Shankar introduced me and I took my place, noting the kind but watchful bearded face of the sadhu and his humble demeanour. I began by asking Garib Dasji about how the lives of the adivasis living in and around Pachmarhi had changed in the time he had spent here.

'It has changed in some ways, but in many ways it is the same,' he said. 'Of course, putting these people in a category removed from other people is not right. Our ancient texts spoke of three different kinds of dwellers — *nagarvasi, graamvasi aur vanvasi* (city dwellers, villagers and forest-dwellers). All should be seen as equal in ability and understanding. This term, adivasi, is an artificial construct and puts them at a disadvantage.'

'Have you lived here all your life? Or did you arrive from somewhere else?' I couldn't help asking.

'This is my *guru sthan*, place of my guru,' he said. 'I was born in Himachal. As a child, I had very high fever once. During that time, I saw this place exactly as it is, in my mind's eye, without knowing where or what it was. When I arrived, I recognized it, and have loved it ever since.'

'Were you already a sadhu by then?' I asked.

There was the glimmer of a smile on Garib Dasji's face. 'I had run away from home, and was doing odd jobs, travelling here and there. I had experienced hunger and thirst, and intense loneliness trying to find my path after leaving the security of home. I reached Pachmarhi by bus one day in 1971, and met my guru as soon as I got off. For some reason, as soon as he saw me, Guruji addressed me as if we had always known each other, and I responded in the same way since I felt I knew him too'. He said, "*Kahin jana to nahin hai?* (Do you have to go anywhere else?)," and I told him, no I only had to go to the police station! A policeman had caught me just as I was about to get off the bus, and wanted to take me to the police station to check if I was carrying any ganja in my cloth bag.' By the end of this story, the sadhu was smiling.

At this point, one of the visitors laughed slightly and said, 'Just think, the police wanted to take you for checking, whereas it was Baba himself who had the miraculous power of pulling out any amount of ganja from his cloth bag any time he liked and no one had any clue about its source!' Shankar and the other visitors laughed at this, making me realize that Garib Dasji's guru had a special affinity with the weed that Mithai Lal and his friends in Varanasi love too.

This shared joke among them made me ask a question that led to an animated discussion of the connection of Shiva to *nasha* or intoxication, that lasted quite some time. 'Doesn't this kind of habit lead to tension between men and women or people from the same family?' I asked. 'When some of them find it easy to escape into some form of intoxication and others are left holding the burden of responsibility?'

The other visitors seemed a little taken aback, but quickly recovered, and one of them said, 'You are taking the whole question of nasha too literally. Because Shiva is associated with bhang or ganja doesn't mean he is recommending or endorsing it for the general population. It has no effect on him, because he is above all intoxication, and in fact, it shows that we cannot be enslaved to any drug.'

'I am sure Parvatiji would have thought differently,' I murmured stubbornly.

Garib Dasji heard our exchange, and said mildly, '*Nashe mein nahin rehte the Mahadevji. Aur bhakti marg mein bhi nasha nishedh hai* (Mahadev never used to be under the influence of any intoxicant. And even on the path of true devotion, being intoxicated is forbidden).'

The men and I may have been tempted to go on arguing in spite of this mild intervention if Garib Dasji had not continued, 'The truth is that if Mahadev came in front of us now, we will not have the capacity to have his true darshan.' He looked at me and said, 'You were asking about change, and how things have changed. The change is in how people have begun to think and feel, the corruption that seems to define us now. It is not necessary to go very far to see how this contamination affects us all. When I first came here, I used to buy sugar for 10 paise from the shop out in front of the ashram, and two packets of tea for 5 paise each. The taste of that tea was unique. Now, even though we have so much tea, and spend lavishly on it, it tastes different. It is as if our intentions and desires have seeped down to the level of even the tea we drink.'

We were listening intently, trying to keep up with the words he spoke and what they signified. 'Baunganga used to be brimming with water,' he said, referring to a waterbody in the Pachmarhi Biosphere Reserve. 'Look at it now, it is unrecognizable. I used to smoke half a beedi, then put it out to do some work and tuck it behind my ear. The taste of that unsmoked half was still good,' he said, his eyes twinkling. 'Now I smoke cigarettes, but it is not the same. It is not one thing, like nasha or ganja that is the problem. It is what we have become inside, how we approach ourselves and others. Why, even I have begun to have occasional thoughts that I should have more money to do this construction, or that ceremony. Then, I catch myself and wonder, from where did this way of thinking start? How did I begin to think about money?'

As we absorbed the import of what Garib Dasji had just said in a moment of silence, it was broken by the loud 'Mm-be-eay' of a white cow, which came briskly trotting in from the open front door of the ashram, and stood right in front of the platform where we were sitting, pointing her eyes and ears straight at Garib Das Maharaj and saying, more loudly now, 'MM-BE-E-EAY!'

He got up from the takhat and went and spoke to her. He stroked her head and ears, then called to someone, 'Has she had her food?' When an attendant sadhu came running up to say she had indeed eaten, Garib Dasji spoke some more to the cow, who now seemed to be intently listening to his every word. Then, seeming to calm down, she trotted right back out the door!

I was intrigued. 'She seems to understand every word you say to her,' I said, when he returned to sit before us once more. He smiled in a slightly self-conscious way, but then turned and looked at the door of his room behind him. 'They all do,' he said. 'Each one understands. *Arre, Ramdas hai* (Is Ramdas here?)' The attendant understood his question to mean opening the door of the inner room to let out a large, very handsome and powerful-looking rhesus macaque male monkey. Ramdas walked out of the room with great dignity on all fours, with his tail aloft, in the manner of proud alpha males. He came and sat in front of us, and looked at us for a moment, before raising his eyebrows and thrusting his face forward to frighten us off in the classic simian gesture. Only when Garib Dasji spoke a few words to him did he, too, calm down and then return to the room, still very dignified. I later learnt that the ashram always had a resident monkey. Ramdas, the present one, had been preceded by Ramrati, another rhesus macaque, a female. But the one who had captured every one's heart was a gentle, bonnet-tailed macaque called Pavandas. 'When he died, I did a proper *terahvin* for him (special rituals after death),' said Garib Dasji.

The door of the room opened again and out came a beige-yellow dog and another black one. They came, slowly wagging their tails and making yawning sounds, plus stretching a little in the 'namaste' pose some dogs adopt before those they love. It was obvious they had been having a nap, but after emerging, they brightened up, began barking at some outside noise, and ran off, but not before they had shown how very fond they were of the Bada Mahadeo sadhu.

His complete affinity with the animals in the ashram definitely made Garib Dasji a much more significant sadhu for me than others I have met. As I had the halwa and tea that had been served to us as prasad, I remarked, 'Bhagwanji sent me to the right place. I am very happy to have met you!' He looked at me, his face showing a calm expression in response to mine, brimming with affection, and said, 'People come here from far-away places, then ask me, how will we get true darshan? How will we ever meet God? It is simple. For true darshan, just be kind to a sick or injured animal, or do some good for an unknown person.'

As I went away from this beautiful ashram, a shelter in the truest sense not only for the humans and creatures who live there, but for the hundreds and thousands of sadhus and pilgrims who have passed through it in their trek to Chauragarh, it was obvious to me that behind the sheer simplicity of Garib Dasji's words, there is great depth and understanding of the mystery that is life.

But just like Shiva who seems too simple and ordinary to really be the ruler of the universe, and unlike so many glamorous preachers on television and elsewhere, he makes no effort to impress anyone.

Chapter 4: Shashigunakara
(He Who is a Storehouse of the Qualities of the Moon)

Sceptics and atheists, of whom I know a large number, may be right when they assert that believing in God makes us susceptible to giving credence to other forms of unproved interpretations of reality. While their criticism usually stems from a dismissal of all such things as horoscopes and old wives' tales, I am bringing this up only because the spiritual path is often a lifelong romance (although one may become aware of it only at a mature stage in life) when one becomes keenly aware of signs that one is loved by God.

Nothing is quite as thrilling for the seeker as those moments of sheer synchronicity that produce a feeling of acknowledgement, or those everyday events that bring great insight in their wake. I can still recall the thrill I felt when I stepped onto the bridge across the Alaknanda river that would take me to the Badrinath temple, and exactly at that moment, the public address system came alive with the bhajan, '*Mata Saraswati Sharada*', enunciating 'Sharada', which happens to be my name. I was convinced that it was a sign of welcome, and nothing that any logical person can tell me about it being just a coincidence will convince me otherwise.

Other memories are thrilling for different reasons. One Sunday morning in late summer, early in the new millennium, my family and I reached the temple at Sriperumbudur, the birthplace of Sri Ramanuja, founder of the doctrine of Sri Vaishnavism. We were four then, my daughter and son, their father and I, well before our divorce. July usually means the arrival of the 'Rumani' mango in Tamil Nadu — a fleshy round fruit with a very small seed, and just outside the temple, a very poor old woman was selling these mangoes from a basket. When I stopped to buy them, I was stunned to find that she gave me five mangoes for the five-rupee coin I held out. It was such abundance, that I immediately gave one to a naked urchin standing nearby, with uncombed hair and a forlorn look. He began to eat it, and as we turned to go inside the temple, two monkeys were climbing down the carved surface of the gopuram, one descending on either side of the entrance. I held out a mango for each one and they took them.

Then we entered the temple and I was entranced by its beauty, by the paintings — rows of large, beautifully painted depictions of Sri Vishnu in the Tanjore and Mysore styles — hanging all around the inner periphery. It was quiet and most satisfying — no festival crowd, no jostling before the deity. We completed an enchanted half hour or more inside the temple to finally reach the tall, golden pillar of the *dhwajasthambham*, straight ahead of the entrance. There all four of us sat down to savour a few more moments. As I looked up at the golden pillar against the clear blue sky I felt great contentment. Just then, the children pointed to a small cow tethered near where we sat.

'Do you think she would like a mango, Ma?' my daughter asked, and of course, we rolled a 'Rumani' offering towards her, then watched in delight as she carefully moved the fruit inside her mouth, and a few minutes later, delicately spat out the tiny stone! Now there was only the last fruit left, and as we four began to share it out of some unspoken agreement, my eyes filled up with the sheer gratitude of being so blessed. I could not recall a single time when five rupees had been able to bring so much satisfaction to so many, beginning with the old lady, and ending with us. It was the clearest and most unequivocal example of receiving prasad, the limitless grace of God.

There is a peculiar happiness associated with sharing such stories and experiences with other believers. In India we are aware of a cultural and aesthetic concept called *rasa*, the bouquet of emotions portrayed by varied genres of poetry and music, dance and theatre. Sharing stories of one's experiences as a devotee produces a similar rasa, but is truly confined only to fellow believers. Trying to share them in neutral circles can have one labelled as a bore or a person who has crossed some invisible boundary of acceptable behaviour. Also, indulging in an endless search for signs from God is a definite danger on the spiritual path. One can then get stuck at a point in one's awareness, where ascribing a divine hand to the most common-place occurrences makes one seem superstitious and becomes an actual handicap in making ordinary decisions.

I was conscious of many such dangers as I negotiated the bends of life in the company of people who shared my belief in varying degrees. Sometimes a spontaneous exchange about what God meant to us would happen with complete strangers. At other times, I had to be careful not to make any mention of God, even involuntarily, to my immediate family. I had to school myself to accept both such situations. Maintaining one's equanimity in the midst of both calm and turmoil is after all, the biggest discipline one has to learn on the spiritual path. Dealing with emotions, which follow cycles similar to the waxing and waning of the moon, is not something that only women need to do. All of us have triggers that disturb the balance of our thoughts, setting us off on a gloomy ride marked by despair and negativity.

Shashigunakara watches our struggles through these phases, finally bringing us relief through a single moment of insight, or a very slight shift in outer circumstances, that help to ground us firmly once again.

By far the greatest emotional challenges most people face are those posed by their relationships, often with those who are closest to them. When one is suffering due to the actions or omissions of someone very close, it is not uncommon to beseech God to bring about some change in behaviour or attitude, something, anything, which will make life better for oneself and others. When I met the women kaanwariyas from Mehrauli in Haridwar, I had asked Dadli and Najo, Reshma, Krishna, Shano and others, if they prayed for Bhola to make their husbands give up drinking, and whether he listened. 'Of course we pray that they should sober up!' they had chorused then. 'But even if they don't stop completely, things do get better for us at home after a kaanwar yatra,' one of them had told me earnestly. I didn't find this statement misleading or untruthful. I knew the truth of it from first-hand experience.

Considering the ebb and flow of emotions in any long-term relationship like marriage, it is hardly surprising that astrologers ascribe the moon as a representation of an individual's relationship with his or her spouse. An afflicted moon can mean ego problems and marital sparring, while a well-placed moon on the natal chart can mean partners purring with contentment. Or so it is propagated. But in more common sense terms, the moon is our closest companion after the sun — but with none of the latter's comforting certainty. Following its own enigmatic pattern of hide-and-seek, affecting moods and temperaments globally through its gravitational pulls and pushes, the moon is a familiar symbol for mystery and magic in cultures around the world.

Possessing all the qualities of the moon whose crescent form he wears in his locks, Shashigunakara is every bit as mysterious and magical, but additionally, he has the power to replace the moon's mystery with reassurance and comfort, calm the fevered lunacy it can occasionally produce with creative insights and transform every lunar influence into benevolent support rather than threatening greyness. One of the forms in which he is worshipped is as Somnath, the lord of the moon.

I had the most magical experience of being in the Somnath temple on the evening of the full moon on 3 July 2012. But this was not before I had clocked many traveller miles at different destinations.

In late June 2012, I was trying to leave Bhopal for Jalandhar and had to return disappointed from the station because a ticket that had been waitlisted at number nine, fifty-five days before my date of travel, had still not been confirmed. There was a huge rush of passengers at the station, all eager to reach their destination on the first day of the annual Amarnath yatra, and all trains to Jammu were therefore running completely packed. The platform was teeming with people and hoardings and posters advertised bhandaras, the community feasts organized to see off groups of yatris leaving for the trek to Amarnath.

The arduous trek to the Amarnath cave where Shiva is worshipped in the form of a naturally formed, large ice Shivalinga makes news as much for the difficulties faced by pilgrims, including the threat from terrorist bullets, as it does for the spiritual experiences of those who visit this shrine. In 2012, ninety-five pilgrims died of natural causes during the annual yatra, down from over a hundred the previous year, but proving that this is an arduous pilgrimage for those in poor health who are not acclimatized to such altitudes.

What are some of the factors that push people into undertaking such hazardous journeys in their search for God? In Bhopal, I had occasion to speak to my cousin Sanjay, a fifty-year-old rebel in my family, with small gold rings in both pierced ears, about his extreme devotion to Shiva and his experience of the Amarnath yatra. 'I turned to Shankarji after my divorce and the death of my father and infant son,' he said. 'All of life, human relationships, everything had begun to seem meaningless to me, and it seemed as if there was no alternative except to turn to him.'

'Why only to Shankar?' I asked. 'Why didn't you turn to Devi, or Rama?'

'Because he has always been my hero, for he is the most easily pleased,' he said. He went on to describe his earliest efforts in his devotion to Shiva – waking in the pre-dawn hours, reading the *Shiv Purana* every day, and always wearing 1100 rudraksha beads. 'That is also when I pierced my ears,' he said, touching one of his earlobes in a self-conscious fashion. Sanjay went to Amarnath in those heady days, when he sought to wipe out the trauma of the repeated losses he had suffered with the satisfaction to be gained from meeting his God. He described to me the journey to the cave – arriving in Jammu and registering for the trek, a process which involved undergoing a medical test. He was then given a time slot for departure, since the narrow mountain paths cannot be overcrowded. 'As soon as you begin the trek, every additional bit of weight begins to appear most cumbersome. It's a tough climb, and even the woollens you wear, any small bag you carry, all of it appears worthy of being thrown away!'

Alongside the track, a long row of tents offer food and refreshments. These have been put up with the help of contributions by people from all over — Haryana and MP, Gujarat and Rajasthan, Mumbai and UP. 'You can get anything you want to eat,' he told me. 'And the best part is, it's all free for the pilgrims. Desi ghee, puris and sabzi, rice and dal, the best halwa, everything,' he said, describing the food with enthusiasm.

The high altitude, the other-worldly terrain of snowclad peaks, wind-blown icy plains, and rocky moonscapes of intermittent valleys, and the focus on meeting 'Barfani Baba' (the Icy Baba as the Amarnath Shivalinga is called) result in transcendental experiences for quite a few on the Amarnath trek. Sanjay described to me several experiences he said he had before, during and after darshan. 'At one point, I had the sensation of being completely drunk, without having touched a single drop. My hands and feet felt as if they were heavy, made of lead. My eyes refused to focus where I wanted them to. All I was aware of was that in spite of all this, I was safe, that Baba would take care of me. I also had a vivid visual experience of Shankarji and Parvati for a few moments. They seemed so real and so close, as if I could reach out and touch them. It is difficult to describe, but at that moment it was a very powerful sensation.'

Amarnath is revered for both the wonder that is the naturally occurring phenomenon of the giant ice Shivalinga in the cave, and the story that explains its existence. It is believed to be the site where Shiva, in his icy mountainous abode, was explaining the secret of immortality to his wife Parvati. Knowing the human greed for immortality and being determined that no one should hear the mantra he was telling his wife, he had banished all his attendants from the cave as he spoke. Unfortunately, Parvati dozed off while listening to this exposition on immortality, but Shiva didn't realize she had gone to sleep. He went on talking because a pigeon that was roosting under the seat where she sat, kept cooing a response to his words. When he found out, an enraged Shiva gave chase to the pigeon, determined to kill it. Chasing it out of the cave and over the mountainous paths, he threw away several of his adornments, such as the snake he wears around his neck. On the Amarnath trail, such spots are marked as sacred, and have small shrines for pilgrims to offer their respects. As for the pigeon, it obviously escaped Shiva's wrath, for a pair of them is to be found to this day, nesting in Barfani Baba's cave.

My conversation with Sanjay gave me much food for thought. Speaking as a casual observer, it appeared as if his passion for Shankarji and other deities was not shared with the same intensity by his wife, who works as a teacher and looks after their two children. Sanjay's elder brother, my cousin Atul, also pointed out that perhaps his brother could better serve

God by just being more responsible towards his duties as a father and householder, rather than seeking to escape reality through an endless quest for God. Valid though such assertions were, they evoked for me those portions of my own life when my relationship with God was the only thing that seemed real, that helped me navigate the other events and developments that passed for reality with calm. A poem I wrote in those years of my life expresses this:

> *'It must be a fairground*
> *where I live*
> *for*
> *every mirror reflecting me*
> *says things I'm loth to hear.*
> *To one I seem*
> *harsh, distant, and*
> *worse, judgemental –*
> *I'm mum because my protests will*
> *shatter this glass,*
> *already brittle.*
> *Others see me*
> *as mournful, or irregular*
> *when symmetry's required.*
> *Others still will hope for a form*
> *that I have never been*
> *nor will be.*
> *I'm a prisoner of distorting mirrors…'*

Nothing has fed my devotion to God more surely and strongly as my challenging relationships with both my husbands. I began seeking God as a friend who would understand me when it seemed no one else did, when it was clear that the man I loved had somehow turned into a permanent adversary, within the familiar and comforting confines of our shared home. Having spent several years now living on my own, I can vouch for the fact that no loneliness stings with quite such a deadly intensity as the loneliness one feels within a marriage. Another poem from the same period, all addressed to Hanuman and published in a collection titled *Seeking Sanjeevani and other Poems'* (Prakriti Foundation, 2005) underlines this state:

> *'Civility*
> *is always an option.*
> *Long after hope's marsh*
> *has dried*
> *into hard, cracked, unyielding mud*
> *and the heart has understood*
> *full well*
> *the futility of further desire*
> *politeness is still possible.*
> *Armed with mild and measured words*
> *and ranting only in my head*
> *I live these days*
> *of desperate calm.*
> *O Hanumate!*
> *It's not as if you do not know*
> *what lies behind*
> *the mask, the ruse.*
> *When will you take me to a place*
> *where I can be*
> *both rude and free?'*

It is strangely ironic that devotion to God should have thus been fuelled, for me, through the difficulties in marriage, when Shiva has declared marriage to be an altogether avoidable nuisance in the twenty-fourth chapter of the Rudrasamhita portion of the *Shiv Purana*. The devas had assembled before him, including Brahma and Vishnu. They were all extremely shaken and terrorized by the antics of Tarakasur, a demon who had received a boon from Brahma that only the offspring of Shiva and Parvati would be able to cause his death. Since no progeny had yet been born to the divine couple, Tarakasur went about unfettered in his mission of mayhem. When the devas beseeched Shiva to get married to Parvati, who was praying steadfastly to become his wife, he rebuffed them. 'Just the act of *panigrahan* (one of the ceremonies observed during a Vedic wedding) by me and Parvati will be enough to cause all of creation to fall into the pangs of desire,' he said. 'Marriage produces desire, desire produces anger, and anger destroys any chances of spiritual advancement. I had done a great service to you all by destroying Kama, the god of desire, following which you each had the opportunity to rid yourself of all desires bit by bit and know the supreme state of self-awareness. But now you come to me with this demand.'

Should this seem like a stinging indictment of marriage, there is more to the story. When the devas persisted in their prayers, Shiva finally relented — but only because he bows to the love of his devotees. At the time, the assembled devas and Brahma and Vishnu were his foremost devotees, and he was bound to do what they asked. Before he gave in to their prayers, he had expressed his personal view, which makes marriage and the desire and anger it produces seem like the biggest hurdle to spiritual growth.

In fact, it is often the other way around. Marriage, or the chances of being happy within it for both partners, is often disturbed by the uneven spiritual needs or inclinations of both partners. Although the pain of being hurt and misunderstood by a partner may be the initial nudge that makes an individual seek greater understanding in God, soon this relationship with an unseen friend begins to eclipse the one with the all-too-familiar-sneer. It throws the 'ego-problem' between the husband and wife in a completely different light.

There was a period in my life, when I got out of some family scrape, that I often sighed and said, 'Thank God we have been able to get over this!' My then husband, the father of my children, would narrow his eyes at me and say, 'Why is it always God? What is there to thank him here? So many crises come and go, but I never hear you say, "Thank ...", referring to himself. (My ex-husband's name, incidentally, is also one of God's names!). Bewildered by his resentment of such a simple and heartfelt sentiment, I would apologize and retreat, smarting under what I felt was an unfair indictment for giving credit to Him who deserved it, and thinking that I now knew just how Prahlad must have felt being taunted by his terrible father Hiranyakashyapa. How could my husband still want me to look adoringly at him and thank him for every little thing, I wondered. Hadn't he grown up enough to even perceive the Higher Power that was helping us along in a myriad ways? God was definitely at the centre of our marital problems, when acknowledging Him seemed to mean not giving recognition to a person.

I have overheard men in north India joke about how their wives have 'gotten God' and it is hard to get any significant attention (or sex) from them in between evenings of satsangs (community prayer) and jagrans (night-long vigils of prayer, such as the one in Damoh, described earlier). Of course, population growth figures from all these regions suggest that men have a way of overcoming the spiritual hurdle, regardless.

But it is not always the wife who gets bitten by the godly bug. An enactment of the saint Tukaram's life in the folk art form called *bharud*, which is a feature of the annual Pandharpur yatra in Maharashtra every year, portrays his wife as an extremely shrill, shrewish woman, constantly taunting him about the rice bin being empty while he does no work except sing 'Jai Jai Rama Krishna Hari'. Any responsible householder in the present day with only a moderate attachment to God might empathize with her plight, while the husband or wife could be moved to tears by Tukaram's abhangs, devotional songs, instead! Goswami Tulsidas' excessive attachment to his wife, which blinded him to every other reality, led her to whip him with such scathing words that they proved to be the catalyst that pushed him into lifelong bhakti thereafter. Men and women, husbands and wives, get pushed apart by many, many factors. Their differing attachment to God is one of the more complicated ones.

When I was growing up, I was gripped by Graham Greene's novel *The End of the Affair* in which it becomes clear only bit by bit that the 'third' presence in a passionate relationship that ended was actually the idea of God. I guess it should have alerted me to how love gets complicated by the looming Higher Presence, but I had to experience my own anguish to really understand it. In my daily struggles with my ex-husband, I used to yearn for a partner who would not worship me, but be a fellow worshipper with me at the altar of life. I fantasized about someone, who, if not a fellow bhakt, at least had such love and respect for all of life's bounty, that it amounted to a deep appreciation of God.

In life's supremely ironic fashion, I next fell in love with, and married, an atheist.

*   *   *   *   *   *   *

The Somnath temple is the first of the twelve 'jyotirlinga' temples named in the Shatrudra Samhita of the *Shiv Purana*. The Shatrudra Samhita extends the scope of Shiva to include all of creation in a number of ways. All his incarnations, across the various eons, are named and described. He encompasses every particle of reality through his *ashtamurti* forms. Shiva as the androgynous Ardhanarishwar, which was the basis for the creation of all living species by Brahma through male and female forms, has been mentioned, as have his earliest appearances as Sadyojaat, Vamadev, Tatpurush, Aghor and Ishaan. The importance of the eleven *rudras* or manifestations of Shiva is explained, and the importance of worshipping Shiva as the fierce, dog-riding Kaal Bhairav is emphasized, in addition to adoring his more benevolent form of Shankar.

The function of so many labels and descriptions of Shiva across the boundaries of time seems to be simply a means to remind and reassure the human imagination that it is never outside the reach and influence of a watchful, sheltering, powerful presence. God is immanent in all that is visible and all that is not. For instance, under the ashtamurti forms called Sharva, Bhav, Rudra, Ugra, Bhim, Pashupati, Ishaan and Mahadev, the earth, water, fire, air, sky, space, sun and moon are collectively ruled. Since Vishwambhar Shiva is the benefactor of all of living creation, he is worshipped as all of existence, the life and breath that inhabits all creatures, and the landscape that holds them. A moving passage in the Shatrudra Samhita is the prayer to Shiva by the virtuous Vishwanar, whose wife, Shuchishmati, has expressed a desire for Shiva to be born as her child.

'Bhagavan! You are the one unparalleled Brahm, this entire universe is your form alone, none of it is alien to you. It is true that yours is the ultimate authority and I, therefore, take shelter in you, Maheshwar! Shambho! You are the provider and the one who takes away; being of one form you are still perceived as millions of forms, and yet, you are finally formless. Just as shimmering water in the heat and silver in mother-of-pearl are mere illusions, I do not want to remain in the illusions of the world, but under your protection alone. You are the cool nature of water just as you are the leaping flames of fire, the warmth of sunshine and the soothing moonbeams, the scent of flowers and the presence of ghee in milk. You can hear without ears, see without eyes, walk distances without feet, and taste every flavour without a tongue. Who can know your true nature? Neither the *Vedas*, nor Brahma nor Vishnu, neither Indra or any of the devas can fathom this secret, but your true devotee understands it! Neither do you have an gotra, nor birth, nor name, appearance, etiquette or country. Yet you rule over the three worlds and have the power to fulfil all desires. You are everything, the whole complexity of existence has emanated from you. You are Gauri's beloved; you wear the sky as your clothing, and are immovably calm. You are seen in the visage of childhood, youth and old age. There is nothing in this world that lacks your essence. I therefore bow at your feet.'

Such a prayer encompasses God across all religions and geographical definitions. It also takes away the taint and falsehoods of man-made divisions like caste and class, pedigree and status. As believers, most people would yearn to have a first-hand experience of just such a God. But, in actual terms, they may spend a lifetime defending their God against another, or ascribing all the divisions and distinctions created by man, to God himself. Shashigunakara is well aware of the half-truths and grey areas that acquire a dangerous edge in the hands of adherents of various religions. He is not a captive of any one label or belief.

My journey to Somnath began from Lucknow, then reeling under the searing temperatures of late June 2012. There had not been a drop of rain in the first six months of 2012, not even the mild showers that sometimes accompany dust storms in Bhopal to a pleasant welcome of overcast skies and moisture-laden cool breezes. Although much of May and June had been dry even here, thankfully the monsoon seemed to have preceded me by a few days. I stopped in Bhopal for a family function, and to complete my visit to Pachmarhi, but since there was a day to spare, my cousin suggested I go to Bhojpur. I later learnt that the Bhojeshwar temple at Bhojpur is sometimes referred to as the Somnath of the north.

Whichever road you take, it seems as if you are still headed for the same place.

The temple of Bhojeshwar in Bhojpur is visible several kilometres before one reaches this village in the Obaidullaganj block of the Raisen district of Madhya Pradesh. There is a bridge across the Betwa, referred to in ancient texts as the Vetravati river, from which one can see the temple clearly outlined against an otherwise plain landscape. It is famous both for being an unfinished structure and for the giant Shivalinga in its sanctum — eighteen feet tall and with a circumference of seven-and-a-half feet. This tall Shivalinga rests on a stone platform, and a metal ladder leads to its top. The priest climbs it to anoint the gleaming rock surface with water, sandalwood paste and other devotional offerings.

For me, the temple on a gently sloping hill in a quiet village was one of the finest locations I had visited in recent years. As I walked up the slope towards the structure, a strong breeze blew. There was no sunshine, only cloudy monsoon daylight, without rain. I felt all sense of urgency leave me even as I stood looking out at the vista of the nearby houses and fields from the courtyard in front of the temple. The breeze ruffled my hair, and lifted my saree to a billowing tent around my legs. I gazed at three dogs, soundly sleeping on the steps carved into the rocks of the hill. It was utterly quiet. An old cliché came to mind, and seemed perfectly true just then. Time stood still.

Raja Bhoj, the most illustrious king from the Parmar dynasty, who is said to represent learning and wisdom through his worship of Goddess Saraswati, and the engineering marvels created in his time, had this temple built in the eleventh century, but it remained unfinished because he was killed by challengers from the Chalukya kingdom of Gujarat in 1060. The temple is a protected structure by the Archaeological Survey of India and no worship is allowed by pilgrims at the Shivalinga itself, but two small stone mandaps in the temple courtyard is where prayers can be offered. Carved stone pillars adorn the extremely tall, wide, imposing entrance to the sanctum where the Shivalinga stands. It is startling in its size and its shiny stone surface somehow conveys a live presence nine centuries after it was carved from a single rock.

The sanctum never had an outer wall built around it and the roof over the Shivalinga, shaped into a dome in the architectural style of the mid-eleventh century, is also incomplete. The noon sun slants directly on to the Shivalinga and further emphasizes its majestic size and shape. Walking around the base of the Bhojeshwar Shivalinga in the dark and cool interior of the temple, I felt dwarfed and humbled. There were few pilgrims, and one or two officials from the ASI. I lingered inside, and on the small wooden bridge leading into the sanctum, without getting in anyone's way.

Flowers and coconuts to Shiva had to be offered at a much smaller Shivalinga in one of the mandaps outside. Here I met Shubham, a young boy carrying out his priestly duties. He wore a bright lemon-yellow kurta and white dhoti, besides a shy smile, and was happy to answer my few questions about the place. Apparently, the temple and archaeological site remain quiet and undisturbed for all the days of the year except the week around Makar Sankranti on 14 January and whenever Mahashivaratri is celebrated in February or March. 'Then there are so many people – lakhs of them come from all over – that they stop the vehicles on the other side of the bridge, and people have to walk the rest of the way,' he said. Shubham is a part-time priest. He attends school too, and has taken up this responsibility out of his own interest, not because it is a hereditary occupation. 'My father and grandfather were not priests. We are not Brahmins,' he said. 'But I love coming here and sitting here for these few hours. Helping people do their puja is something I like to do. I started coming here when I was a very small child. Now it has become an important part of my life.' True to his description of the job as a labour of love for him rather than a means of earning a livelihood, he did not try to convince anyone to part with extra money for puja or *dakshina*. He just sat, silent, attentive, helpful — the perfect person to play the role of a priest in a place as peaceful as Bhojpur.

I walked around the temple and admired its carving and masonry, and the ramp which had been used centuries ago to transport rocks to build the structure. Raja Bhoj had many dams constructed in the area around Bhojpur, and created a lake in one with supposedly medicinal properties. But in the fifteenth century, the Persian king Hoshang Shah of Malwa had the dam broken, acting on complaints from the local traders that thieves hid themselves in the forest around the lake. The remains of the dam can still be seen in the area, as can the ruins of the palace of Raja Bhoj. I didn't venture to explore it because the still, calm landscape around the Bhojeshwar temple seemed like a place I wanted to linger in for a much longer time.

I sat on the rocks in front of the temple for quite a while, drinking in great lungfuls of the fresh breeze, and allowing myself to wonder about great kings like Raja Bhoj and Rajarajeshwar Chola, both known for the giant Shiva installations at Bhojpur and Thanjavur. Yet neither had left much in the name of a palace to speak of their personal glory. How much of the world's violence and misery was caused by a desire to be remembered by posterity, I reflected. Raja Bhoj and Rajarajeshwar Chola were exceptions. The stark, unadorned Shivalinga at Bhojpur was an unaffected and implacable witness to the wars which finally destroyed Raja Bhoj's kingdom and claimed his life. Another definition made its way into my consciousness — what is God, if not a witness to the many destructive follies of mankind?

The saffron pennant on the mandap where devotional offerings are made fluttered constantly in the breeze, leaning slightly towards the main temple and reminding me of Bandakpur. It bore the words 'Har Har Mahadeo' and I silently said them to myself. Thanks for offering me this balm of a place and time, away from the relentless heat and isolation of Lucknow, made its way from my heart to the giant, looming Shivalinga in the half-finished temple.

*   *   *   *   *   *   *

When I reached Vadodara to make my way to Somnath by road with a couple of my friends, I remembered my last visit to Gujarat a decade ago. It was in April 2002, when the burnt shells of buildings that had borne the brunt of the riots could be seen in Ahmedabad, with many streets and colonies suddenly cordoned off in selective curfew clampdowns. My earliest memories of Gujarat dated back to the early 1980s, when I visited Porbandar and other cities. Since then, every association with the state had become tinged with tragedy or controversy.

As my friend Chitra took me towards the old city areas of Vadodara for a short tour of discovery, I experienced one of those pleasant moments of ambush that happen from time to time. Suddenly, we were driving around a small lake in the centre of the city, and there, in the middle of it stood a towering statue of Shiva. I was quite taken aback at this unexpected endorsement of my 'Bol Bam' quest. I had never seen this trident-holding giant before. It was both startling and reassuring at the same time to see him suddenly loom up in the middle of city traffic, after I had spent so many of my waking moments reflecting on him.

The lake is the Sur Sagar lake, a popular recreational spot for tourists and locals in the evenings. Apparently, the 120-foot-tall Shiva was installed by the Vadodara Municipal Corporation 'some years back' (no one could tell me exactly which year, but I assumed it must have been after my last visit of 2002, else, how could I have missed seeing such a large and significant landmark?) and is illuminated with special lighting on Saturdays and Sundays and festive occasions. Several fountains spray out of the statue, making it seem as if streams of water are rushing out of Shiva's locks.

We left early the next morning for Somnath. It had rained in the night and the air was crisp and cool in the darkness before dawn when we set out. We were driving to Somnath on the western coast via Rajkot and Junagadh, and expected to be there in the evening. The largely pastoral vista of Gujarat, interspersed with distant chimney stacks of industrial units, unfolded before us as we sped along. Majestic Kankrej oxen, with their distinctive curving horns, walked in straight, dignified lines across fields, while Kathiawadi shepherds, wearing their short frock-coat-like kurtas, boat-shaped woollen caps, and baggy-bottomed churidars herded precious flocks of *desi* goats out to pasture. The goats' horns were very interesting too — neat spirals ending in points. I had spent so many years in Tamil Nadu, where indigenous breeds of cattle have been indiscriminately diluted with Holstein or Jersey or other foreign breeds, resulting in large, ungainly animals without horns, that seeing these original desi animals was a delight.

When we stopped for breakfast, it was *fafda*, curving flakes of fried besan (gram flour), served with a chutney that looked like *kadhi* but was actually sweet, and *poha* (cooked rice flakes) topped with *sev* and chopped green coriander. Long fried green chillies accompanied every order, lest we think that the Gujaratis were getting away with making everything sweet.

We drove into Junagadh town around 11 o'clock in the morning. Chitra, an avid photographer who has captured many historic sites all around Gujarat, was keen to take pictures of the Mahabat Maqbara. We had to stop only once for directions before we reached this building, the mausoleum built for the tombs of Mahabat Khanji, the Nawab of Junagadh, and Bahauddin, the minister of Junagadh's erstwhile ruler, Nawab Rasul Khanji. Construction of this charming building began in 1878 under the direction of Mahabat Khanji and it was completed in 1892 by his successor, Nawab Bahadur Khanji. When we reached the spot, we just stared, dumbstruck for a few minutes.

Four minarets with spiral staircases curving around them stand beside this extremely embellished and beautiful structure. Giving a fairytale feel in the cloudy daylight which casts no shadows, the Maqbara's surface is yellowish stone. It is topped by a single onion-shaped dome, with many smaller domes clustered in front of it. Adorned with intricate floral patterns on its arched doorways and all along its turreted width, it was a spellbinding sight. Both Chitra and her friend Usha got busy shooting this edifice from every conceivable angle. I too, took some pictures before wandering off to explore the place.

Next door to the Maqbara, presenting a complete contrast in colour and style, is the more modern building of the Jama Masjid — an architectural confection painted bright green and yellow. Opposite the Maqbara, across a narrow road, is the cluster of buildings housing the District Court. The compounds of both the Maqbara and the courthouse are encircled by low walls. A cart in front was selling roasted peanuts and gram weighed into small paper cones. There were one or two benches in front of the courthouse wall. As I began walking from the Jama Masjid towards where my friends were still exploring the Maqbara, a small group of urchins began following me. They called me 'Aunty! Aunty!' and I turned around to see a few boys, a couple of them with runny noses, and two girls, all between six and ten years old. They were just curious, not begging, but I decided to buy them some treats anyway, from a shop across the road. When I had distributed the biscuits and peanut brittle I had bought, some was still left in a small paper bag in my hand. I reached the cart selling roasted peanuts and decided to treat myself to something, too. Behind the peanut-seller's cart, on a bench, sat two older women and an elderly man with two bright-eyed children, a boy and a girl.

I asked for the peanuts, then decided to offer the bag with the sweet biscuits to these children. Smiling and holding out the bag, I watched them look wary, then turn for approval from their older companions, and only then come forward and accept the packet. The elderly man got up from the bench, and went into the courthouse compound. So I sat on it to wait for my friends with the women and children.

The younger of the two women was Shahnaz, and these were her grandchildren. Her son was in jail, and it was in connection with his case that they had come there from their home in the outskirts of Junagadh town. They asked where I had come from, and I told them. I asked if I could take their picture, and for some reason they found this hilarious, but then agreed. I gave my camera to the boy to take my photograph, and he clicked with complete confidence. They were happy moments. I was completely unprepared for what happened next.

Shahnaz put her arm around my shoulder and asked, 'Do you do your own cooking at home?'

I was startled. 'We-ell, not exactly,' I said, feeling slightly guilty. 'I mean, I used to, while my children were growing up, but now, for several years, I have hardly cooked.'

'You have help at home, isn't it? Someone who cooks and cleans for you, keeps your house running while you work,' she gestured in the direction of my friends taking pictures — an expansive turn of the hands meant to include a whole world of 'outside work', not the more humble vocation of keeping house.

'Yes, I do,' I admitted, thinking of dear little Kapil, alternately cycling off to buy fruits and groceries, or sitting in front of the television chuckling at a Salman Khan film. I looked at Shahnaz, wondering what was coming.

'Take me,' she said, and I had to look deep into her eyes to make sure she was not trying to pull my leg.

'What?' I asked. 'Why? You have your family to look after. Where I stay is very far away. Why would you want to leave your home?'

'I am fed up of endless rounds of this *court-kacheri*, having our bread-earning boy in jail for months without any reason. For an ordinary fight and someone filing a false complaint against him, we have to keep coming like this, spend money without any hope of getting justice. What do I do for my poor daughter-in-law, these children? Take me. I will do everything — cook, wash clothes, clean your house. You won't have any worries. Just give me some peace.'

A young black-coated lawyer, overhearing her over the low wall, and seeing my obvious discomfort, said to her in a scolding tone, 'Now why are you bothering this lady? We are doing what we can, right?' But when she turned around and shot some sentences at him in rapid-fire Gujarati I found hard to follow, he relented, then looked towards me and said, 'They are suffering. That is why she wants to go. They don't have any hope of getting justice for their son.'

'I understand,' I said. 'But I don't have a place to offer immediately.' He nodded, grimacing in agreement. We arrived at a compromise by exchanging phone numbers. I promised to call, if there was any chance of offering Shahnaz boarding and a modest salary in return for 'cooking, cleaning house, washing clothes'.

Chitra and Usha had concluded their exploration of the Mahabat Maqbara by then, and I waved to Shahnaz and her family till our car had moved away down the street. I found it hard to shake off her look and the plea, 'Take me.' Junagadh is a place which comes up in the rhetoric of right-wing groups when they want to denounce the Nawab of Junagadh, who, in 1947, refused to sign the Instrument of Accession that would make his kingdom a part of the Indian republic, and fled instead to Pakistan. The ethereally beautiful Mahabat Maqbara, although still recognizable as an architectural treasure, was looted of its silver fittings by angry mobs when the Nawab abandoned his country.

But does it make any sense to try and seek revenge for the Nawab's divided loyalties from the likes of Shahnaz and her family? Sabre-rattling politicians would have us think so. But Shashigunakara knows that this is like trying to steal from one's own house in the light of moonbeams...

*   *   *   *   *   *   *

As we made our way to the region of Gujarat around Somnath which is known in the ancient texts as the Prabhas Kshetra, we passed the cluster of seven peaks of the Girnar mountains. It is at the base of these mountains, known as the Teleti area, that an annual fair is held, attracting thousands of Digambar sadhus on the occasion of Mahashivaratri. Vimla Patil, in her outline of the script for the sound-and-light show at Somnath, refers to the importance of this area as the site of the shrine of Ashtamurti Bhaveshwar, where a very important prayer to Shiva, the Shiva Mahima Stotra, was composed by Pushpadanta, one of his devotees in medieval India:

> '... Here, Shiva is the powerful deity with three eyes – the sun, the moon and agni or fire...Pushpadanta, legend says, was a Yaksha in the service of Shiva, and assigned

to collect flowers for the worship and rituals of Shiva. He once became struck with the arrows of cupid and was lax in his duty. The flowers he brought contained bees, which stung Shiva. He was cursed that he would be born as a mere mortal and go through the cycle of life and death like all human beings. Upon prayers and prostrations, Shiva relented and said that as a human being, Pushpadanta would become a poet and would write one of the greatest songs in praise of Shiva. Thereby, he would be restored to Kailas, the realm of Shiva. Shiva Mahima Stotra, a unique Sanskrit composition… is a rich treasure of imagery and beautiful language…'

Before going to Somnath, we stopped at the fishing village of Veraval, in which a temple marks the spot where Sri Krishna left his body after he was accidentally hit by a hunter's arrow as he lay resting under the shade of a tree. Veraval is famous for its distinctive fishing boats made out of wood curved into long slats for the body, and shaped into narrow, pointed prows. We drove through the village and towards the small harbour. Giant logs were being loaded onto wooden flat beds with wheels that were to be towed by camels. These tall and supercilious animals waited patiently while the loading went on, looking down at us with their special heavy-lidded look as we took photographs. The sight of the harbour was unforgettable. Miles and miles of pointy prowed Veraval boats with spiky masts reaching upwards were visible from the roadside. There was hardly space to insert a thin razor blade between them, and we wondered how they would be taken out into the open sea unless they were in the front row. From where we watched, the water was merely a figurative presence. It could only be seen gleaming at a distance, not between the tightly packed boats.

It was afternoon as we drove into Somnath, and the outline of the temple shone brightly against the monsoon clouds and seascape. We were to stay in a new residential block built right behind the temple along the shore line. As we drove into the courtyard of this place, the sight of the Arabian Sea – a grey-blue-green expanse capped with white breakers was a delight. I have lived next to the sea for a very large portion of my life, first at Mumbai, then at Chennai, and seeing it again after a long gap spent in land-locked Lucknow evoked emotions I had forgotten. We spent a happy half-hour here before freshening up and heading to various sites around Somnath.

Somnath is the site where faith has always been challenged by the might of invaders and those who have sought to prove their force as conquerors. It first came into existence since before time as we know it began to be measured, built by Soma, or the moon, in gratitude, after the curse afflicting him was lifted by the grace of Shiva. Daksha Prajapati, the fiery father-in-law of Shiva, had married his twenty-seven daughters to Soma, a celestial being born out of the churning of the primordial ocean. These twenty-seven daughters were the twenty-seven different constellations of stars known to ancient astrologers. Unfortunately, Soma showed himself partial to one of them, Rohini, to the exclusion of the others, which angered Daksha, and caused him to curse him to die.

When Soma beseeched him to withdraw his terrible curse, Daksha relented slightly, and advised him to bathe in the confluence of three rivers that empty into the ocean near Somnath – the Triveni Sangam of the rivers Hiran, Saraswati and Kapila, and pray to Shiva for salvation. It was Shiva who, moved by the plight and prayers of the moon, lightened his sentence, changing the total extinction of Soma to being a waning and then waxing moon. Immense gratitude towards his benefactor impelled Soma to construct a temple for Shiva, by all accounts the most luminous and remarkable temple of all that were ever built on the site.

When we reached the Triveni Sangam, we were disappointed to find the water had receded to a few kilometres away from where we stood on the ghats. It was too shallow and green with algae just under the ghat steps. Chitra remembered that she could feed fish here on her last visit, but the tiny local biscuits we had bought to crumble and offer the fish could not be given this time, because there were no fish. The spot looked desolate and swampy.

We drove then to the Gokul temple, a peaceful spot alongside a gently flowing portion of the river. Three old men sat at the gate, one, a shabbily dressed flautist playing his instrument for money, another a bespectacled man wearing bright red sadhu robes, with his long grey hair piled up in a tall heap on his head, and a third man in orange robes, with his eyes shielded by a very dark pair of glasses with attachments on the side to shut out the light completely. While the flautist continued to play some well-known bhajans in a relaxed kind of way, I spoke to Jeevanand, the bespectacled man, a former school teacher from Kolkata, who had become a sadhu twenty-six years ago. He told me he lived in a small hut that he had built for himself outside the temple compound. There was a small aluminium pot in front of him, and he sat accepting whatever coins pilgrims put into the pot with a slightly sad and gentle expression on his scholarly face.

'I have been to all the holy spots, to the Kumbh Melas in all the four places, but finally feel most peaceful and content here in Somnath,' he told me. 'Shiva is everything and everywhere. His presence can be clearly seen.'

'What made you become a sadhu?' I asked.

'I was born into a Brahmin family. My family used to do a great deal of puja,' he offered, by way of explanation.

The man sitting next to him, who seemed to be recovering from a cataract surgery, was Kanchan Singh, from Jabalpur (my birthplace). 'This place is very good to live in. There's no *chori-chalaaki* (thievery and cunning) here,' he said. Although he sat right next to Jeevanand, both of them vehemently denied being friends. It made me wonder at the social and economic distinctions that persist even after one has taken on saffron robes.

I was charmed by the sight of a young boy in a white kurta and yellow dhoti speaking to a cow and feeding it some rotis inside the temple compound. He was Ruturaj, a young boy who comes to do temple duties after school hours, much like Shubham in Bhojpur. 'I cycle here immediately after I have returned from school and eaten,' he said. 'Only after coming here, do I feel I have actually reached home! It feels good to be here, because this is such a peaceful place.'

The approaching evening was drawing us back to the vicinity of the temple, where we wanted to be present for the aarti at 7 p.m. and the sound-and-light show at 8 p.m. We left the Gokul temple and reached Somnath town after a short drive. It was tea time, and while enjoying a splendid glassful at a tea stall with my friends, I was treated to the sight of a young man wearing an enormous amount of gold jewellery on his slim person. Several thick chains, some with medallions, hung around his neck, a very thick bracelet adorned one wrist, while large gold rings could be seen on the fingers of both hands. He had large, long-lashed eyes, frizzy hair, and a thick black moustache. He passed us, with two or three men walking a few paces behind him, obviously aware that we were covertly studying him. I decided I must talk to him too.

I waited till he had gone behind the counter of the Kathiawadi Bhojanalaya before approaching him for a chat. He was the owner of this eating establishment as well as several others in Somnath. I greeted him and told him about my book, then began with some general queries about Somnath. His name was Laxman Dodeja, and he was a local BJP functionary. Even as we were talking to each other, Narendra Modi's voice boomed out of a television screen in the background, talking about how his government had brought internet connectivity across Gujarat, among other things. 'You are well-prepared for the elections,' I remarked (the Gujarat assembly elections were held in December 2012) and he gravely nodded in agreement. 'Is that a television channel?' I asked. It wasn't. Dodeja was then playing a DVD. The NaMo channel had not begun test telecasts till October 2012.

Dodeja took pains to emphasize the facilities enjoyed by pilgrims at Somnath — part of Gujarat's development story. He pointed out a block of guestrooms put up by Keshubhai Patel, former chief minister of Gujarat, to counter Narendra Modi's influence on the Shree Somnath Trust. His voice was slow and measured, stopping just short of slurring, for he was giving off a not-unpleasant but unmistakable scent of someone who had managed to beat the prohibition that is Gujarat state policy. We talked for some more time about Somnath's history. 'The soil of Somnath is soaked with the blood of those who sacrificed everything to protect their faith and their country,' he told me. From him, I learnt that a shopkeeper three doors down from his restaurant had financed a feature film on the local hero Hamirbhai Gohil, who had resisted Muslim invaders in one of the battles to save Somnath.

'Is NaMo getting ready to abandon Gujarat for the bigger task of becoming India's PM?' I asked him. He fixed his large eyes on me in a serious look. 'Gujarat will never abandon NaMo,' he said firmly, giving me only an oblique reply. I nodded. It made sense. Why speculate about the national scene when the assembly elections were the first priority? Narendra Modi won these elections very convincingly in December 2012. I thanked him for his time and got up to go. I had only gone a little way from his shop front when I heard him call me again, and wondered why.

Emerging from behind his counter, and with the slow grace of one who is being very carefully conscious of his movements, Laxman Dodeja bent to near where I had been sitting talking to him, picked up a half-full bottle of mineral water I had left behind, and handed it to me with exquisite courtesy. I took it and thanked him again.

If he had only known that I was more sympathetic to his apparent fondness for soma (as liquor is mentioned in ancient texts) than to his politics, perhaps we could have been more frank and open with each other, and examined more topics. Or who knows? He may have been tempted to come after me with a sickle, a lunar curse on his lips.

The passage of time must have dimmed the famed lustre of the very first Somnath temple described in mythology and caused it to sink into dilapidation. For by the time it entered recorded human history, it was already a second temple built on the same site by the Yadava kings of Vallabhi in Gujarat around 649. The temple was also grand enough to attract the marauding armies of Junayad, the Arab governor of Sind in 725, who destroyed it. The third temple had to be built by the Gurjara Pratihara king Nagabhata II in 815.

The worst looting and desecration at Somnath was at the hands of Mahmud Ghazni in 1024, who let his men break the Shivalinga into several pieces in a barbaric manner that surpassed even the looting of valuables. The invader carried one of the pieces home with him to Ghazni and used it as the stepping stone to a mosque, so that the 'true faithful' would walk on it every day. Two years later, King Bhoj of the Parmar dynasty of Malwa (builder of the Bhojeshwar temple at Bhojpur) and the Solanki king Bhimadev I of Anhilwara, from the present-day Patan region of Gujarat, came together to rebuild it between 1026 and 1042. Apparently, this was a magnificent wooden structure, which lasted till the next century when it was replaced by a stone temple by a local ruler — Kumarpal — between 1143 and 1172.

Another invading army was to target the temple in 1296, led by Sultan Allauddin Khilji. This operation was also marked by great violence and the enslavement of locals, besides the looting of their homes and livestock. The next ruler who invested in this holy site was Mahipala Deva, the Chudasama king of Saurashtra who had it rebuilt in 1308 and his son Khengar installed the Shivalinga there some time between 1326 and 1351.

History marched on with the temple being razed in 1375 by Muzaffar Shah I, the Sultan of Gujarat, in 1451 by Mahmud Begda, another Sultan, up to the time of the Mughal emperor Aurangzeb, the biggest philistine of the Mughal dynasty who had the temple destroyed in 1701, and had a mosque built on the site, using some pillars from the Hindu temple, with their unique inscriptions and carvings. It does seem as if flattening this particular temple had become a point of honour for conquering armies, a competitive display to prove their might to fellow invaders, as much as it must have been to quell and terrorize the locals.

As competitive as the conquering armies were to show their might, so it appears, were local rulers to prove their faith and win back the support of their people. The temple was always resurrected from the ruins into which invaders had thrown it by the efforts of kings from various parts of India, assisted by sculptors, artisans and architects from Gujarat, Malwa and other regions. After Aurangzeb's assault, the Peshwa of Pune, Raja Bhonsle of Nagpur, Chhatrapati Bhonsle of Kolhapur, Queen Ahilyabai Holkar of Indore and Shrimant Patilbuwa Shinde of Gwalior joined hands to rebuild the temple in 1783 at a site adjacent to the ruined temple, which had been converted into a mosque. This smaller temple still stands adjacent to the large compound of the Somnath temple, and is visited by crowds of pilgrims.

We went to this smaller temple on our second day in Somnath and were rewarded by an intimacy with the Shivalinga that couldn't be hoped for in the main temple, with its much bigger crowds and the rush of pilgrims. The large black granite Shivalinga was being washed by some devotees from Maharashtra, and we could touch its wet, gleaming surface, or even place our foreheads against it if we wished. There were no priests to shoo or chastise us. The Maharashtrians, after washing the Shivalinga, tenderly anointed it with some sandalwood paste and offered flowers. We shared in their special moments with complete contentment.

Sardar Vallabhbhai Patel's statue stands in the foreground of Somnath inside the large temple courtyard. He is commemorated here because he played a decisive role in the construction of the present temple. Patel ensured the integration of Junagadh into the Union of India after the Nawab had fled to Pakistan. When he visited the region as deputy prime minister, he made sure that the transition of the former kingdom into the Republic of India was peaceful. Saddened by the ruins of Somnath, he issued orders for its reconstruction on 12 November 1947 and also ordered that the mosque, which then stood on the site, should be shifted to another place a few miles away.

These orders were presented as part of a larger plan for the area by Mahatma Gandhi, Sardar Patel, K.M. Munshi and other leaders of the Congress. Although Mahatma Gandhi was not against the restoration of Somnath, he added a rider which reveals his conscious desire to keep administrative matters free of associations with any religion or community. He approved it on the condition that the funds for the reconstruction should be collected from the public and the temple should not be a government-funded project. Unfortunately, when work was still under way on the Somnath project, both Gandhi and Patel died. The task of reconstruction was continued under the stewardship of K.M. Munshi, who was the minister for food and civil supplies under Jawaharlal Nehru.

The newly constructed Somnath temple was ready for Rajendra Prasad, the first President of the Republic of India, to perform the installation ceremony at the temple in May 1951. In a stirring speech on this occasion he declared that, 'The Somnath temple signifies that the power of reconstruction is always greater than the power of destruction.' He also invoked the glory of the original temple as the ideal towards which the newly independent, modern India should direct its drive for prosperity. While such an idea can be considered inspirational, it was treading on sensitive territory in a multi-faith republic, and no one could have been more aware of this than the then prime minister, Jawaharlal Nehru.

President Rajendra Prasad and K.M. Munshi considered Somnath to be a successful attempt to reverse the injustice done in the past to Hindus. On the other hand, Prime Minister Nehru considered that the executive should not be seen to be identifying with one particular religion or community in a secular democracy. Some coolness between the PM and President on this matter was, therefore, inevitable. Both viewpoints have remained alive within the Congress party, without any attempt to reconcile them. The Congress has ruled the country for the maximum number of years, either with its own government, or as the dominant ruling partner of an alliance. Its ambivalence on sensitive issues like the Somnath one is the reason why the Congress has pursued the dual policies of soft Hindutva on one side, and minority appeasement on another, using one as an alibi for the other, in a completely cynical interpretation of its professed secularism.

Somnath has been managed by the Shree Somnath Trust since it was completed. Being a trustee is a point of prestige for political bigwigs of the BJP, as can be seen from the composition of the trust in August 2012 — Keshubhai Patel, who quit the BJP to protest against the high-handed tactics of Narendra Modi and floated the Gujarat Parivartan Party, Gujarat chief minister Narendra Modi, BJP veteran L.K. Advani, former chief secretary P.K. Laheri, Professor J.D. Parmar, former member of Parliament, Prasannavadan Mehta, Harsh Neotia, an industrialist from the Ambuja group, and business magnate Rajen Kilachand. However, in press releases the trust makes appropriate noises about being an 'apolitical body'.

My first hour in the Somnath temple was dominated by an awareness of the temple's close relationship with the ocean. The sound of the waves, the salt- and moisture-laden sea breeze, the unmistakable scent of the ocean – all this pervades one's consciousness inside the temple periphery. The Shivalinga is a large black one, which was then decorated with flowers and sandalwood paste, in preparation for the evening puja. Darshan was being strictly monitored on both sides of the railings marking a path to the deity. Women were on one side, and men on the other, and both were being urged to keep moving by temple marshals of both sexes. 'Hurry now, no loitering, keep moving!' they were saying, and tapping those women on the shoulder who were staring rapt at the Shivalinga, forgetful of time. Chitra and Usha became quite indignant at the sight of a couple of women getting pushed in front of them by an overzealous marshal woman. However, we realized that the trick to get more time to gaze at Shashigunakara in Somnath was joining the queue once again just as soon as one darshan was completed. Then we just had to wait till our turn came around again!

We completed a few such turns, then moved to sit outside for a while and wait for the call to the evening aarti. While my friends walked into the garden and sat on the lower steps leading up to the temple, I chose to sit quietly on the stone platform just outside the temple entrance. It felt strange, reaching here after so many years, and so many temples. 'What is behind my meeting you at such a mature age?' I wondered to Somnath, the timeless one, my eyes welling up as I began to dwell on the circumstances of my failed relationships. 'My moon is surely afflicted, and you have been more witness than champion in all my struggles,' I was saying to him. This feeling often occurs in places that represent an emotional or spiritual threshold. One may be let down by nobler emotions, but one can always count on self-pity.

As I sat, with the strong sea breeze blowing against my face, the sight of the vast ocean and the sounds of the temple behind me began to have a hypnotic effect and I felt myself calming down. The ebb and swell of the tides, in synchronization with the phases of the moon, the periods of upheaval and calm, violent destruction and careful reconstruction – all the frenzy and furore of humanity, everything seemed to have been effortlessly absorbed into what Somnath represented. For just a tiny, tiny moment, I had a glimmer of something so large, so still, that it did not matter what danced, dwelt, dared, dreamed and died within it.

I was finally able to register what was happening around me, as I regained control over my feelings. A middle-aged man, ordinarily dressed in a pant and shirt and looking like a government servant was sitting close to where I sat, giving an impromptu discourse to an elderly couple who were hanging on to his every word. 'All is Shiva, it is all Shiva,' he was saying, and his words were an echo of Jeevanand, the sad-faced sadhu, saying, 'Shiva is everything and everywhere.' The man seemed keen on making the couple understand what true devotion was. 'Why do we come to a temple? To experience Shiva or to open up a long list of our demands and needs? Most of us come not as devotees, but as beggars. Is this worship?'

He allowed the import of his words to sink in for a few moments, before beginning another thread. *'Jahan jeev hai, wahan Shiv hai* (Where there are living beings, there is Shiva),' he said, gesturing expansively at the temple garden around us, where two adolescent dogs were playing rough and tumble together on the cropped grass. 'When we come to a temple it is not only to stand before the stone image or idol,' he said. 'God is in every creature to be found here, just as he is everywhere else. The other worshippers, the dogs playing, the pigeons, all are a manifestation of Shiva.' His listeners perked up when he mentioned pigeons. It was obvious that they were thinking of the pigeons in the Amarnath cave, as I was. The man acknowledged this with a nod. He may have continued this way for much longer, but the call for the aarti made us rise and get ready to enter the temple for the evening puja.

*   *   *   *   *   *   *

That night, we were treated to the spectacle of a large, resplendent full moon in the sky, its reflection glittering on the waves of the ocean, and the tall temple shikhara (spire) outlined against the sky, even as its shadow fell across the ground and on the water. The Somnath sound-and-light show had the ocean as a narrator (through the voice of the late actor Amrish Puri), the eternal witness to every one of the temple's incarnations. It could not have asked for a better setting than a full moon night. Although some of the script was pretty standard stuff, it was not without its magical moments. From the celestial encounters of Soma and the twenty-seven constellations who were his wives, to the love story of a dancer and King Bhimadeva, there was enough romance to keep the narration fairly lyrical. But even in this narrative, it appeared, the dancer loved Shiva himself more than her lover (familiar complications), and subsequently, the story became a long list of conquests and seeming defeat, destruction and rebirth.

Halfway through, my mind began to wander and form those half-questions that occasionally result in fresh realizations.

Are all relationships too polluted by the quest for power, Shashigunakara, just as human history is?

Is one being more courageous by relinquishing power, or by staying firm and guarding one's turf?

And, most importantly, if you are present in both, the one who surrenders, and the one who demands surrender, then whose is the pain of defeat? Whose is the joy of victory?

Chapter 5: Sarvatapana
(He Who is the Scorcher of All)

The vast courtyards of temples in Tamil Nadu are paved with stones that become searingly hot under the summer sun. Walking on these in any dignified manner becomes near impossible, forcing the visitor to race across, hop, or completely ignore the burning sensation in one's soles — in the manner of firewalkers. On many occasions, reaching a distant temple like Kalahasti, or Ekambareshwar at Kanchipuram just before its closing time of noon, because of the time it had taken us to travel from Chennai, I have grimaced and run across the stones to reach a comparatively cooler spot of coir matting, or mud, thinking how Sarvatapana is gathering us into a fiery embrace. Whether or not one's soul becomes open to receive Shiva as Sarvatapana's grace, the sole is always vulnerable.

Since I had become aware of being on a spiritual journey, I had realized that there are different stages in one's own feelings for God. There was a time in the beginning of my growing attachment, when my eyes filled up with tears and I felt goosepimples along my arms every time I stood in front of the deity in a temple, sending out my love and prayers, and very aware of being blessed. Since then, I had settled down to darshan in most places with much more equanimity. It appeared as if my growing security in God's affections resulted in less emotional reactions inside places of worship. As the years passed, I rarely shed tears before God.

One April morning in 2001, before the sun had gathered its late morning's ferocity, I was headed for the Brihadeeswar temple in Thanjavur with my mother, daughter, son and my children's father. As our taxi drove through the streets of Thanjavur town, then swinging into a day of bustling commerce and activity, my mother pointed out a small shop to me with the name 'Jabalpur Hardware & Electricals' painted on its front. Since Jabalpur is my birthplace and her married home, and we were far away from MP, we were both startled. 'Some Jabalpur man must have come here and set up his store,' I remarked to her, and she smiled.

We reached the Big Temple and it lived up to every description I had ever heard. The grand sweep of its precincts, the sheer sight of its distinctive vimana and shikhara above the structure housing the main deity, its vast scale and awe-inspiring aesthetics — were all felt keenly by even the children. Since the temple is a world heritage site and under the strict supervision of the archaeological authorities, its carved stone structures have been left unpainted. This contrasts hugely with the multi-coloured visages of nearly all temples in Tamil Nadu, and underlines the uniqueness of the Big Temple. The well-tended gardens prevented us from falling prey to the scorched feet syndrome, and the smaller shrines and deities all around the central structure each had their own charm. We lingered over murals depicting Shiva's acts of grace for his devotees, and gazed with wonder at the enormous Nandi leading up to the sanctum.

By the time we entered the sanctum to stand before the largest Shivalinga I had seen till then (in spite of seeing the Bhojpur one since then, I still have a sneaking feeling that Brihadeeswara is the tallest!), we were in a kind of daze from the sights, and the drone of the guide giving us the history of the nearly thousand-year-old temple (its millennium was celebrated in September 2010). I stood before the tall black granite form of Brihadeeswara, unadorned except for a thick garland of white flowers along its length, and for some reason, my eyes welled up, my throat felt all choked, and I could feel the goosepimples along my arms again. The guide was explaining how Rajaraja Chola was intrinsically tied up to the ceremonies of the temple, and what role he had played in the construction of this wondrous site, completed in a record five years. '…the stone for the shikhara on top of the temple was carried up on a slope,' he was saying. 'It was brought from a quarry in the king's mother's village…' I was listening with scant attention, completely focused on Brihadeeswara, wondering what it was about this particular Shivalinga that had caused me to be overcome with emotion once again. Something made me suddenly interrupt the guide and ask, 'What about the stone for the Shivalinga? Where did that come from?'

Pausing slightly at my interruption, the guide quickly recovered his poise and said, 'Oh, that is from the Narmada riverbed. I believe it was brought from Jabalpur.'

He could not have imagined the effect his words would have on me. From merely making my eyes glisten, the tears began to fall unashamedly down my cheeks as I gazed upon Brihadeeswara, feeling him give me a little pinch that said, 'So you thought you knew all the ways you are connected to me, did you? Well, I will always have more surprises for you…'

The mystery of 'Jabalpur Hardware & Electricals' was explained in a flash. In plain factual terms, the discovery that Brihadeeswara was crafted from stone that came from Jabalpur, a town in MP, was merely something to know. But for a devotee from Jabalpur, it seemed like a particular blessing.

I have explained earlier the danger of looking for such 'signs' on the spiritual path. It is possible to lose one's reasoning and common sense if one reads omens in perfectly ordinary happenings, and one must scrupulously avoid doing this. But there are certain moments when it is impossible to stay convinced about the ordinariness of that instant – moments experienced as a sort of alignment with the Almighty – and it takes time to recognize these for what they are, after one has begun to be more observant and appreciative. If I had learned about

Brihadeeswara being made of stone from my birthplace when, say, I was twenty years old, it would have meant nothing to me.

He knew when to tell me.

*   *   *   *   *   *   *

In Tamil Nadu, the path to spirituality definitely lies through the senses. As one takes more and more delight in the myriad ways in which the presence of God is daily celebrated, one cannot but help becoming a devotee. I arrived there in 1984 from Mumbai — when it was still called Bombay and Chennai was still Madras — as a primarily English-speaking, non-vegetarian Brahmin from MP with no particular fondness for temples or holy sites. My senses were immediately assailed by the strong aroma of coffee and sambhar from neighbouring kitchens, which still quintessentially represent south Indian homes in other metros. But over and above these domestic imprints on my senses, there were others.

The mingled scent of camphor and of the *kumkum* that is largely turmeric-based, with overtones of the seasonal *malli* (jasmine), every time I passed a place of worship, soon began to have an effect on me. The sound of T.M. Sounderrajan's voice on loudspeakers, singing romantic, devotional or patriotic songs from the films of Sivaji and MGR and Gemini Ganesan conveys those early years better than any verbal description can. I began to be fascinated by and attached to the freshly drawn patterns of *kolam* or rangoli in front of houses and huts alike, on neatly swept and watered doorsteps or patches of earth. This visual treat was considerably enhanced during the December–January period (which is the Tamil month of Maargazhi) when the designs became larger and more elaborate, and were completed in the pre-dawn hours.

Finally, the physical lure of the temples themselves — awe-inspiring structures with vast courtyards to wander, sit, dream, or sigh in, the temple tanks and towers, with flocks of birds flying away and towards them, the sound of *nadaswaram* and *thavil* to herald the opening of the doors in the mornings and afternoons — all of it was enough to draw me completely into an enjoyment of worship that engaged all my senses. Here, temples are still spaces where the tired spirit can go and return home feeling physically refreshed. On sweltering hot summer evenings, groups of people sit in the courtyard of most temples, letting the odd gust of breeze blow over them, sharing the small leaf-bowls of curd rice, tamarind rice, or whatever prasad has been bought or handed out at the temple, finally rising to go home several degrees calmer.

The gradual accumulation of devotional feeling or bhakti in the heart of a devotee is described in the basic text of the Saiva Siddhanta philosophy, the *Siva Jnana Bodham* by Meykanda Deva written in the thirteenth century. This treatise encapsulates the main beliefs that have contributed to the worship of Shiva in the Tamil-speaking region. Although references to Shiva are found even in the earliest Tamil literature, well before Meykanda Deva's work, the *Siva Jnana Bodham* emphasizes that Shiva is not just one of the deities in the trinity of Brahma-Vishnu-Mahesh for the followers of Saiva Siddhanta. He is the supreme one who has defined and sustains this universe, and who releases the human soul from the bondage of earthly suffering. It is because of this that he is called Pashupati by the Saiva Siddhanta followers, with the human soul, or *jeeva* being seen as bound by a *paash* (rope). The rope comes into place due to ignorance and the accumulated causes of past lives, and Shiva is the *pati* or master of such souls.

Saiva Siddhanta prescribes a four-fold path to overcome the suffering of human bondage and achieve union with Shiva. First, a devotee may perform acts that are described as *Sariyai*, willingly performing the chores for Shiva's worship, such as cleaning the temple, gathering flowers for worship and cooking prasad for fellow devotees. This Dasa Marga or the path of the servant leads one to *Salokya* or becoming a part of God's abode. A more intimate service to God is called *Kriyai*, and considered the Satputra Marga, or path of the good son. This can be considered the more ritualistic and well-defined form of worship, performed diligently and with devotion. Travelling on this path takes one nearer to God, a condition described as *Samipya*. The advanced devotee achieves the third stage or *Yoga*, which includes meditation and being internally focused on the names and qualities of Shiva. This is the path of friendship, or Sakhya Marga, which can bring one near enough to begin attaining the form of God, or *Sarupya*. The most advanced path is that of *Jnana*, or the path of Sanmarga, which leads directly to *Sat*, which is God himself. The union of the devotee with Shiva is referred to as *Sayujya*.

In the twenty-four years I spent in Chennai I had plenty of opportunity to observe the various paths in practice. At the Ratnagirishwar temple, the foremost Shiva shrine in the residential neighbourhood of Besant Nagar, I saw senior government servants, corporate heads, lawyers, doctors and other professionals arrive at the temple in the early morning clad in dhotis and shirts which they would fold and put into a cloth bag. Then they would join enthusiastically with other friends and regulars in the day's worship, the men sitting with bare upper bodies on the temple floor in their dhotis, singing the bhajan '*Shambho Shankar Umapate, Shyam Sundar Pashupate,*' at the end of the prayers. When required to do so, these men would not hesitate to wield a broom to sweep up a portion of the temple. They also volunteered to stand and hand out the *pongal* or *kesari* that had been made as the temple prasad on festive days, mornings in the month of Maargazhi, Tuesday evenings or any other such time.

It was obvious that these individuals took the *Sariyai* portion of the four-fold path very seriously.

On *pradosh* days, the temple would be overflowing with men and women who had come to offer special prayers marking the hour which is supposed to correspond with Shiva's intake of the resinous black poison *halahala*, which came up to the surface at the time of the churning of the primordial ocean and posed a threat to all living creatures. Gathering in large numbers to commemorate Shiva's sacrifice, these crowds melted away after the pradosh time was up, hurrying off to their routines with complete composure. The entire exercise of staying abreast with Shiva's lunar calendar of *pournami* (full moon), *amavasai* (new moon) and pradosh besides, of course, the significance awarded to Mondays, Shiva's own day of the week, was a part of their lives.

I never became a full-fledged member of this temple-going community of mainly upper-caste and upper-middle-class individuals in my neighbourhood, perhaps because I had come to Madras as an adult outsider. My children had more opportunity to join this mainstream if they desired. But my continued observation of the practices of my neighbours, and my participation in some of their most cherished occasions offered me a window to get naturalized into the 'Madrasi' lifestyle. On an intellectual level, I was also aware of the social contradictions that simmer in Tamil society just as they do everywhere in the country. I knew that many of the pradosh and pournami regulars carried a feeling of persecution in a state where anti-Brahminism has been part of the political discourse for decades. In the homes of my childrens' friends and classmates, this translated into an excessive exhortation by parents, 'Perform or perish! Study hard, harder, or the competition will have you eliminated! Don't you know that there are only … seats in the unreserved category? GET MORE MARKS!'

I didn't engage in discussions for or against reservation with these families – some of my best-loved friends. What was the point of vitiating the smooth and happy flow of personal relations with political questions unlikely to be solved in a hurry by our government? It was quite likely that I would find VHP sympathizers and anti-reservationists among friends and neighbours, just as I would find steadfastly liberal and unprejudiced proponents of the secular viewpoint. I lived politically incognito nearly all the years I spent in Chennai, although my politics emerged in the vision of our republic and democracy that I communicated to my children.

One way in which my children learnt about the larger society they lived in, the different categories of people and their skills and needs, struggles and triumphs was when we attended occasions like the annual *ther* procession of the Sri Kapaleeswar temple at Mylapore, Chennai.

The ther or chariot festival of the Kapaleeswar temple is held in the month of Chithirai, or March–April, and followed the next day by the Aruvathimoovar festival or the festive procession of the sixty-three revered saints of Tamil Shaivism. The Tamil Shaivite songs and hymns written by these sixty-three saints constitute what is referred to as the twelve-volumed *Thirumurai*. The four tallest pillars of Tamil Shaivism are Sundarar, Appar, Thirugnanasambandar and Manickavachakar. The first three volumes of the *Thirumurai* are the hymns of Thirugnanasambandar, the next three are the hymns of Appar or Thirunavakkarasu, the seventh volume contains Sundarar's hymns, while the eighth volume consists of the *Thiruvachakam* and *Thirukkovaiyar* by Manickavachakar. The ninth and eleventh volumes are by various saint-poets, while the tenth is the work of Thirumoolar and the twelfth and final work is the *Periya Puraanam* by Sekkizhaar. This work is an account of all the sixty-three Shaivite saints, collectively known as the Nayanmars, and highlights the beauty of their hymns as well as the major turning points in their lives that emphasized their closeness to Shiva. Sekkizhaar was the prime minister of the eleventh-century king Kulothunga Chola.

The celebrations of the ther and the Aruvathimoovar festival bring traffic restrictions to the densely packed area of Mylapore for several days. Bus routes are diverted, and people throng to thousands of temporary stalls that sell everything from plastic toys and household goods to pictures of gods and goddesses, bead necklaces and woven mats. It is a proper mela in the old-fashioned sense for people to come out and market the skills and goods that are in danger of going extinct due to the relentless pressure of mechanization and the marginalization of poor craftsmen. Potters, weavers, toymakers, gypsy bead-sellers can be found, as can fortune tellers with parrot companions, solitary nadaswaram players or groups of child acrobats with their adult family members. Rounding off all these are the men who operate rides like miniature ferris wheels with small wooden bucket seats or portable merry-go-rounds. The lanes around the temple are packed with temple-goers and shoppers, vendors and mere gawkers. It is usually the early days of summer, and it is impossible to be unhappy in the bright sunlight and the bustling, lively ambience of the Mylapore mela.

On any non-festival day, when one enters this large, landmark temple for a relaxed darshan, one can read a plaque at the entrance which describes the confrontation that the keepers of the Shaivite faith had with St Thomas, one of the apostles of Jesus Christ, and later the Portuguese. The Kapaleeswar temple, which marks a spot described in the *Puranas* where Parvati is said to have adored Shiva in the form of a peacock (*mayil* is the Tamil word for peacock), is said to have been originally built by the Pallava kings in the seventh century on the seashore in the nearby area of Santhome. Its gradual ruin and final destruction by the Portuguese led to it being reconstructed by the Vijayanagar kings in the sixteenth century at its present location, around a kilometre and a half from the seashore.

Shaivism pre-dates both Jainism and Christianity, the two faiths which clashed and competed with it for followers in the south. The clash between St Thomas and the Shaivite orthodoxy didn't have happy consequences — he died on 21 December 72 AD at St Thomas Mount, a hill that can now be seen on the way to the Chennai airport, when he was stabbed by opponents of his faith. The Santhome basilica stands in commemoration of his life and martyrdom. As for the Jain challenge to Shaivism, it is repeatedly referred to in the context of the life of Appar, or Thirunavakkarasu, one of the four great Shiva-worshipping saint-poets who was tortured and hounded by Jain monks after he left a Jain monastery and returned to his original faith of Shaivism. An enraged Pallava king, advised by the Jains, ordered his execution and Appar was tied to a stone and thrown out to sea; when he didn't die, he was kept in a container of lime for seven days in the hope that his body would dissolve; when that didn't work, he was trampled by an elephant, but to no avail. He survived all such attacks in miraculous ways, and continued to sing of the glory of Shiva so that the king finally admitted defeat, and himself returned to the fold of Shaivism.

The Kapaleeswar temple in Mylapore is among the 275 temples of Shiva that have been extolled at various times by the sixty-three Nayanmars, and are, therefore, referred to as the Paadal Petra Sthalams. It is the quintessential Tamil temple, with all the characteristics that are especially pleasing to the devotee. A large idol of Vinayaka or Ganesha greets the devotee at the main gate. Shiva and Parvati's other son, worshipped across Tamil Nadu as Murugan, or Shanmugha, has a sepa-rate shrine to himself on the way to the adjoining shrines of Sri Kapaleeswar and Karpagambal, as Parvati is referred to in this temple. The dim smoke-filled sanctum of the main deity, redolent with the fragrance of camphor, incense and flowers, houses statues of Shiva and all the sixty-three Nayanmars. Genial and generous priests complete the happy experience at Kapaleeswar. Karpagambal's sanctum is lined with portraits of various facets and forms of the Devi. The dominant scent in this chamber is that of the deep red, turmeric-based kumkum, and the form of Karpagambal, dressed in brilliant silks and jewels, never fails to comfort those that stand before her. Peacocks call aloud in the compound, cats sun themselves or stroll in the courtyard, and calves and cows seem content in the temple goshala. From the gate directly opposite the main shrines, a view of the large temple tank, brimming with water in the last months of the year, is a treat, especially in the evenings when the breeze blows as one gazes at the peaceful tank, all a contrast with the city traffic beyond it. Other popular draws in the temple are the shrines for the Navagraha deities and the separate small mandapam for Shaniswara (Saturn). A long, pillared hall provides space for dance and music recitals on the temple premises, adding to its charm.

For the annual ther, the *utsava murtis* or portable images of Sri Kapaleeswar and Karpagambal are carried in a huge, wooden, intricately carved chariot. This chariot is usually parked behind upright corrugated tin sheets diagonally across the road from the famous Rasi showroom of silk sarees. On the day of the ther, it is hardly recognizable as the same ancient vehicle with blackened wheels standing silently in its tin shed the rest of the year. Decorated with flowers and towering tall and resplendent above a sea of devotees, it is a striking sight.

When we attended the ther, my children and I would take up a position on the street, along the route that the chariot would follow as it was pulled along by thousands of devotees. Corporate sponsors would set up booths dispensing buttermilk or water along the procession route, as did social service organizations and the VHP. People were ranged on both sides of the road, behind ropes that reined them in, and marshals drawn from temple volunteers assisted policemen in keeping the crowds in check. The air would be thick with excitement and anticipation. Children blew on toy trumpets, toddlers were perched on their fathers' shoulders, and everyone assembled would have their eyes fixed on the bend around which the chariot would be seen before it passed before us. It is always taken in a circumambulation of the temple tank and brought back to the main entrance of the temple.

The flower-bedecked chariot had thick ropes attached to it, which snaked over the shoulders of the thousands of devotees ahead of it, who were pulling it forward. A heavy weight at the back of the chariot, manned by a temple veteran, provided a leverage that served as a kind of steering. The height and width of the chariot posed problems where overhanging cables, under-construction buildings, or awkwardly positioned shop awnings obstructed its movement. At such times, it would have to be manoeuvred out with skilful coordination between the priests and staff atop the chariot, the main group of devotees pulling it, and the traffic-minding volunteers and police.

But this only describes the physical conditions under which the chariot moved in the procession. Its emotional impact was a different story altogether. As the huge vehicle rumbled forward a few feet, it was accompanied by a roar from the onlookers, the beating of drums, and the joyous blowing of conch shells, trumpets and nadaswarams heralding its onward march. Immediately after it had moved those few feet, it paused, giving devotees ranged alongside the chance to rush forward and touch the ropes reverentially, to make offerings and receive prasad. Then, after a few minutes, a signal from inside the chariot would make the men pulling the ropes gather their strength for the next move. They were not only being cheered on by roars and trumpets — many of the people who had gathered on the rooftops of houses along the street, mainly women and children, would throw water to refresh the sweating rope-pullers and restore their enthusiasm. It felt good to have some of those cold drops land on us too, as we stood in the summer heat.

There was something about the sight of the huge vehicle trundling forward amidst a sea of humans that never failed to spark a sense of wonder and happiness. For the children and me, it represented being a part of something much larger than the social milieu we were accustomed to. As we rubbed shoulders with onlookers and rope-pullers, vendors and volunteers, it truly did not matter who was which caste and whether they were taking advantage of reservation or against it. It did not matter if we were local or global, Tamil or non-Tamil. Like any true gathering of faith where people have gathered only to affirm their love for God, the ther of Mylapore's Kapaleeswar destroyed pretension and levelled distinctions.

When you participate in occasions like those, it is hard to remain focused on your separateness or superiority — it is much easier to accept how you are and feel at one with all humanity.

*　　*　　*　　*　　*　　*　　*

'Arunachala! Thou dost root out the ego of those who meditate on Thee in the heart, O Arunachala!' This affirmation, printed on every single cloth bag from the Sri Ramanashram bookshop, is one of the ways in which Bhagavan Sri Ramana Maharshi, the great seer, addressed Shiva as Sarvatapana, the scorcher of all *ahamkara* or ego.

Thiruvannamalai is around 190 kilometres from Chennai and the Arunachala hill that marks the spot is an embodiment of Shiva himself as *agni* or the element of fire. Described in the *Skanda Purana* and the *Linga Purana* in the episode wherein Brahma and Vishnu were both baffled and defeated by the endless column of light, Arunachala represents that jyoti or light that banishes forever the darkness of ignorance or *avidya*. It is also referred to as the centre of the earth by Tamil elders, and there is a widespread belief that it serves as a magnet that attracts *siddhar*s or realized souls. This is borne out by the presence of many enlightened seers and saints in Thiruvannamalai during the last century, the foremost of whom was Ramana Maharshi. The Sri Ramanashram, an ashram built around Ramana Maharshi's quarters at the foothills of Arunachala, is still the best known and most frequented centre for seekers and devotees.

I began going to Thiruvannamalai on short, solitary trips from Chennai in late 1997. My attraction to the place came after I read Canadian author Paul William Roberts' book *Empire of the Soul* describing the years he spent in India. I had then been living in Chennai for thirteen years, but had never been to Thiruvannamalai. After my very first visit, I began feeling an urge to go there again and again. In fact, there was a period when, driving my scooter on the busy Chennai roads, I would feel my heart skip a beat in happy recognition if I caught a glimpse of the State transport bus No. 122 ahead of me in traffic. 'Thiruvannamalai' was spelt out in bold Tamil script on the board that showed where the bus was headed. Whenever I left Chennai for Thiruvannamalai, the 122 PP or point-to-point service was my preferred means of transport.

For millions of people, going to Thiruvannamalai to circumambulate around the Arunachala hill in a form of worship known as *girivalam*, is a monthly affair, coinciding with every full moon day. Many famous and creative personalities also make regular visits to this town. Ilayaraja, the noted composer and music director from the Tamil film industry is known to have a tonsure and shave every full moon day at Thiruvannamalai. Rajnikanth, the beloved screen idol of Tamil and Hindi films, who is perceived in Tamil Nadu as a spiritual seeker and a simple man not unduly attached to his wealth or fame, regularly goes to Thiruvannamalai and is even said to have contributed to lighting up sections of the path that goes around Arunachala. This is locally referred to as the girivalam or 'hill-round' road.

There is a topographical twist in the way the road approaches Thiruvannamalai that makes the hill appear ahead only when one is almost in the town. The road is positioned in such a way that both sides appear as flat terrain after the rocks and boulders of Gingee, the site of two historical hill top forts, have been crossed, around 27 kilometres before one reaches Thiruvannamalai. Meanwhile, the hill is straight ahead, hidden by the trees that line both sides of the road. Then suddenly, one crosses a rail track to enter the town that lies around Arunachala, where the tallest structures are the four gopuram towers of the Arunachaleswara temple. You peer out of the bus at a hill now suddenly so close that the ridges, plants and bumps on its textured face are clearly seen, and it feels strange to not have noticed it coming. From the first glimpse, it occupies one's attention perhaps because there is always an interesting play of light and shade around it, some movement of the sun, or clouds that float in wisps around its peak.

I developed a routine of my own each time I visited Thiruvannamalai. While I never went there on the days of the full moon when lakhs of people walked barefoot around Arunachala, I made the girivalam offering on many occasions. Each trip therefore, always involved circling the mountain by the entire stretch of 14 kilometres, which includes the town roads and the 'hill-round' path, visiting the Arunachaleswara temple, and going to Sri Ramanashram. In addition, on some trips, I climbed the hill on the path that Ramana Maharshi used to walk on, which starts from his ashram and goes up to the Skandashram where he meditated and the Virupaksha cave where he lived for seventeen years. As one gazes down on the town from the mountain, and looks at the vast expanse of the temple courtyard, the perfect symmetry of its four towers and the central structure housing the deities, there is a feeling of being in the right place, a great gratitude that grips one for having reached there. It is indescribable, but palpably felt on the spot.

My frequent trips to Thiruvannamalai were always attempts to overcome the inner turmoil and confusion I was experiencing in those years. I would be feeling torn apart by questions like 'Why can't I be happy with the shape my life has taken? Is there something wrong with me? What is it that I am searching for, and is there any chance of my finding it without hurting the very people I care about? ' Early on in this phase of my life, on perhaps my second trip to Arunachala, I began walking from Sri Ramanashram, completed the girivalam in the afternoon, and returned to a spot right opposite where I had started, from where a road led to the Yogi Ramsuratkumar ashram. I had read about this saint in Roberts' book, where he describes meeting Yogi Ramsuratkumar when the saint was still a long-robed, wandering personality in the market lanes of Thiruvannamalai, smoking cigarettes and fanning himself against the oppressive heat. This is how he had received his name from the locals who called him Visiri Baba, *visiri* being the Tamil word for fan. He was hailed as a siddhar who had been attracted to Thiruvannamalai from as far away as UP, and had come all the way from there to stay at Arunachala's feet.

In those days, the Yogi was still present in his body and gave darshan to long queues of people who had gathered to meet him. I joined the queue, my mind full of fanciful notions of what could happen should the saint cast his eyes on me, recognize me for being a great seeker, and take me under his wing to become his favourite disciple. Like millions and millions of people who first became aware of their spiritual leanings, I had devoured *Autobiography of a Yogi* by Yogananda Paramahamsa some years ago, and the scene where he meets and recognizes his guru Sri Yukteswar Giri had made a powerful impression on me. Yogi Ramsuratkumar sat in an ordinary plastic chair in a huge hall then under construction, and the queue shuffled silently up to him and out of the door. He merely glanced at each person. There was no further acknowledgement. 'I hope there is a spark of recognition in his eyes! Maybe he will even smile at me,' I was silently hoping, somehow convinced that there would be such a miraculous moment.

I reached the seated figure on the chair and bowed, then folded my hands and looked up at his face. It remained expressionless, neutral. He moved neither eyes nor hand in any acknowledgement. The person behind me gently nudged me forward and the moment was over. I made my way outside the ashram in a daze, profoundly disappointed, even hurt. I was physically exhausted from the 14-kilometre walk, my mind was in its usual turmoil around my existential questions, and I could not believe that the all-knowing seer that Yogi Ramsuratkumar should have been, had carelessly tossed me aside without a second glance. The familiar tears of self-pity began to prick my eyes.

Just then, I reached a fork in the road, and without any thought, I blindly walked on ahead, not the way I had come, but deeper into the houses around the ashram. Dimly, I remembered a dear friend telling me her parents lived very close to the Yogi Ramsuratkumar ashram. Stumbling on the uneven surface of the road, and still wrapped up in my recent non-encounter, I had walked only a few steps when I saw an elderly man sitting on the steps in front of a house. His gentle, handsome face, the kind eyes crinkling up in a smile as I looked at him, made me exclaim all of a sudden, 'You're Uma's Appa!' He slowly nodded an affirmation, and I saw his wife, my friend's mother, come out from the door behind him and invite me in.

I walked up the steps and entered their home to spend over an hour in their warm, welcoming presence. The kind gentleman was the renowned sculptor Kalasagaram Rajagopal, creator of the lifelike statue of Bhagavan, as Ramana Maharshi is also known, in Sri Ramanashram, among others. Sipping tea that tasted like nectar, I felt completely overwhelmed by the affection and acceptance extended to me by my friend's parents. Unhurried, gracious and dignified, they were perfectly at ease with my awkward, tearful, abrupt speech and manner, till I could sense myself calming down, healing from the afternoon's hurt without any effort on my part. When it was time to go back to my room, I kept looking back to wave at both of them, reluctant to tear myself away from their love.

Later, as my tired limbs slowly drifted into the leaden state of sleep, I understood that the miracle I had hoped for had indeed occurred. The grace of God touches us in ways that are not immediately apparent, but always significant. Bhagavan Ramana Maharshi and Yogi Ramsuratkumar had both sent me love and reassurance in my troubled state. Only, it came through the kind sculptor and his wife.

*　　　*　　　*　　　*　　　*　　　*　　　*

Sri Ramanashram at Thiruvannamalai is one of the most serene and soul-satisfying spots I have been in. As a casual visitor from Chennai, I never got counted as one of Bhagavan's steadfast devotees, but this did not prevent me, or anyone, from tasting the peace that pervades the place. The large meditation hall, with a seated statue of Bhagavan and his portraits lining the walls, is undoubtedly the biggest draw. People sit, sometimes for hours, and while each is engaged in solitary contemplation, there is something very soothing about being among other seekers. The two rooms that represent Bhagavan's living quarters have been preserved as they must have been in his time, with a lit lamp and fresh offerings of flowers every day. This is a wonderful spot in which to pay homage to him, and I have pressed my forehead to the glass dozens of times, in prayer or gratitude. The bookshop is a treasure trove of books, pictures and digital media, where one can be sure of picking up something new each time. Monkeys, peacocks, and feisty puppies have completed my sense of being in a haven for all creatures, while, leaning into the large well just outside the dining hall, one can spot contented fish! The memorials for Lakshmi the cow, a crow and a deer behind the other buildings reinforce how Bhagavan's life was lived in utmost harmony with all of them.

After spending a morning at the ashram, it was always wonderful to sit on the dining room floor and partake of lunch, the prasad that represented the culmination of another successful trip to Thiruvannamalai.

For millions of Tamilians, Sri Ramanashram is not the primary draw in their journey to Thiruvannamalai. They arrive on the day of the full moon to complete the girivalam and darshan of Arunachaleswara, one of the *pancha bhootam* Shiva temples representing Shiva as the elements. Thus Shiva is agni or fire at Thiruvannamalai, *akasha* or space at Chidambaram, *vayu* or air at Kalahasti, *varuna* or water at Thiruvanaikaaval and *prithvi* or earth at Kanchipuram. He is Arunachaleswara in Thiruvannamalai, Nataraja at Chidambaram, Kalahastiswara at Kalahasti, Jambukeswara at Thiruvanaikaaval near Trichy, and Ekambareswara at Kanchipuram.

Every one of these temples and holy places has their own significance, but Arunachala and Arunachaleswara, whom the faithful call 'Annamalai' enjoy a special place in the hearts of their devotees. As Tamil elders are wont to put it,

'Kasiyil iranthaley mukti
Thiruvaruril piranthaley mukti
Thiruvannamalaiyai ninaithaley mukti'

(By dying in Kashi, one attains salvation
By being born in Thiruvarur, one attains salvation
But merely thinking about Thiruvannamalai, that brings one salvation.)

A mental picture that always comforts me when I am feeling low is the memory of how I have been around Arunachala in the heat of the afternoon, and the middle of the night, in a fine drizzle, in pouring rain, on foot, on a bicycle, and in an autorickshaw, walking alone, or accompanied by my happy, skipping children. Apart from the fact that one is walking past field and forest, village and town, there are many attractions that make girivalam eternally appealing to many.

One of my favourite pauses is at a Hanuman temple 3 or 4 kilometres past Sri Ramanashram, where the priest has a lovely, singsong way of intoning '*Sitaram, Jai Jai Ram, Sri Krishna, Sri Venkateswara...*' Entering the little temple redolent with the smell of tulsi leaves, one is rewarded with a darshan of Hanuman carrying the mountain decked with Sanjeevani, the medicinal, life-infusing herb. The small idol is actually an embossed figure on a wall, and always beautifully decorated. Behind the deity, there is a large rock, where one can rest one's back and take in the vista of Arunachala across the fields, while the breeze removes any trace of fatigue.

There are eight separate smaller Shiva temples on the path, like the Agni Lingam, Kubera Lingam, Patal Lingam and others. The village of Adi Annamalai has its own Shiva temple — not as imposing as Arunachaleswara, but with all the charm and grace of typical historical shrines dotting Tamil Nadu. A high point of the girivalam is when one has walked around the path from the town and reached the other side of the hill from which five separate points or peaks of Arunachala are clearly visible. These represent the *panchamukham* or five faces of Shiva as Satyojatam, Vamadevam, Tatpurusham, Eshaanam, and Aghoram (reference to whom has been made earlier in the context of the Shatrudra Samhita of the *Shiv Purana*). Close to this is an intriguing Ganesha temple with a very narrow opening inside the small stone mandapam. The strange thing about this is that the fattest people have been able to pass through it without getting stuck. While not claiming to be the fattest, I can certainly vouch for having somehow slithered through this narrow aperture.

The towering gopurams of the Arunachaleswara temple dominate the township, as they should. In ancient times, the Tamil belief was that the tallest structure should always be the house of God, so trying to build a private dwelling taller than the temple would have been construed as a sign of a monstrous ego, and frowned upon. This is one of the largest temples in the country, and it is best to have enough time to appreciate what it offers. Craning one's neck to see the top of the gopuram at the main entrance, one sees the ascending vista of hundreds of small deities telling their various stories. Shaivite Iyers hold that Arunachaleswara's are the tallest towers, but Vaishnav Iyengars believe that the honour belongs to the Sri Ranganathaswamy temple at Srirangam.

Entering the temple, one crosses the tank to the left, the smaller mandapams with the installed deities of Ganesha and Murugan or Kartikeya, then through the Kili Gopuram, or tower of parrots, marking the inner periphery. Rukmini, the temple elephant, is usually standing here to bless devotees, and I had to duck so that she could gently brush the top of my head with her trunk. When one finally crosses the threshold into the innermost courtyard, one faces the heart of the temple where Arunachaleswara resides, with a smaller shrine to the right, where Parvati is worshipped as Unnamalai Amman. This is a fine moment to pause and gaze at the sight, because Arunachala towers behind the temple, and both mountain and main deity merge perfectly in one's consciousness.

When I first stood before Annamalai in late 1997, the heat inside the chamber caused the sweat to pour down into my eyes and mingle with the inevitable tears. Annamalai was highly decorated on that day, being worshipped with many lamps and offerings. Since then, I have seen the deity in many moods – once as a simple black Shivalinga covered only by a white dhoti and three horizontal stripes of sacred ash. One evening, I could hear the refrain:

'Arunachala Siva! Arunachala Siva!
Arunachala Siva, Arunachala!
Arunachala Siva! Arunachala Siva!
Arunachala Siva, Arunachala!'

being sung with great devotion by a gifted singer. It was Subha, a well-known artiste from Tamil films and pop, who has been a Ramana devotee for years. I am indebted to her for the sound of these lines resonating forever in my heart and memory.

Together, the girivalam and the worship at this temple give millions of devotees each year a chance to slake their very real thirst for God even as they have their egoistical thoughts and desires burnt away by Sarvatapana, just as camphor burns before the temple, leaving no residue.

*   *   *   *   *   *   *

The Karthik Deepam festival in Thiruvannamalai is celebrated on a scale that makes it comparable to the Jagannath Yatra at

Puri. Occurring each year on the full moon day of the month of Karthikai or November–December, the festival culminates with the lighting of a lamp on the peak of Arunachala. It is fed by over ten tonnes of ghee and oil offered by lakhs of devotees and is aflame for weeks. On the day before the lamp is lit, the annual procession from the Arunachaleswara temple is carried out, on the lines of the Kapaleeswar ther I have described earlier.

Lakhs arrive to complete the girivalam, pray at the temple, and even climb up the hill with offerings to be poured into the *deepam* flame. The festival brings all the qualities of Shiva as the ultimate jyoti to the fore. It also underscores the seeker's offering of the self into the greater light that is God. The flame atop Arunachala, reaching up into the heavens, is a thrilling sight, manifesting as it does all the elements of a devotee's wish to reach a higher consciousness, and finally, liberation. Even those who do not travel to Thiruvannamalai, can watch the Deepam festival on television in Chennai and Madurai, Salem and Trichy.

But, of course, celebrating the festival is not about watching it on the small screen alone. When I travelled to Thiruvannamalai, Chidambaram and Vaitheeswaran Koil with my daughter in December 2011, we had the opportunity to see thousands of small clay lamps lit in homes in villages we passed through. For me, seeing these *aghal vilakku* (earthen lamps) was very gratifying, unlike the sight in UP where even village homes had engaged their friendly neighbourhood electrician to string China-made coloured fairy lights across their modest dwellings.

The aghal vilakku lamps are lit singly or in twos throughout the month of Karthik or October-November in the evenings. In the following month of Maargazhi, a single lamp is lit in the pre-dawn hours, and placed on the threshold. On the Deepam evening, these lamps are arranged in great profusion on large kolam designs drawn on doorsteps or just outside the home. As we passed villages that were dark except for hundreds of these flickering lamps, we saw children lighting crackers and playing with what seemed like a flaming rope that was swung round and round in interesting patterns. Thinking of the Deepam treats brought a smile to my lips. I have always relished the crunchy *pori urundai* or laddoo made with puffed rice and jaggery and the *masala vadai*.

Before this evening ride through the Tamil countryside, we had reached Thiruvannamalai on the morning of Karthik Deepam after an early morning start from Chennai. Entry into the town was being very strictly regulated, and we saw the landscape transformed into vast parking lots along the highway and a huge police presence ensuring that no vehicle entered the town except the local autorickshaws that were ferrying people from their buses, cars or taxis from well outside the town to an area within walking distance of the temple.

We got into the autorickshaw of R. Kuppuswamy who had been driving one in the town for a decade. He was happy to make three or four times his daily earnings by merely making the repetitive trip from the outer periphery to the town and back for twenty rupees per passenger. 'It is only on Deepam day and on pournami that we can earn decently,' he said. 'This is when all of Tamil Nadu and even people from abroad come to Thiruvannamalai. Rest of the days, we just manage.' As if to substantiate Kuppuswamy's statement about people coming from all over the world to see the festival, a lady from Malaysia and her daughter were sharing our autorickshaw 'We have always dreamed of coming here for Karthik Deepam,' the Tamil-speaking lady told me. 'This is our first visit during the festival.' Like me, she had been here on numerous other occasions.

My daughter and I alighted from the autorickshaw, marvelling at the sheer numbers of people everywhere. We had never seen Thiruvannamalai as crowded as it was then. Pilgrims carried their belongings in small bags on their shoulders or heads. They had either completed the girivalam or were headed there. Some had tonsured heads, and the bald heads of little children who had also had their hair offered at a temple could be seen bobbing up and down in the crowds, riding on the shoulders of their fathers or uncles. The purple flowers worn at this time by the women in great profusion were the appropriately enough named *December poo* or December flowers. The familiar vendors and mela performers were there. Groups of tribals, their foreheads painted with bright red sindoor and carrying long whips with which to lash themselves and ask for alms, were enjoying a break, laughing among themselves, and eating pongal from a big earthen pot.

We moved effortlessly, swept along by the crowds, towards the centre of the town, close to the temple. All the shops were open, although they had their fronts nearly obscured by stalls that had been put up for the mela. We walked in through the open doors of the Poompuhar Cloth Centre on Car Street, welcoming an opportunity to sit in its bright and calm interior, away from the crowds for a few minutes. The owner, Mohammed Iqbal, a native of Karur, had been here for thirty years, although the shop was older, about forty-three years old. There were pictures of the opening of the shop showing his father with Gemini Ganesan, then a reigning screen idol.

'Earlier, girivalam was not this popular,' said Mohammed Iqbal. 'Every year, the numbers are increasing. We have very few customers at this time, though we do not close the shop. This is the time for the street vendors to do business!' he said with a smile. I asked him about the arrangements for the festival in town. Were they satisfactory? 'Oh yes! Very good arrangements have been made,' he said. 'There are around 10,000 policemen, the municipality is active, and the private trusts, especially people from Salem and Karaikudi are working as volunteers to help in the arrangements.'

'What about the caste tensions that keep erupting in different parts of Tamil Nadu?' I asked him. 'Has that affected the town or this festival in any way?' He considered my question, then said, 'There are no caste tensions affecting Deepam in Thiruvannamalai. The scheduled castes are numerically strong and dominant here, they cannot be exploited. The trading community is united. We all do business together. For instance, we also make donations to the temple,' he said, referring to his being of a different faith. 'Not only do we donate to all the important festival ceremonies, we know about all the rituals too. Anybody who starts a business in Thiruvannamalai will look to start at an auspicious time that is acceptable to all faiths. There is no other way to operate here. It is only by keeping the temple and its festivals in mind that we can have our own trading calendar.'

From Mohammed Iqbal I learnt of another way in which caste differences are accommodated without conflict by the temple administration. Apparently the Deepam festivities are spread out over a ten-day *thiruvizha*, the celebration during which each community is assigned a separate day to take out their own procession or ther.

All this while, I was conscious of a huge hoarding across the road showing the faces of seventy-two regular con artists, pickpockets and thieves. It had been put up by the police to warn pilgrims to be careful of their belongings, not accept food or any offers or invitations by those featured in the rogues' gallery, and inform the police if any encounter with them actually resulted in a loss. Since I am a veteran at having my belongings stolen while on pilgrimage (on one such occasion, I had my bag picked while my eyes were closed in ecstasy before the Kamakshi Amman temple dedicated to Kamakshi, a form of Parvati, at Kanchipuram), I thought this was a very good idea indeed, provided one had the time to stand and examine the whole hoarding with care, noting each of those seventy-two faces. The multitude milling about on the street obviously had no such moment, it seemed.

However, the hoarding did lead me to the police control room at Thiruvannamalai, where I met Sub-inspector (Crime) R. Sekar and his team. 'The police is at its full strength at present,' he said. 'No one is allowed leave at this time, unless they are very sick. We have men and women personnel from thirty districts, totalling more than 10,000. Our biggest head-ache during this festival time is thieves. They will be all over. In very crowded areas, we have to place men and women in mufti.' As he was explaining this to me, a very burly, bearded man in a steel-grey safari suit, with a bandage on one ankle, came up on a motorcycle. This was Sampath Kumar, the sub-inspector from the nearby village of Kizhpanathai, whom his colleagues described as 'well-versed in the law against criminals'.

'Criminals also like Shivan, because he is too kind,' said Sampath Kumar, using the name Shivan like all Tamils. 'They pray to Arunachala to give them good earnings during this period. It is our job to stop those earnings.' There was a danger-ous glint in his eye as he spoke.

'You must be familiar with all the regular offenders here,' I suggested.

'Yes,' he agreed, in a voice that was a deep rumble. 'Crimi-nals see me and get afraid.' I nodded. I could see the truth of his words without further elaboration.

The control room was highly organized, with charts show-ing the duty allocation of personnel across various locations. Besides the drive against thieves, the police had their hands full with protection for VIPs. An additional director general of police (ADGP) law and order, a director general (DG), an inspector general (IG), five deputy inspector generals (DIGs), sixteen superintendents of police (SPs) and fifteen additional superintendents of police (ADSPs) had been assigned with the task of ensuring the smooth progress of VIP visits. Every gopuram of the temple was under the supervision of an SP and there were three SPs inside the temple to make matters doubly secure. All temporary bus stands were under supervision. As I heard these statistics, they seemed to be abundant and well thought out.

A different viewpoint was provided by one of the younger men, Inspector Velliyan. 'Providing first aid to locals who get injured in accidents while doing girivalam or climbing the mountain is also our responsibility,' he pointed out. 'The people who come for this festival are all villagers, they don't come equipped with anything. We have to take care.'

'So are they unaware of rules to be obeyed?' I asked.

'No, no, nothing like that,' he said. 'Everyone obeys the rules here. They cooperate fully.'

The policemen and I had a short discussion about the siddhars or enlightened souls who lived in Thiruvannamalai. There were many, and each had his own followers. For instance, Seshadri Swamigal and Yogi Ramsuratkumar were two siddhars who lived at the same time as Ramana Maharshi and their ashrams too exist, close to Sri Ramanashram. In recent years, I had heard of a swami who lived on top of the hill and was a *mauni* or a saint who never spoke. Locals sustained him with fruit, I had been told. 'No, no, Mauna Swami left for his home town and passed away,' said a policeman when I asked about him.

'These days there is a Lakshmana Swamy,' someone added. 'What about Nityananda?' another asked, and there was a snort of derision that greeted his query. 'He is not a siddhar!' said several of them. Since I knew about a scandal that had erupted in 2010 about this person and a female devotee, I understood the reaction.

It was time to thank the police team and move on to explore the wider canvas of Deepam. The huge temple chariot, which had already been used to carry the utsav murtis of Annamalai and Unnamalai Amman around Car Street the previous day, was parked nearby and had become the focal point before which offerings of flowers, coconuts and camphor were placed, the camphor burning steadily atop the heap of offerings. Devotees who were unable to reach the temple because of the rush chose to place their offerings here, even though repeated announcements urged them not to do so. We paused in front of the chariot ourselves, before moving into the crowd once more.

At a tea shop, we met Vadivel Murugan, sixty-seven, originally from Trichy, who was one of the saffron-clothed sadhus seen in such great numbers in Thiruvannamalai. This is a place associated with renunciation and spirituality, and it is not uncommon to find perfectly educated men, who have led long lives as householders, taking to the streets of Thiruvannamalai in saffron robes in the evening of their lives. Vadivel Murugan told us he had become a sadhu after 'settling' all his four children, two sons and two daughters twenty years ago. When he first became an ascetic, he had travelled across the country to Kashi, Ayodhya, Haridwar, Rishikesh, Badrinath, Amarnath and Kurukshetra.

He described his experience without any attempt to appear saintly, 'I didn't know Hindi, didn't know what was waiting for me, I just went around. All along the way, I encountered only *anbu, paasam, dharmam* (love, affection, good deeds),' he said. 'People who had lakhs and crores sustained this beggar.'

'So would you say that north India is a good place to become a sadhu?' I asked him. His expression turned guarded.

'I don't know about that,' he said. Then the real reason became apparent. 'In the north you only get roti to eat,' he said. 'They don't understand the meaning of *saapaadu* (food, meaning rice).' My daughter and I were hard pressed to hide our smiles at this. It seemed as if he had taken a real shine to us, particularly Shivani and he wanted to talk about many things, mainly 'about Shivan, for your book.'

'For Shivan, there is no caste or creed,' he said, and I agreed. 'He has great love for everyone. He likes both good and bad people. Else why would Manickavachakar sing in this vein about him?' He then launched into a musical rendition of *Shiva Puranam*, the first verse in the saint Manickavachakar's *Thiruvachakam*. When we strained to hear his voice above the din of the market, he had a bright idea. 'Come and sit by my side,' he said to my daughter. 'Let me tell you what he said about our Arunachala.'

The next half an hour or more saw my daughter sitting on the pavement next to him, valiantly struggling to copy what he recalled from *Thiruvachakam*, *Thiruvembavai* and other works of one of the four great proponents of Tamil Shaivism — the saint Manickavachakar of the tenth century. '*Thollai irumpiravi...*' she wrote, or '*...Nama Shivaya vaazhka...ena epozhudum...*', with only a very faint idea of what she was transcribing from classical Tamil into English. Her innate courtesy forbade her from interrupting his flow, and Vadivel Murugan waxed more and more lyrical, till, in response to one of her more desperate glances in my direction, I finally thanked him profusely, and ended the tea-time interlude.

'Ma, I am not getting into anything like that, again,' Shivani said to me through gritted teeth, taking a very dim view of my obvious amusement at her recent struggles.

Devotees of Ramana Maharshi recall how he was moved to tears of devotion whenever he listened to the works of Manickavachakar. Unlike the other three saint-poets Sundarar, Appar and Gnanasambandar, who, between them went to hundreds of Shiva temples around the Tamil countryside and extolled

Shiva under many different names, Manickavachakar visited and wrote about only seven shrines in his life, out of which the hymns to Arunachala and Arunachaleswara are the most significant. It is to him that all later devotees owe the feeling of being in a personal relationship with the mountain itself.

During the month of Maargazhi, which is the month just before the 14 January festival of Pongal, devotion reaches a peak in Tamil Nadu as millions bathe before dawn and reach the temples when it is still dark. Small children, their voices sounding like the chatter of hundreds of birds, congregated in the Ratnagirishwar temple in my neighbourhood for an hour of community singing of classical Tamil songs followed by a hot breakfast of pongal served in small leaf-bowls. It is in this season that the hymns of Manickavachakar, from a collection called the *Thiruvembavai*, are sung in Shiva temples all through Tamil Nadu. In Vishnu temples and Vaishnav homes, there is a corresponding recitation of the *Thiruppavai*, the hymns of the saint-poetess Andal.

In his account of the sixty-three Nayanmars in the *Periya Puranam*, Sekkizhaar describes the words of Saint Manicka-vachakar as he speaks of Shiva: 'Behold the God whom every-one is entitled to apprehend!' From this, he concludes that if only one lesson were to be learnt from the lives of the sixty-three saints, who represented every strata of humanity from a prince to a plebeian, a hunter to a priest, it would be that everyone is entitled to live a life of the kind that saints led — every human soul is free to know closeness to God, and Shiva is accessible to all. But this freedom is exercised in uneven ways. In my wander-ings to Haridwar or Thiruvannamalai, Deoghar or the Maha-kumbh Mela, it seemed as if the poor and less sophisticated among my fellow humans are much better represented than the rich and privileged. Those who have nothing, or very little, seem to feel it necessary to prove their devotion, while those, who have every comfort that money can buy don't seem to feel it necessary to give thanks to God in equal proportion. It used to make me wonder — does money and sophistication always increase one's distance from God? Would I lose any sense of intimacy with God and become a mere nodding acquaintance should I actually receive the million dollars that were promised to me in phishing emails of lottery wins? I also wondered whether I would like to be tested with riches, or with increased deprivation. And then, of course, I knew that such thoughts were merely self-indulgence. I am where I am through the grace of God, and I even love Him as I do because He would have it no other way.

Whenever I carried my troubled thoughts to Thiruvannamalai, I always wondered how, on my return, I somehow knew how to approach my life in a better way. Nothing was changing overnight, yet I was always growing stronger and less fearful. I did not read every last word in the books I bought from Sri Ramanashram, neither did I make any great strides in meditation. I just did the girivalam, had the temple elephant Rukmini bless me, partook of prasad in Ramanashram, and it seemed as if welcoming doors had opened. And most importantly, each time I stood wordlessly before Arunachala, seeing its rocks and slopes, its shrubs and trees, its well-remembered shape, I could understand perfectly what Manickavachakar was referring to when he sang, 'O flawless hill, how have you claimed me as your own?' The reason I, or anyone else, returns to Thiruvannamalai time and again is because it is a place where one can be soul-naked before a mountain that knows everything, nothing need be said. In the *Thiruvachakam*, Manickavachakar describes this quality of Arunachala as being the source of love greater than the love of one's own mother. Sarvatapana — the scorcher — burns away all that is inessential and an obstacle, but He never fails to give us the feeling of being completely protected.

On Deepam day in December 2011, I talked to Marimuthu, forty-three, a scrap dealer from Coimbatore, who was in Thiruvannamalai for the 127th successive full moon. 'Thiruvannamalai is special. I don't go anywhere else,' he told me. 'The siddhars here have power. One can still feel Ramana Maharshi's power, isn't it?' he asked, and I nodded.

'What do you do when you come every month?' I asked him.

'I go to the temple and Sri Ramanashram, and try also to climb the hill up to Skandashram, unless I am very pressed for time,' he said.

'Do you have a regular spiritual discipline like meditation?' I asked him.

He smiled in a self-deprecating fashion. 'Meditation is good. It prevents bad habits from forming. But I am not a regular meditator or anything.' Then, considering the matter in the space of another breath or two, he added, 'Actually, *aasai* (desire) recedes around places of Shivan worship. We feel at peace.'

K. Raghothaman, a farmer and barber from Thirukoiloor, endorsed this and said, 'I don't know any other means of finding peace than coming here. *Shivan amaithi thaan* (Shivan equals peace),' he said.

While we were thrilled to be in the town for Deepam, it was obvious to my daughter and me that getting a room to stay overnight in Thiruvannamalai was nearly impossible. The crowds were increasing, and were expected to peak in the evening when the lamp would be lit. We made our way to the municipal office, in which the lower floors were being used by tired pilgrims as a resting or sleeping area. Even though Deepam is a week-long holiday for schools and other institutions in Thiruvannamalai, it is a measure of the efficiency of the administration in Tamil Nadu that we found a responsible person to answer our queries.

Nagendran, a junior assistant, informed us that the budget for the Deepam mela in December 2011 was one crore rupees, excluding contracts, and covered sanitary works and cleaning, drinking water, fire fighting, temporary toilets, electrical works and lighting, food arrangements at several public places, lodge facilities, medical camps and first aid, and transport. When I recalled the Haridwar Kaanwar Mela municipal budget of a mere 25 lakhs that same year, this seemed a much more realistic outlay. Cleaning before and after the crowds had been to the town was a big issue in the successful completion of the Deepam festivities. The municipal assistant described a process of separating waste and its transport and disposal.

'Do people cooperate in the cleanliness drive?' I asked him, thinking of UP where every person doesn't think twice about throwing litter wherever they please. 'Of course, madam,' he replied, in a slightly rebuking manner. 'Without cooperation, such a festival can't happen.' Mohammed Iqbal, the policemen and the young municipal assistant were all praise for the north Indian IAS officer who had arrived in Thiruvannamalai five months before the festival and taken charge of it in an extremely capable fashion. 'Meetings were held with various departments more than one month before the festival began to make sure all the arrangements are properly carried out,' said Nagendran. We thanked this sincere young man and moved outside once again.

As we deliberated on what to do next, the smell of delicious sambar rice drew us to where it was being handed out to people who extended their hands to get some. Both of us received our share and ate it standing in the street. It was during my trip to the Mahakumbh in 2001 that my gurubhai Indresh Pande had taught me the ego-destroying importance of receiving alms. 'The idea that one can be closer to God only by being in the position of a giver must be abandoned,' he had said to me. 'We have to learn to receive, as well as give.' As we ate the hot and tasty prasad, we decided to go on to Chidambaram, and spend the night there, rather than try to find a place in Thiruvanna-malai. Even though experiencing the magnitude of the festival had been eye-opening, neither of us could reconcile the presence of noisy crowds with the peace and unhurried worship we usually associated with Thiruvannamalai.

And so we sped along on the Deepam evening through villages lit with hundreds of lamps, and children gathering to burst crackers. The early morning start, and the long day spent with the crowds had been quite tiring, and I was longing for a good rest. As I thought of the next day, with its promise of a darshan of Nataraja, Shiva in the form of a cosmic dancer, in the golden, loaf-shaped sanctum known as the *kanagasabai* at Chidambaram, I was cheered in spite of my fatigue.

We reached Chidambaram when it was already past 9 p.m, finding a part of the town that was unfamiliar, and not as populated as the dense area I remembered just outside the main gate of the temple. One of the halfway decent lodges had a room, and we stopped. As the clerk handed me the keys, I asked, 'Is the temple far away, or is it within walking distance?' and he replied, 'Madam, we are just outside the temple. Tomorrow morning, you can walk in through the gate at the end of this lane.' We retired to our room for an early night's sleep.

The next morning, just as the man had suggested, we walked to the end of the lane after a bath and coffee for our morning's darshan of Nataraja. The tall gopuram we passed through was nearly deserted. Remembering that the four gopurams at Chidambaram represented the four different directions from which the great Shaivite saint-poets had approached the temple, I stopped a bespectacled Dikshitar priest who was hurrying past us on his way out of the temple. 'Please, sir, this is the first time I have come to this side of the temple,' I said. 'Can you tell me which of the four saint-poets passed through this particular gate?'

Without a moment's pause and perfectly pleased to be answering my query, the priest replied, 'Manickavachakar.' Then he was gone.

Shivani and I stared at each other. Why were we completely unsurprised by this reply? Because, after the way he had dominated our previous day in Thiruvannamalai through the endearing persona of Vadivel Murugan, it would have been strange if the great saint-poet had directed us to the gopurams of either Sundarar, Appar or Gnanasambandar. He led us to his own gate.

We walked into the temple, feeling doubly charged and blessed.

Chapter 6: Mahaaushadhi
(He Who is the Great Medicine)

It was the hottest day of summer 2012, and I was not headed for a Shiva temple, but Amritsar, home to the Golden Temple, the seat of Sikhism. The bus I caught in the morning from Jalandhar was an air-conditioned one. The rising temperature across the wheat and mustard fields, villages where houses had aeroplane-shaped water tanks on their roofs, and dusty highways, could not be felt through the sun-filmed windows. All illusions of coolness were dispelled however, as soon as I got off in Amritsar at a late morning hour when the sun was close to reaching its zenith. I could feel myself burn as I waited a few minutes to be picked up and taken for darshan to the temple.

My first experience of the Golden Temple did not disappoint, in spite of the extreme heat. In fact, the glittering water of the pool of nectar refreshed both eyes and spirit with its inviting blue-green expanse. Every moment I spent in the temple was salutary, conveying the inherent self-discipline that Sikhism communicates to its followers. There was no shoving and pushing in the queue for darshan, even though there were hundreds of us. No intrusive security checks with khaki-clad women policewomen frisking my person and peering into every bag and purse — a contrast to what I had been through at Kashi Vishwanath, Ram Janmabhoomi or Mathura, at the Sri Krishna Janmasthan.

Anywhere in the Golden Temple, willing hands of an ever vigilant army of volunteers continuously cleaned up puddles of water or muddy footprints right in front of us. The gleaming steel vessels for use by pilgrims — bowls to drink water in, plates and spoons for the 'langar' meal — all were scrubbed with dark-grey ash kept in long wooden troughs, by twin lines of orderly men and women who sat on opposite sides. Other groups could be seen cutting and peeling vegetables, while some men had taken upon themselves the role of calling diners for 'langar'. They invited us in, holding aloft a gleaming thali, welcoming us into the huge dining halls, where dal and roti, some sabji and even a helping of kheer were assured to whoever sat down to eat.

From the moment I stepped onto the moist coir matting laid out to protect the feet of pilgrims from being scalded on the hot marble floors, and washed my feet by stepping into a dip in the stone path fed by running water that flowed through carefully designed holes at the sides, I did not experience a single jarring, discordant note the entire time I spent in the Temple complex. The queue moved in an orderly fashion right up to the time we entered the sanctum. Here 'gurbaani' was being sung and people were sitting and praying all around the central platform on which the holy book is kept. Although some sat longer than others, there was no pushing, shoving, glaring or ill-will here either. I paid my respects and made my way outside into the 45-degree-plus heat. The long verandahs around the large sarovar or temple tank served to shelter families who had travelled many miles to reach this holy spot. People sat, or slept, or just quietly rested in the shade of these cool verandahs, contrasting so strongly with the blazing sun glinting off the roof of the Golden Temple.

I could not help thinking of the troubled times the place and its faithful had gone through not so long ago when a military operation was launched in 1984 against Sikh militants inside the Temple. I was also conscious of the challenges to the overriding authority of the Akal Takht that have emerged in recent times in the form of the various 'Deras' (such as the Dera Saccha Sauda) led by charismatic preachers. And yet, the security and serenity one feels in Amritsar is undeniable. Challenges and difficulties within the faith have not translated into paranoia.

If I had been humbled by the disciplined devotion I witnessed at the Golden Temple, there was much more the land of the five rivers was about to teach me. The journey back to Jalandhar was vastly different from the one I had undertaken in the morning. This time there was no air-conditioned bus, but an ordinary one through which the searing afternoon heat blew strong gusts of wind. I was sapped by the heat, and tried to close my eyes against the onslaught of wind and dust. The bus was making good time on the highway, till we reached the Beas river, and the bus stood for an inordinately long time on a bridge, filling up with many more passengers till the aisles were full, and people were standing on the steps climbing up into the vehicle.

I woke from my nap and saw huge crowds on the highway. It was the hottest day I had experienced that summer, and perhaps my entire life — 1 July 2012. Yet, I saw men women and children carrying their belongings in little cloth bags, travelling in open tractors, on the roofs of crowded mini-buses, in jeeps and tempos. Bewildered by the sudden rush, I enquired what the occasion was, and learnt that lakhs of people had been attending the Sunday satsang at the Radha Soami Satsang headquarters at Beas. The sect seemed to have an awesome reach, at least in rural Punjab. The highway was jampacked with vehicles, all heading away from Beas, and our bus driver decided to take a detour to avoid the worst of the rush and still keep to his arrival time at Jalandhar.

We now began travelling on narrower roads through fields and villages. At some villages, pandals had been put up offering travellers cold water in steel tumblers — the most welcome gift on a day like that one. Our bus did not stop in such villages, merely slowed down a little, but this did not deter the villagers from urging us passengers to accept water. They held up trays filled with brimming tumblers to the sides of the bus, and a few of these were taken by thirsty passengers as the bus slowed. Seconds later, the empty tumblers were thrown back onto the road. But what was most remarkable for me was that the people offering water didn't seem to care if they got their tumblers back or not. Offering water was their priority, not guarding tumblers. 'How would they have managed in UP?' I couldn't help wondering. Prasad and beverages in disposable containers, yes, that could happen in UP. But giving someone a steel tumbler without knowing if it would come back — that was too big a leap of faith in a state where deep distrust of another's intentions is second nature to most people.

In fact, while faith in God is still the biggest motivator for people in most parts of India (for example, the extreme hardship that pilgrims travelling on rooftops of mini-buses in the blazing sun are willing to suffer to carry out a religio-spiritual task), faith in other humans seems to be lessening for us every day. Not a day passes without some glaring examples of corruption, cruelty, or greed for power being given prime time coverage in the media. The cynicism this breeds has become part of the modern Indian psyche in a way that even the great big Indian wedding is not.

Reflecting on faith and the way it shapes our society on the way to Jalandhar, I was reminded of the words of Bhupinder Singh, a driver in the army, who had driven me through the impeccable Jalandhar cantonment. When he heard I was writing a book about faith, he offered me some insights of his own. '*Pehle dharm aur bhagwan logon ki raksha karte the. Ab log inki raksha karne chale hain* (Earlier religion and God used to protect people. Now these people have set out to protect their gods!).' Agreeing with him and somewhat amused at his description, I realized that we have become a hysterical society where one of the prime occupations of those seeking recognition from their peers or those in authority was to wage battles on behalf of their deities.

In the last few years, some group or individual has always been in a state of outrage and 'hurt sensitivities' have become the mantra by which courts and the government have been petitioned to curtail another citizen's freedom. While someone like Bhupinder has the wisdom to put it so succinctly — is God such a fragile entity that He requires our protection, or are we, in fact, under His? People and institutions who should know better have fallen into the habit of cravenly pandering to those who make it a habit of protecting their deities and practices. In 2013, this has become the biggest threat to the freedom and creativity of artists, filmmakers, actors, event managers and academics alike.

In 2012, not only was faith being invoked to fuel all kinds of campaigns against books, festivals and films, but it was also being repeatedly tested by the doings of men and women who had acquired cult status, promoting themselves as emissaries of God, or God himself. As Bhupinder Singh described it, '*Bharat desh mein pata nahin kitne Baabey hain. Ek khatam nahin hota to doosra chala aata hai. Janta bhatak rahi hai.* (Who knows how many 'Babas' are there in India? One hasn't yet gone out of fashion, and another one comes along. People are misguided and going astray).' One of the big stories of 2012 was Nirmal Baba's trial by the Hindi electronic media – the same channels that raked in money through his sponsored programme, 'Nirmal Darbar', projecting him as a modern-day Shiva. For months, people had been tuning in to repeated telecasts of occasions where Nirmal Baba interacted with hundreds of people in different cities. Entry into these venues was strictly on a monetary basis, and troubled attendees could be seen on television, being blessed by Baba. On one of the programmes I saw, Nirmal Baba asked all those present to open their wallets and receive the grace of Shankarji. They did so in solemn silence. TV channels went to town about the arbitrary prescriptions he gave to those who went to him for help once they had banded together to discredit him. 'Why does Baba ask a devotee to have green or red chutney/*gol gappa*/pumpkins?' some channel promo would scream in the weeks when the Nirmal Baba exposé was airing. This was regardless of the fact that it was this very channel that promoted Nirmal Baba for months when he was buying airtime.

Does faith in God on the scale that it exists in India make people more susceptible to the likes of Nirmal Baba? In fact, it's the other way around. When everyday life gets so ugly, cruel and stressful, the poor get poorer, the unjust richer, and survival is beset by all kinds of complications, it is difficult to believe in a flawless, omniscient, all-conquering God who will put matters to right. Faith wears thin, and people get desperate enough to be willing to experiment with those who seem to have a direct channel to God, who seem to have tapped into a source of power that seems distant and removed from them. Unshakable faith in God releases one from the need of middlemen. Nirmal Baba and his ilk are those who have discovered the profitable business plan of being middlemen for God in an age of anxiety and stress. Millions were and are seeking Mahaaushadhi, or the great healer that is Shiva, and if a Nirmal Baba arrived to say he would take them to the ultimate Baba, people would be ready to give him a chance.

I watched Nirmal Baba only a couple of times on telvision, but my impression of his meetings with people was not all negative. I liked the calm way he told people to have gol gappa, or chutney, or cold drinks, or a particular vegetable. While the television channels kept bringing these up as examples of how Nirmal Baba was encouraging superstition by ascribing extraordinary powers to *pani puri* or coloured chutney (and it did serve that purpose for a vast multitude of his followers), I saw it from a slightly different perspective. It seemed to underline for me something that I personally hold true about God — that he does not distinguish one person from another — they are all one to Him. If Nirmal Baba's followers were strengthened in their belief that Shiva's grace was raining down on them, it wasn't a bad thing, I thought. I am completely convinced that my Bhagwanji is watching over me, whether I am eating an ice cream at a street vendor's or satvik food cooked in my own home. The key is the affection in which I hold for my God, only a particle of the love He has for me. When that is understood as constant, the food is a non-detail. People who ascribe superior or inferior status to one or the other dish, and its consumers, need to rethink their idea of God.

In 2005, I made reference to this in a poem entitled 'Clean Inside':

'Today's idlis
soft as fresh blossomed flowers
made me forget
to bathe, then pray.
First morsel I did think of you
but guilt, at dereliction
of puja with a clean body
came unsought.
Now, distraught,
I paused,
and saw a man with unkempt hair,
grey beard, long teeth
in my mind's eye.
He sat on a bench,

sipped tea from a saucer,
broke a bit from bread
held in dark, gnarled hands.
When had I truly set eyes on him?
I forget
he was with me today.
O Pingakshe!
I'm now surely old enough to know
You love the unwashed
as much as the bathed.'

(From *Seeking Sanjeevani and Other Poems* by Scharada Bail, Prakriti Foundation, 2005)

Unfortunately, the virtues of eating gol gappa or a particular dal or sabji were never explained in quite this manner by Nirmal Baba, or any of the television channels that were in the forefront of the campaign against him. Overall, the hype generated by the Baba, and the counter-propaganda unleashed after his downfall, contributed only to more hysteria and shrill emotion-mongering. There was another personality, a she-Baba, who blessed devotees by hitting and kicking them, and the channels got after her act, too. While the merits or demerits of these personalities can be endlessly discussed, what stands out is the need felt by so many millions to seek an outside source of blessing and benediction in the times we live in, where we have exhausted ourselves with our own meanness.

On another of our rides through the Jalandhar cantonment, I remarked to Bhupinder Singh on the 'Pir baba' shrines that had come up at some places, where people offered green chadars over the graves of fakirs who had lived frugal lives and blessed many. He had some pithy words to offer on this as well. '*Soch lo* (Just think),' he said. '*Jab yeh zinda the to koi inhe kapde dene wala nahin tha. Ab log chadar chadhane aate hain* (When they were alive, nobody could be found to give them clothes. Now people come to cover their graves with chadars).' This point was made effectively in *OMG* (Oh My God!) the run-away hit film of 2012 starring Paresh Rawal as an atheist, with Akshay Kumar playing a New Age Krishna who discourages the deification of his own symbols, and helps his atheist friend fight all those who have set up shop in the name of religion.

The greatest paradox in our country is that God, who is above all controls, who cannot be captured or pinned down, should be the reason for so many people offering us a route to God on which they hold the copyright.

When I reached Jalandhar that evening after my visit to the Golden Temple, my eyes were red, my face was burnt red too, and looked unrecognizable in the mirror. I had a throbbing headache that lying down, cool drinks and a palliative could do little to counter. Remembering the men travelling on the rooftops of mini-buses, or the heads, arms and legs of children sticking out of tempos and jeeps on the highway, I shuddered and wondered whether they had reached their homes safely, and how the heat must have affected them. My hosts, Shailesh and Seema, coaxed me into a dinner outing to 'Haveli', part of a chain of popular vegetarian restaurants across Punjab, where the Sunday crowd was immense and the final effects of the Radha Soami Satsang and other similar preachers could be seen. Lakhs and lakhs of people are turning vegetarian in a land associated with tandoori chicken for most non-Punjabis.

*   *   *   *   *   *   *

At Dashashwamedh Ghat in Varanasi I met Gopal Mallah, a living embodiment of the Laughing Buddha.

In March 2012, it was already hot enough in the afternoon to produce a raging thirst. A small booth stocked from top to bottom with gleaming bottles of mineral water was perched right at the top of the steps of this ghat, and Gopal Mallah sat inside it, shirtless, and wearing a white dhoti. I bought a bottle of water, and as I thirstily drank it standing at the shop, I thought it appropriate to begin a conversation about the river — the mighty Ganga — that may at one time in this very man's life have had water potable enough to drink.

'Feels strange to be buying water in front of this symbol of purity,' I remarked. 'Have the attempts to clean the river gathered any momentum in recent years?'

'It's riddled with politics just like any other issue connected with people's welfare,' he said. 'They take some effective measures, then go back several steps. The river takes care of itself.'

'Have the sadhus' fasts for the river had any impact?' I asked. In 2011, Swami Nigamanand, a young sadhu from Uttarakhand died after keeping an indefinite fast against stone quarrying and crushing along the ecologically sensitive riverbanks of the Ganga, and the failure of the government to prevent its pollution by industries and municipalities. Another sadhu had also been repeatedly hospitalized for the same protest.

'Yes, they have,' said Gopal Mallah emphatically. 'That is because we have also stood behind them.' He slapped his chest as he spoke, identifying the community of boatmen and fishermen with the cause of cleaning the Ganga.

'So are more fish seen in the water now? Is it clean enough to sustain them?' I asked. 'And what about turtles? When I came twelve years ago, one could see them in the river.'

'Yes, turtles used to swim around us,' said Gopal Mallah, nodding. 'And some years back the government wanted to have a special turtle sanctuary here.'

'What happened, then?' I asked. 'Did the numbers of turtles increase?'

'First of all, they released the wrong species of turtles, not the ones that are native to these parts. Then, they marked out boundaries in the river to show the limits of the sanctuary. But the released turtles merely swam away in different seasons and currents. Who knows where they are now? *Kachhuon se kaha ja sakta hai, ki sirf yeh ghat se yeh ghat tak jaaya karo* (Can you ask turtles to swim only between X and Y ghats)? They did not plan their project properly, and kept blaming the motorboats of the Mallahs.'

'Hmm…' I said. All issues of conservation of the environment are invariably tied up to livelihood issues in our country. Shortsighted policies and ill-thought-out strategies at the administrative level are further handicapped by protests that invariably follow when steps *are* taken. Outreach and communication are given such a low priority that people cannot be faulted for opposing what they do not perceive to be of any benefit to them. On the other hand, those who live in daily contact with rivers, forests and lakes understand very well the importance of preserving these natural resources. But administrators are often engaged in thrusting some project down their throats, rather than taking them into confidence and making them true partners in any process of conservation. The death dance of development has been repeated too often in so many different regions of our country to be unique to any one place. Varanasi and the Ganga just seemed to be another site of the same feeble and ineffectual commitment to environmental issues.

When we turn to God as the medicine to heal the wounds of humanity, we are actually asking that He reverse all the processes that have landed us in the mess we are in. But will God intervene to repair every human-created ugliness? And does He even want to? On 5 March 2013, the *Times of India* carried a report on how 80 per cent of sewage in India was being discharged untreated into rivers, ponds and lakes. Mahaaushadhi is always on hand to heal us from the worst pain of being human. But He is not endorsing our negligence and greed by enabling us to continue just as we always have. The irreversible processes of damage to the national and global environment have to be understood by us, and care taken for them not to be repeated. Unfortunately, not much exists at present to offer us the reassurance that this will indeed be so in future times. As they offer water to Shiva, or take a dip in the Sangam at Prayag in the Mahakumbh, millions of our people show a very real respect for the natural elements that sustain us. But their leaders, who they have been putting in place for sixty-five years and more, seem to operate in a vacuum untouched by either the concerns of faith, or those of sheer scientific evidence.

I continued to talk to Gopal Mallah for another few minutes. 'What will happen to the *masti* (carefree spirit) of Varanasi?' I asked him. 'If the Ganga dries up in another thirty years as many are predicting, will this place and its people be the same?'

The man with the dark, round face widened his brown eyes and told me, '*Kuch nahin hoga* (Nothing will happen). It will remain as *mast* as ever. Remember one thing, it will serve you well. *Jo sukh ke peechhe nahin bhaagta, usse dukh ki chinta hi nahin hai* (He who does not run after happiness is never worried about being unhappy)!' Saying this, he lifted both hands in the air and laughed aloud, 'Ha, ha, ha!' looking exactly like the Laughing Buddha, which indeed he was at that moment, for me.

I was struck. This was such an interesting assertion. Truly, is it only the fear of unhappiness that keeps us from becoming truly happy? Does running after happiness produce its own unhappiness? Gopal Mallah's laughter was meant to underscore his unconcern, and I envied him at that moment. He had stated a philosophical point in a positive, elliptical form that seemed very liberating. However, those of us placed at advantaged positions in life, who need not endlessly worry about survival, tend to grapple with its negative connotations — fear of unhappiness and trying to stave it off by satisfying a series of cascading desires. When we become exhausted by this whole process, that is when we turn to God to heal us.

Another encounter at the Gupt Mahadeo cave in Pachmarhi where I met miner and part-time priest Sanju Vishwakarma from Chhindwara, a town in Madhya Pradesh, made me ponder about Mahaaushadhi's intervention in matters of environmental degradation once more.

The cave is a mere narrow slice between rocks at several places in the approximately forty feet one has to walk inside to reach a small shrine lit by a lamp where Sanju sat, dispensing prasad next to a small Shivalinga. My girth made it imperative for me to walk sideways at several points, in absolute darkness, my bare feet sinking into the soft, fine sand that covers the bottom of the cave. Only seven or eight pilgrims at a time are let into the cave, and the rest have to wait outside till all the people inside have come out. I exchanged a few words with Sanju when I was inside, and he discovered that I had met Garib Das Maharajji. This prompted him to ask me to wait outside, where he emerged into the sunlight a few minutes later, for a break.

When we began talking and I discovered that he worked as a coal miner for most of the year, and as a priest in Pachmarhi for some months, I realized that he was perfectly qualified for spending hours inside the narrow Gupt Mahadeo cave without feeling overcome by claustrophobia. We stood before a bright orange figure of Hanuman with a raised mace, in front of the cave, and Sanju urged me to come to Chhindwara also, as part of the travels for my book. '*Ma Hinglaj Bhavani ki kripa se Chhindwara mein poore Bharat ke liye koyle ki virasat hai* (Through the grace of the divine mother Hinglaj Bhavani, Chhindwara has coal reserves for the entire country),' he said.

He was young, enthusiastic, and thirsting for recognition like many people from smaller towns and less developed regions of India. I told him that Chhindwara was not on my present itinerary, but it may turn out to be a future destination, since I had relatives there. He again emphasized that I should go there, since it was blessed with natural resources, and famous for its Devi temple. When I said my goodbyes to him, and was walking back through the forests towards where Shankar's jeep waited, my mind was a jumble of thoughts.

To Sanju Vishwakarma, a native of Chhindwara, coal was a symbol of God-given bounty, and his life was intrinsically tied up with it for the major portion of the year.

To millions of poor households, both urban and rural, coal was a precious commodity, often very hard to come by to keep their meagre home fires burning. To a significant section of the political class and administration in Delhi, Raipur, Bhopal, Kolkata and other power centres, coal was an important ingredient to be looted in a sophisticated and systematic fashion for purely personal gain. To millions of Indians whose only contact with coal in 2012 was through newspaper headlines, it was another example of our democracy — wounded and bloodied by corruption.

If God is the source of all natural riches as most people in our country believe, is He also to be their only protector? Somehow, I couldn't see Mahaaushadhi bringing any hope to matters affecting the environment without committed volunteers. We are mistaken if we believe that seeing God as the ultimate medicine absolves us of the responsibility to perform those acts that must necessarily involve healing ourselves.

*   *   *   *   *   *   *

In large regions of our country, the presence of a particular god is felt by many in the very air they breathe, the water they drink, the soil that nurtures their crops. They identify so closely with their deity that he or she is invoked in virtually every other word and deed. I have travelled in Madhya Pradesh's Malwa region in summer, around Ujjain, just before the harvest, to see a dusty, sun-bleached landscape filled with golden wheat stalks, where every other child in villages is called 'Shankar' or 'Mahesh' or 'Bhola', and it is hard not to associate the place with the fair, ash-smeared body of Shiva. On winter evenings, driving through the darkening green Kerala countryside, filled with mysterious scents, and lit with the lamps of evening aarti, it is as hard not to conjure up Devi in one's imagination.

Even just looking at the names of shops, the legends on trucks and tourist cabs, and the calendar images on roadside stalls can tell us when we are entering a territory infused with the presence of a particular deity. Thus 'Jai Badri Vishal' reveals one is in Uttarakhand and 'Manimekhalai' shows one is driving through Tamil Nadu, while 'Tulja Bhavani Prasann' means one is in Maharashtra. Mahaaushadhi comes in many different doses and appearances, under many different brand names. But He is, finally, the same healing and restorative formula.

Garib Das Maharajji of the Bada Mahadeo Sthan at Pachmarhi explained this to me in an unexpectedly lyrical fashion. When I was sitting before him discussing spiritual matters, and the aspects of Shaivism and Vaishnavism that differed on certain points, he told us, 'If we take all the vegetation on the earth to make quills to write with, and use all the water in the great oceans as ink, we will still be unable to write down all the names by which God is known. He can be called and loved in countless ways.'

I had found this a very beautiful and compelling image to describe the infinite variety of the relationship between the human heart and the friend it seeks. I also understood the logic inherent in this image. If every one of the names to call and seek God is a valid one, then why do we defend the names we choose with such vehemence and violence? Taking up cudgels to defend or promote one or more of God's names is actually just serving to exacerbate the pain of the human condition.

Returning to Bhopal from Pachmarhi is another bus journey of several hours. The driver of the bus I travelled in was young, in his thirties perhaps, very cheerful and popular with many of the regulars who got on from villages on the route. At Pipariya where the bus had stopped, another young man had got on, a serious, bespectacled, neatly dressed youth whom I took to be a mere friend of the driver till I heard their conversation more closely. The youth was a collection agent or creditor for a personal loan that the driver had taken some months earlier.

The two exchanged banter, then the driver turned serious and said he had not received some dues and had faced a couple of really bad months. He promised to clear the amount he owed as soon as he could. Then he said, 'If my situation continues to be so tough, I'll take a *kamandal* in hand and set off on the Narmada Parikrama!' His young creditor laughed in response. The conductor signalled that the bus was ready to start, the spectacled man got off with a wave, and the driver drove off once again.

I continued thinking about this encounter and what it revealed for another few minutes. The driver was thinking of becoming a mendicant or ascetic carrying a vessel known as a kamandal, which is also one of the symbols of Shiva the yogi. Going on the Narmada Parikrama means undertaking a pilgrimage on foot along one bank of the Narmada, and back along the other, covering hundreds of kilometres. The good-humoured manner in which the young creditor listened to the driver shows how the mention of God pervades a lot of common discourse in our country. In this instance, the worldly had given way without protest to a mention of the spiritual. As the bus drove past Pipariya, Budni and Hoshangabad, there were many shops alongside named after Ma Rewa or Ma Narmada. Cars, buses and trucks went past with 'Jai Bholenath' or 'Jai Mahakaal' painted on them. It reinforced for me the feeling of how natural and intrinsic to our population are concepts like faith and devotion, asceticism and spirituality, and a reaching out for the great healer that is God.

*   *   *   *   *   *   *

I discovered the countryside around Baidyanath Dham, a little before reaching Jasidih, the station where I was to get off, was a gently rolling green landscape, dotted with small ponds, small hills, small fields and even small animals. Moving past my train window, it looked like the kind of scene children love to draw and paint. The neat dwellings, also small, and the clouds passing overhead that cast a pleasant pattern of light and shade, added to the overall beauty.

Baidyanath Dham is in Deoghar, a town that is the district headquarters of one of the five 'Santhal Parganas' districts of Jharkhand, formerly part of Bihar, and a part of Bengal during the British Raj. Naturally, this makes it a melting pot of several different languages – Santhali, Hindi, Bengali and Bhojpuri, to name the major ones.

When I got off at Jasidih, a mild shower had turned the air cool and inviting. It was the first Monday in the lunar month of Bhaadon, immediately following Saawan, when lakhs of kaanwariyas arrive in Deoghar, to pour water over Baba Baidyanath, at the ninth of the twelve jyotirlinga Shiva temples. Even though Saawan had officially ended a few days ago, there was still a vast overflow of pilgrims arriving for the Saawan Mela at Deoghar. A huge number of saffron-clothed men, women and boys, all carrying small plastic kaanwar pots on brightly decorated sticks, could be seen on the platform of Jasidih station. I navigated the crowds, a happy feeling of anticipation making me smile as I emerged outside to find an autorickshaw to take me to Deoghar.

The autorickshaw driver, Dhananjay Jha, was a keen conversationalist. When I told him that it was my first visit to this part of the country and asked him about the local attractions, he said, 'Baba Baidyanath is the only attraction. He is the reason we are able to live peacefully. Look at the lakhs of people who come to see him! They are still coming, and will go on arriving for some more days. At least, today we are able to drive without any problem. At the peak of the Saawan Mela, this road between Jasidih and Deoghar is jammed with vehicles and pedestrians.'

I murmured something about having been to several jyotir-linga temples, except Baidyanath, and he continued.

'You may have visited this place late, but you have come, isn't it? Those who have darshan of Baba are indeed fortunate. Baba fills our stomachs, Baba protects us.'

It was obvious that this homily was part personal belief, part marketing spiel. I resigned myself to listening, even as I delighted in the surrounding sights and the fresh, rain-scented air. 'Baba hates *chalaaki* (cunning),' Dhananjay Jha continued. 'Clever people are actually unable to understand anything about life. They try to poke, they try to analyse, they try to criticize. But can they tell us who put the fragrance in the flowers, who turned the mangoes sweet, who breathes lives into the young ones of all species? *Bam banna hai to chalaaki chhodna padega* (If you want to become a Bam or devotee of Shiva, you have to abandon all cunning).'

'Absolutely right,' I said. He was in full flow, needing only the slightest of agreement as punctuation. He deposited me at a guesthouse very close to the temple, charming his way past a police barricade, with a promise to return the next day to take me for sightseeing.

Five minutes later I was in my room, transfixed by a local cable television channel on which Kaanwar Mela music videos were being continuously telecast. The feel, the visual and audio effects of those videos can perhaps not be adequately described here. They were in Hindi and in Bhojpuri, featuring local boys and girls enacting scenes from Shiva and Parvati's domestic existence in appropriate costumes, interspersed with shots of groups of kaanwariyas making their merry way across a rural landscape of fields and forests, roads and rivers. I was completely fascinated by the actors in the videos, who, to me, seemed the last word in rustic 'cool'. They wore loud make-up and lots of glittering jewellery and clothing, but their dance and expressions were nowhere near suggestive or vulgar. Instead, they enacted innocent scenarios showing Bhola and Parvati having domestic arguments, or a man leaving for the Kaanwar Mela being asked by his wife to bring bangles home for her, or a girl entreating both parents to accompany her to Deoghar.

The actors playing Shiva were dressed in tiger-striped cloth and fake cobras around their necks ending in a spread-out hood to one side of their cheeks. Shiva and Parvati argued mostly about bhang or chillums it seemed to me. In one video, a small girl playing Parvati said she was going to her mother's house because she was tired of constantly having to grind the green bhang leaves on a flat grinding stone for Shiva. In another scene, they fought because she stopped Shiva from smoking that one last chillum. It wasn't at all hard to know where the creators of these videos were getting their ideas from. Similar scenes must be enacted all over the country, in both rural and urban areas, all round the year.

The tinny sound of the songs is specially recorded with microphones that produce that weird Kaanwar Mela effect. And yet, in spite of so many no-nos, I was immeasurably cheered by these songs and even did a few dance steps in the privacy of my room. This was techno-folk, and as awful as that sounds, it still had the power to amuse and delight. Purists may shudder at the way in which Shiva and Parvati, Ganesha, Kartikeya, and even Rama and Sita were depicted in some of the videos. But I know my Shiva is not in the least threatened by being presented in a tacky way. In fact, I am sure He must be pleased that personalities like Pappuji, Guddu Jhamela, Kallu and Sunaina (from towns and villages that could be anywhere between East Champaran to Ballia and Gorakhpur) should be getting a chance to shine and strut their stuff in an India otherwise dominated by Bollywood, such as Kareena Kapoor's declaration of being a leg of tandoori chicken in *Dabanng 2* (December 2012). I watched a full hour of those videos with intense enjoyment.

Baidyanath Dham is the ninth jyotirlinga of all the twelve jyotirlinga Shiva temples, and its establishment in Deoghar is attributed to Ravana, the ten-headed Lankan king who was a great Shiva devotee. The *Shiv Purana* describes Ravana worshipping and meditating for years at Shiva's abode in the Himalayas, but being unable to please him. Feeling that he needed to make further efforts, Ravana decided to sacrifice his head, and since he had ten heads, he ritually began offering them one by one, till only one was left. He was about to offer this too when Shiva appeared before him, and stopped him from this final sacrifice, further blessing him by granting him a boon.

Ravana asked his Lord to accompany him to Lanka, where he wished to instal a Shivalinga in a grand temple. Shiva agreed, on the condition that Ravana should personally carry the Shivalinga for worship, and not put it down anywhere on the ground along the way from the Himalayas to Lanka. If it was kept down anywhere, it would establish itself on the spot. Ravana agreed to this condition, and joyfully imagining his

Lord in his own kingdom, set off at once. This displeased the devas in the heavens, since they did not like the idea of Ravana being further empowered by Shiva's presence in his territory. Vishnu then convinced the mighty Ganga to enter Ravana's body, so that he, in his travels, would feel the uncontrollable urge to urinate.

Asking a young cowherd, who was actually Vishnu in disguise, to hold on to the Shivalinga while he answered nature's call, Ravana stopped at Deoghar. Imagine his horror when he returned and found the cowherd had fled and the Shivalinga had established itself in this scenic spot for good! The gods and goddesses in the heavens above were so pleased at this development that they all assembled to establish Shiva in the site with appropriate prayers and worship.

Interestingly, there is a near identical story describing how Sri Ranganathaswamy or Vishnu as established at Srirangam, on the banks of the Cauvery river, when he was being carried to Lanka. In that story, the mischievous boy who dropped the idol on the ground so that it stayed forever at Srirangam was actually Ganesha in disguise. Sri Ranganathaswamy consoled Ravana by telling him that although he was established in a lying down position atop the coils of Sheshanag at Srirangam, his gaze was directed towards Lanka, and the king would, therefore, always have his blessings. Some Tamil old-timers believe that the ethnic strife in Sri Lanka which began in the early 1980s was due to the fact that Sri Ranganathaswamy's gaze was obscured by the height of a particular gopuram raised under the instructions of a Vaishnavite religious head.

At Baidyanath Dham, the ancient Shivalinga established by Ravana and the gods was rediscovered for history by a cowherd called Baijnath, which resulted in its being named after him. The temple itself is very distinctive, with many whitewashed shrines clustered together, offering devotees the chance to worship Shiva and Parvati, Ganga, Vishnu, Bhairav Nath and other deities. An ancient well on the premises provides another focus of worship.

Devotees at this shrine are referred to as 'Bam' which is a combination of the syllables of Brahma, Vishnu and Mahesh. Some consider it a mantra that generates energy and enthusiasm for carrying out the kaanwar yatra, which is why it is chanted along the way as the distinctive cry, 'BOL BAM!' Since most of the lakhs of kaanwariyas walk 105 kilometres from Sultanganj to Deoghar with Ganga water, the psychological strength they gain from saying this and hearing it chanted by their fellow pilgrims cannot be underestimated. The mantra gains further importance from the *Skand Purana*, which describes those who complete the holy journey by reciting 'Bam' as obtaining the virtue equivalent to performing an Ashwamedha Yajna or the great ritual sacrifice of yore.

Just like at other destinations, the kaanwar yatra at Deoghar is growing in numbers every year. Although it was always the biggest congregation of kaanwariyas compared to any other Shiva temple, it is increasing in size with each passing Saawan. En route from Sultanganj, where the devotees bathe in the Ganga and collect water for the shrine, there are many dharmashalas before the final destination, Deoghar, where *bam log* (devotees) can rest. Throughout the town and along the route of the yatra, the cries of 'Bol Bam!Bol Bam!' can be heard in thousands of voices, resonating with power and affirmation.

I had my bath and got ready (in spite of the lure of the music videos) and went out to explore the possibilities for lunch. The market was a pleasantly bustling place with many shops selling the famous *peda* sweet of Deoghar, puja items, plus the usual household goods, clothing, cosmetics and costume jewellery. The bangle shops were so bright and dazzling that they threw out light into the already sunny setting outside.

Some of the older buildings in the market area were of British Raj vintage – private dwellings with elaborate façades that were now in a state of disrepair, but pointed to a time of prosperity at the turn of the last century.

My progress, ambling though it was, began to be handicapped by the pesky attempts of two young beggars. These boys were not asking for alms on the basis of their poverty, but their religious clout. They were dressed in full costume as Brahmin priestly apprentices, wore dhotis and carried cloth bags, sported the Vaishnavite tilak mark painted on their foreheads, and several tulsi malas around their necks. They stopped me in my tracks, and insisted I take them out for lunch. Since I had just then set out and wanted to spend some more time exploring, I declined. I might even have come back and offered them the lunch later, but they began to wheedle, not allowing me to walk even a few steps, and this made me see red. Wondering at the 'sucker aunty' tag that must be making me a prey to such people, when a hundred other potential lunch-givers on the road were being overlooked, I began making my way forward, resolutely ignoring these two. For a time, life became a grim struggle to avoid their imprecations and still maintain my dignity and interest in the bustling bazaar. Then I reached a point on the road where their territory must have ended, for they just melted away.

After a restorative post-lunch nap and tea-time enlivened by some more of the music videos, I was ready for my first visit to the Baidyanath temple, accompanied by Ramji Pande, the priest whom the guesthouse had assigned for my darshan. It was a Monday, so the temple was going to be very crowded, he told me. We walked to the temple, a mere minute away from the guesthouse, and I entered the courtyard with the white-washed structures where the stones were slippery with water spilled from thousands of kaanwar vessels. The staircase that

Ramji Pande took me up to the first floor office, was also wet, as were the marble floors. It reminded me of the wetness in Rameshwaram, the temple where devotees bathe twenty-two times before darshan at many wells and tanks within the temple periphery.

We went to the office for me to meet some officials of the temple and ask them questions if I wanted to. There were a couple of men, very well-built Brahmins with paan-stained mouths and red tilaks on their foreheads, supervising some small, slim and slight temple minions who were counting and sorting a huge pile of coins. They provided a visual contrast in size that revealed social and economic differences better than any explanations could. The office had a huge screen showing images captured from CCTV cameras at several points around the temple. I watched, incredulously, at what looked like 500 people inside a tiny room engaged in a struggle involving flailing arms and legs, a flurry of flowers, leaves and water, people getting pushed and jostled and nearly falling. This was the view of the sanctum sanctorum around the Baba Baidyanath Shivalinga. For the first time in Deoghar, I felt a wave of nervousness. Was it possible to have darshan in these circumstances?

Just then, Ramji Pande appeared a few feet ahead of a priest wearing a red silk dhoti and a red cloth thrown over his upper body. Several assistants walked behind him, indicating his seniority in the temple hierarchy. He walked in and occupied the chair behind the big official desk in the office, and nodded at my namaste in a preoccupied fashion. Ramji had introduced me as a writer documenting the Saawan mela. 'He is our head,' Ramji whispered to me. 'I will take you for darshan along with him.'

The head priest did not spend more than two minutes in the office. After a quick word of enquiry from his assistants, he pulled the cloth off his upper body and, twisting it, began to form a tight turban around his head. When this was in place, he picked up a bunch of thin bamboo sticks that had been tied together. 'Oh, will you be using that? I was wondering what it was for,' I blurted out.

'Yes, I will be using these,' said the priest, nodding emphatically. Then he added in an ominous manner, 'You write.'

I had no time to wonder what he meant as I scrambled to get up and follow him along with Ramji as he left the office and began walking extremely fast down the corridor and stairs. We literally raced past the crowds that scattered at our approach, till we were in the open area right in front of the entrance to Baba Baidyanath's sanctum. This was packed with people, and a number of policemen were trying to regulate the crowd.

The priest in the red dhoti began using the bunch of bamboo sticks indiscriminately on the crowd. 'Thwack! Thwack!' came the sound of cane meeting flesh as people began to flee from his blows. I was horrified. They were poor, rural people who had walked miles carrying water and were waiting for their turn inside with Baba. Yet, no one protested. As if reading my mind, Ramji said, '*Bam log lathi se nahin darta hai. Unko maloom hai ye yahan ka prasad hai* (The 'Bam' devotees don't fear the lathi. They know these blows are the prasad of this place).' This was hardly the justification I wanted to hear. The caning went on for another few seconds, till an area in front of the entrance was cleared of people.

Now Ramji asked me to ready myself for darshan. Completely rattled, I wondered what was to come. The policemen had gathered at the front, where they were calling for the inside crowd to be released. Men came out at a run from inside, spilling out at odd angles, some tall, some crouched, some pushing hard with their elbows. I suddenly remembered that on the CCTV camera clips, I had seen one crowd completely made up of women. So, if women and men had separate timings, what was I doing in a completely male crowd? I remembered being groped in the Badrinath temple at the crowded time of the evening aarti. But this was not the time to quiz Ramji Pande. He was totally focused on the moment that would be the right time to enter the temple. The shouting of officials, the 'thwack-thwack' of canes beating people who were coming out, and the general din, unnerved me further.

Then all of a sudden, Ramji took me by the elbow and said, 'Go!' and I was swept by the crowd pushing me from behind to a very narrow doorway, beyond which people had assembled in a packed queue. There was an even narrower stone doorway with a raised threshold to the right of this entrance, which was the entry into the *garbha griha* or sanctum. As people rushed out of the sanctum, we in the queue had to go in. It was so narrow that two or three people would get stuck together for a second or two, then disengage and go their respective ways. The sensation of chaos was absolute, yet I was somehow inside the sanctum holding tightly to my small plastic pot of water, flowers and leaves, with my handbag tucked under one arm.

Inside, there was an extremely small chamber and right at the centre of the floor was the Shivalinga, Baba Baidyanath himself. The crowd of over two hundred people was jostling to make their offerings. Leaves and flowers were piled so high on Baba that I could not see the stone. I was pushed close enough to it to make some attempt at pouring water and offering the bilva leaves and flowers. A single priest near the Shivalinga spotted me and started making loud demands for dakshina in the midst of it all, till he was silenced by a signal from Ramji. Then the hysteria inside the sanctum reached a crescendo, the crowd surging within, the place completely packed. Ramji gave me a push and asked me to stand inside one corner, with my back against the wall, while he stood facing me, pressing the walls around him with an arm on each side, forming a protective shield. Water was flying everywhere. People slipped and stumbled as they ran to make their offerings. Suddenly, the call from outside asked the place to be emptied for the next wave. Even though we waited till the place was nearly three-fourths empty before making a move to go out, we still had another breathless, panicky exit through the two narrow doorways — until, at last, I stood outside in the evening light, dazed, confused, momentarily unable to comprehend that I had come out unscathed. Only my saree was wet, but my bag was unharmed. No one had tried to touch me oddly in the crowd, and I was grateful. I had never before had such a chaotic darshan of any deity, and I was hard put to describe what I felt. I had a similar experience when I looked in the eyes of Kali, at Kalighat in Kolkata, in an extremely crowded sanctum with my feet trampling a sticky, flowers-leaves-sugar-water covered floor. That now seemed like an easy, disciplined outing.

'You had Monday evening darshan,' said Ramji, smilingly reminding me of my good fortune, and I just nodded. Then he looked serious and said, 'But today the temple is too crowded. It will be better if you come back once more, in the daytime. Are you going to be staying long enough for that?' I was. We arranged to meet once more on Wednesday morning, then I left, still dazed by what I had been through.

*   *   *   *   *   *   *

My autorickshaw drove steadily through the charming countryside I had seen from the train window before getting off at Jasidih. I had decided to spend Tuesday out of Deoghar town, and passed through the villages, ponds and rice fields filled with women in colourful sarees folded up to their knees who were bent over in ankle-deep water, planting seedlings. The weather was tranquil, the landscape lyrical. Even the goats

I saw skipping in the villages were perfect creatures. Every once in a while, our vehicle was overtaken by jeeps or vans carrying saffron-clothed 'Bam' devotees.

Before leaving Deoghar, I had spent some time at the entrance of the town where the road from Sultanganj reached. It was lined with arches put up by local businesses and institutions. A long line of saffron-clothed kaanwariyas could still be seen, approaching the town. I spoke to several groups who were resting at roadside tea shops and found a large number were from Nepal. Some of them had been coming for years. It took them a week to complete the yatra, and each person spent around 5000 rupees. What did they pray for? Longevity of their husbands or providers, for offspring, for curing an illness — the list was long. A man from Bara zilla, Adhapur, in Nepal grinned up at me and said, '*Baba audhar daani hai, sab kuch deta hai* (Baba is a complete giver, he gives whatever one asks).'

A young boy in a school uniform, with gleaming dark skin and a smile revealing very white teeth was selling coconut slices. This was Ujjwal, fourteen years old and studying in Class VIII. He helped his poor family by selling his tray full of coconut slices during the Saawan mela. 'I break the coconuts myself, cut and wash the slices,' he told me, and I bought half a dozen. He was so neat, shy and serious, and I couldn't help contrasting him with the wheedlers I had met the previous afternoon, who felt the world owed them lunch after they had donned priestly clothing.

As the autorickshaw took me to a hill called Tapovan, considered holy because a special spot in the rocks resembled Hanuman tearing his chest open to reveal 'Sita Rama', we passed a long line of solar panels winking in the sunlight. This example of harnessing an alternative energy source was as soothing as the picturesque surroundings, so that I arrived at the hill feeling quite content. 'Will I have to climb much?' I asked the autorickshaw driver. 'No, the climb is only about 40 feet or so,' he said. A slim middle-aged priest with a pencil-thin moustache walked up and we set off to see the Hanuman stone with 'Sita Rama' written on it.

The first part of the climb was up clear steps cut into the rockface of the mountain, and I made it with relative ease. We paused at one spot, where, under some overhanging rocks, half a dozen enterprising locals had set up computer printers on batteries. All over Deoghar, including inside the Baidyanath temple, men walk up to you with cameras, selling each picture they take of you for twenty rupees. This is usually delivered within minutes of your posing, printed out on the battery-operated printers. I thought it wonderful that this assembly was sustaining so many families in these parts. As I smiled at the vista of fields spread out before me and felt the breeze blow through my hair, I had my picture taken by a couple of shutterbugs.

That was the end of my serene outing. Reaching a temple that had been the meditation spot of Sri Mohanananda Brahmachari, one of the disciples of the great yogi, Sri Balananda Brahmachari, I first had to climb into a kind of loft, then exit it through another tiny hole in the floor. I managed this, but there was no time for self-congratulation. After that we had to reach the spot among the rocks of the mountain where a cluster of tall bamboo poles with saffron pennants was clearly visible from many kilometres away. If I had been under the impression that it would be a gentle climb that I would manage with a few steps, I was sadly mistaken. Apparently, Rani Charushila of the Pathuria Ghat royal family of Kolkata, who had been kind enough to have the steps built at Tapovan, had subsequently had a dream that prevented her from completing the task. So all the devotees who reached all the way up to the meditation spot, had to start climbing over large boulders, unevenly tossed by the forces of nature onto the hillside. This was not only the single way to reach the spot with the pennants, it was also the only way to go down.

I climbed the first few rocks with the false confidence of one who believes the steps are only around the corner. When there was no sign of them and the way became increasingly difficult — a loss of footing could have meant a fall and a fracture — I began to wonder. The priest kept encouraging me in the manner most people do at pilgrimage spots, 'Not much to go, now. *Aaraam se* (Easy does it). Say "Har Har Mahadeo!" Say "Jai Hanuman!"' and I would negotiate a big rock by sitting and sliding on it.

Wild thoughts rushed through my brain. This was surely Baba Baidyanath's revenge on me for not undergoing even a fraction of the physical discomfort and difficulties of actual 'Bam' devotees. He was ensuring I paid up my full quota of physical effort, I thought. A moment later, I was having an attack of hysterical giggles. 'I may not have become a bonafide "Bol Bam" devotee, but I am surely now entitled to be known as "Aunty bum",' I thought, negotiating another big rock on the seat of my salwar. The ground, with its beautiful chequered surface of fields, dotted with small animals and people, looked very far away, and I was wondering if I would ever reach it. Arthritis, osteoporosis, and pelvic fractures had already overtaken me among the rocks, or so it seemed. But the truth was, nothing happened. I was safe and unscathed till the end.

We reached the spot with the pennants, and I touched my head to the Hanuman rock, covered in sindoor. 'Please see I make it back safely!' was the only prayer that came to my mind just then. I rested a couple of minutes on a rock below an overhanging branch on which two langurs were sitting, one grooming the other. For some reason, this sight and the breeze revived me. 'We are almost there, just reaching,' said the priest gently, and this time he spoke the truth. A few more boulders later, we had reached the steps.

I met the senior superintendent of police, Deoghar, Subodh Prasad, at his office in town in order to get a perspective of the arrangements made by the administration for the Saawan mela. Knowledgeable about the town and its people, he not only belonged to a neighbouring district, but this was his second tenure at Deoghar. He had earlier been the deputy superintendent of police from 1994 to 1998. 'Conditions then contrast with what they are today,' he said. 'The crowds have grown tremendously. When I returned to this posting, I could see the difference and immediately requested for more personnel. In 2009, for instance, there were only 2500 police personnel available. The next year, in 2010, I got 500 more on hand. In 2011, this number increased to 4500 policemen, till this year, in 2012, we have 6000. We also allot the supervising officers according to the traffic seen at the festival. In the first phase, when more numbers arrive, we have thirteen DSP level officers assigned to the mela. In the second phase, it reduces to eleven DSPs. Of course, now we notice that the mela is not confined to Saawan alone. For instance, it is now Bhaadon, and numbers are still high.'

SSP Prasad was in close touch with the temple authorities about crowd control within the campus, and visited it every day, sometimes more than once. When I mentioned the caning by the head priest, he smiled and said dryly, 'Our policemen do not cane like the traditional priests. They are not supposed to. That method is part of the priests' means of crowd control. It has been going on for generations.'

'The temple has instituted new systems for darshan, and these have helped to some extent, but what about facilities for pilgrims?' I asked. 'Shouldn't these be augmented?' SSP Prasad agreed, and told me about the arrangements for first aid, water supply and sanitation that had been added in his tenure. He was also personally on hand to welcome the first wave of kaanwariya arrivals every year, he told me, and he went on regular visits to ensure facilities were extended to them on the Sultanganj route.

I made note of this, but it was routine stuff that I had no means of checking, since my visit was after the Saawan mela. Instead, what I found riveting was the *janta darbar* or hearing complaints from people that went on for nearly three hours as I sat in the SSP's office. It was here that he discharged his duty as a virtual instrument of Mahaaushadhi or Baba Baidyanath himself. Nearly all the cases presented before him were of a domestic nature. A man who asked him to rescue his daughter from the home to which she had eloped with her boyfriend, and put her in a remand home instead, was sternly asked, 'Have you seen the conditions in the remand home? What lesson do you want to teach her? Are you angry that she is happy where she has gone? If she was not happy, you would have some information from her friend or your neighbour, is it not?' The man began to wilt under this questioning, finally agreeing to give his daughter the chance to be happy in her new home, even though the boy she had fled with belonged to a different caste.

The large, frightened eyes of a very thin young woman holding a baby, accompanied by her father and mother, also leading two very small girls, are seared in my memory. This woman was being threatened with death by her husband for giving birth to three daughters. She was now living in her parents' home, and the poverty of the couple made one wonder how they survived. But her husband had arrived there too, once accosting her in the dead of night when she had gone out of her hut to relieve herself, and tried to strangle her. Here Subodh Prasad took immediate action, ensuring that the man was brought to the police station.

A middle-aged woman who had been waiting with me, had paid money to a man for property which he refused to register in her name after taking the cash, and did not return the money, either. Details were also quickly collected from her for a follow up. I began to see the pattern of the darbar. By the time anyone began to tell the SSP what their problem was, a constable already stood at the officer's elbow, holding the papers relating to the case. As soon as he had decided what was to be done, he made a note on the papers and passed it back. Women representatives of two political parties — the Congress and the Janata Dal (U) — had also come to present the problem of protégés. The SSP was polite, but slightly cool to them.

I was quite taken aback to find that almost the entire three hours had got taken up with issues relating to women. As if anticipating my comments, the SSP said, 'This is the bulk of my work — protecting the rights of women. No great lowering of the crime graph or dealing with murderers or Maoists. Here it is all about women being tortured, or threatened, or abandoned, and the SSP is the first stop. Mandal, Muslim, Das and Yadav, these four communities are a real headache in terms of the feudal approach they have to women. Men marry, have one or two children, then abandon the wife. Worse, they will go on to marry again. I really wish sometimes women's groups would highlight such problems on the national stage, instead of making a huge fuss about an incident in a nightclub.' His words may have sounded patriarchal to me had I not been witness to his work of the previous three hours.

'Is every day like this?' I asked.

'Most days are,' he said. Some days I rise for lunch at 4 p.m. because there are so many cases. And the bulk of them are always these domestic matters. Women's empowerment — if it is needed anywhere, it is here, in rural and semi-urban India.'

Born and brought up in Deoghar, Alok Santoshi was a senior journalist I met on my third day in Deoghar to piece together some more details of the Saawan mela. With over fifteen years of writing for papers like *Dainik Jagran, Sunday Nai*

Duniya, Ranchi Express and others, Santoshi had finally turned to the electronic media and started his own local cable television channel. 'The Baba Baidyanath temple used to be administered by one particular family – that of Sardar Panda,' he said. 'When he died, there was a succession war among his relatives and descendants, which was going on in court. It was during the pendency of the court proceedings that the Mandir Prabandhan Board was set up some three to four years ago. Since then, the mela has been organized more systematically. A Panda Dharmarakshini Sabha, like a union of the priests, has also come into existence, to give better service and prevent exploitation of both the pandas and the public. For instance, there is now a 'Sheeghra Darshanam' (quick darshan) facility being offered for 500 rupees. Out of this money collected, 60 per cent goes to the government and 40 per cent to the pandas, with the allocation being 20 per cent to the individual panda and 20 per cent to the Sabha. This has brought some transparency to the matter of huge collections during the Saawan mela.'

Santoshi was very clear that the single most important factor in the increase in numbers at Baidyanath Dham was the improved means of communication, particularly television serials, audio and video CDs, and the playing of both music and videos on mobile phones. 'T-Series, for instance, is a single company that has contributed hugely to the "Bol Bam" phenomenon, with hundreds of videos and songs being produced every year. Films have also contributed their share. *Ganga Dham* was shot completely in Deoghar, with Arun Govil, Shakti Kapoor and Namita Chandra as the cast. *Jai Baba Baidyanath* is another one that comes to mind. After people see these movies, they wish to come to Deoghar, to see Baba Baidyanath.'

The increased numbers of kaanwariyas have very specific characteristics, according to Santoshi. 'The first type of kaanwariya comes with complete surrender (*poora samarpan*) in his mind,' he said. 'The second type is the one who has found inspiration from seeing someone else who has done the yatra. And the third one is the kind just arriving for the picnic and fun. This is how it is in these times. Earlier, we remember very severe *hatha yoga* performed by kaanwariyas, such as the *dandavat kaanwar* or rolling on the entire route from Sultanganj to Deoghar, sometimes even from their homes in nearby districts. They would take two and a half months to reach. The other was the *khada kaanwar* where the person remained standing the entire time, even during the nights, when they paused for rest. Now it is more common to have the dak kaanwariyas who run and complete the entire stretch in twenty-four hours, with a vehicle following them, or the *phalahar bam* who consume only fruit and food meant for fasting.'

*   *   *   *   *   *   *

'Baba ka ghar hai door,
Par jaana hai zaroor!
Bol Bam ka naara hai,
Baba hi ek sahaara hai!'

(Baba's home is far away, but I absolutely have to go. My slogan is 'Bol Bam!' and my only refuge is Baba.)

At a relatively early hour on Wednesday morning, I kept my assignation with Ramji Pande at the temple. 'Bam log' were continuing to arrive even now. Many reached the temple and poured water over themselves at the well, before going for darshan. Ramji Pande wanted me to do a proper puja at the temple, and asked me to wait while he went to make arrangements. I sat and watched hundreds of kaanwariyas walk past me. Completely intent and focused on their minutes with Baba, these men and women walked past me in silence, occasionally breaking into a 'BOL BAM!' or a 'Har Har Mahadeo!'.

One could sense that this time represented a culmination for them of many weeks of effort, and they wanted to savour it in all seriousness. Some had reached a stage when it was clear that just putting one foot before another was costing them great effort, yet they did so with total determination. Some still had the energy to run, the final dash towards Baba.

An old drummer was beating a drum and its throbbing rhythm was heard above the bhajans being played on the public address system. Incense and camphor smoke was rising from many aartis being performed by devotees at different places in the courtyard. The sound of conch shells and the clang of temple bells added to the ambience of worship.

The crowds were marginally lower than on Monday evening, but I was determined not to let the process of entering the sanctum make me lose my serenity. I waited patiently for Ramji to come with all the materials for puja. The tremendous faith and patience shown by the kaanwariyas over their pilgrimage on foot was a salutary example for me. When he arrived with flowers and water, a lamp and incense, we spent a few minutes saying the obligatory mantras that recorded my name, my attendance on that particular day at the shrine and my prayers for my family. Then we made our way towards the entrance. Today, the caning was sparingly done by a few temple officials, and our entry was also accomplished without the kind of panic and bewilderment I had felt the last time. Inside the sanctum, I was taken to the Shivalinga, which was at that moment, bare, except for a few bilva leaves on top. I poured water on Baba, and touched the Shivalinga reverently. It made me feel that Baba Baidyanath was the brother of Omkareshwar, the Shiva I prayed to on an island in the Narmada in the jyotirlinga temple there. The Baidyanath temple filled with people again, but even though I began to be jolted and pushed, I felt at complete peace.

We exited Baba's sanctum, and Ramji took me to the shrine of the twin figures of Durga and Parvati, where I again had an intimate and satisfying darshan. Then we were out in the sunlit courtyard, where I was introduced to a special feature of Baidyanath Dham. Here, the twin shrines of Shiva and Parvati are linked by devotees' offerings of long strips of red cloth, which are tied first to the shikhara of Baba's temple. A man brought down one end of the strip and gave it to me to hold and carry for some time. He then took the other end, climbed up with it, and tied it to the shikhara of the Devi temple. Once this was done and my prayers completed, I was given the entire red length to coil and take home. I felt very happy linking the two — Shiva and Shakti. The whole experience concluded with an aarti to Baidyanath Dham expressing gratitude for having brought one here. I performed the aarti in perfect contentment. Everything was just as it should be.

Ramji Pande was most anxious that I should not go home with any negative memories. 'Are you happy?' he asked me several times. 'Yes, of course!' I replied, thinking, 'How could I be otherwise?' For finally, that is the shape of God we each have the chance to know most intimately — the pure happiness that arrives unexpectedly in our hearts.

Returning home to Lucknow from Deoghar, my train was arriving close to midnight at Jasidih station. When I reached there a couple of hours earlier, I found thousands of kaanwari-yas resting on the platform, or attempting to board trains. I had seen them in the past few days at many places, exploring the countryside and tourist spots around Deoghar just as I was doing. Jeeps with banners proudly proclaiming that the occupants had come from Bhagwatpur Puraina, or Muzaffarpur, or Motihari, tractors with tarpaulin shades providing temporary living quarters to a group of 'Bam log' could be seen every-where. The tractors would have their sides festooned with the decorated kaanwar pots. Vans, mini-buses, and long coaches, all with many kaanwariyas travelling on the roofs of these vehicles, crossed us every few minutes on the road. Solitary men in orange cotton vests and shorts, an orange cloth twisted around their heads, the kaanwar pole with its two small pots balanced on their shoulders were intriguing sights. I admired their courage and focus in travelling alone. But of course, I also knew that the courage primarily stemmed from the fact that they felt they were never alone — that Shiva, the great healer, was with them every moment and every milestone of the way.

At the station, while I was waiting for my train, I saw some poignant scenes of the returning 'Bam log'. Some were limping, some being helped by their fellow travellers as they placed their hands on the shoulders of their friends and took slow steps on blistered feet. A great weariness was apparent on the faces of many of the men and women, lying on small scraps of cloth or plastic sheets or newspaper on the platform. Seeing them in this state, my mood turned slightly melancholy. I knew what dragged them down was not just the physical exhaustion. It was what waited for them back in their homes. Relationships that tested and tired them, authorities that exploited them or remained indifferent to their requests, living conditions perhaps so dreary that the rigours of the 'Bol Bam' march seemed better in comparison. 'O Baba Baidyanath! Bring what improvements you can in each of their lives. Please don't let their journeys go to waste!' I found myself silently urging Mahaaushadhi. But of course, I also knew that He would do this anyway.

On incredibly crowded trains, hanging on by the skin of their teeth, with their kaanwar poles tied to the train windows, some of the 'Bam log' began leaving in front of me. They took the extreme discomfort of the trains in their stride in the same way that they had taken the 'thwack-thwack' of the bunched canes. I saw their silent resignation as a vast ocean of opportunity for the political leaders who have robbed them of their basic human dignity and rights — men and women they have trusted with their votes. 'O Baba Baidyanath! Heal the wounds of this republic. Make this a democracy in the truest sense, by empowering every one of these people,' I prayed.

My train arrived, and I got on, but for a time, I was unable to sleep in the comfort of my berth in an air-conditioned compartment. Stray thoughts and memories chased themselves in my head. In Lucknow, I recalled being driven in a tonga in the Imambada area by Shakeel Hussain. 'I drive a tonga some months of the year, when it is not the wedding season. Otherwise, there is a demand for my horse for bridegrooms to ride on,' he had said. 'And of course, in the month of Saawan, I stop both horse and tonga work.'

'You do? Then how do you manage?' I asked him, astonished.

'Oh, then it is all Bhole Baba's work,' he said. 'I am an ice sculptor. For years, I have been making ice Shivalingas for various neighbourhoods. *Hamaare Barfani Baba bahut mashhoor hain* (My Barfani Baba or ice Shiva is most famous).'

Of course, Shiva counts Shakeel as one of his own. How could He not?

'*Bam naam grahan karne ke baad aap ki jaati nasht ho jaati hai. Phir ek hi dharm hai — Bol Bam* (After assuming the name *"Bam"* your caste tag gets destroyed. Then there is only one religion — Bol Bam).' Alok Santoshi's words to me had the ring of absolute conviction when he described the nature of the 'Bam log' in Deoghar. As I lay in the darkened train compartment, tears crept across my cheek as I thought of the implications of this declaration. 'How easily the divisive nature of caste can evaporate before Shiva! Then why are we in a hurry to assume its abhorrent cloak once again as we reach home?'

As I struggled to shake off the melancholy induced by exhaustion and the scenes of the returnees I had witnessed, another memory came to my rescue – the smiling tribal woman at Pachmarhi saying to me, 'I always say Na-Mah-Shi-Va-Ya!'

'Yes,' I found myself thinking, feeling my limbs relaxing at the very thought. 'Always say, "Namah Shivaya".'

'Har Har Mahadeo'

'Bol Bam!'

Epilogue: Suffering as Offering

All the challenges to faith described in the Introduction of this book pale before the colossal calamity that began unfolding from the night of 16 June 2013. In the Garhwal Himalayas of Uttarakhand, at the very sites from where this book begins to explore the facets of Shiva, cloudbursts, floods and landslides flattened whole towns and villages, obliterated roads and infra-structure, and left thousands dead, with a greater number stuck in the open without food or transport, or rendered homeless.

The Uttarakhand floods in 2013 represented the worst natural disaster in living memory for us as a nation. They also resulted in a rescue operation on the scale of which no attempt has been made before. The floods coincided with the peak of the pilgrimage season to the Char Dham or holy sites of Kedarnath and Badrinath, Gangotri and Yamunotri, besides the journey to Hemkunt Sahib, the holy lake which is the destina-tion of thousands of Sikhs in the same period. This is why those raging, tumultuous waters so shook the faith not only of those who experienced them first-hand, but also those who waited for weeks to have some word of their missing loved ones, or watched the horrifying images of the 'Himalayan tsunami' on millions of television screens in homes across the country.

The aftermath of the floods brought up all the famil-iar aspects that have defined us as a nation for the last several decades. Politicians trying to grab credit and headlines, horror stories of looting from pilgrims who were thousands of kilo-metres away from homes and down to their last resources, an account of official apathy in disaster-preparedness, or in the planning and prevention that could have lessened the environ-mental impact of what happened. Alongside this, there were, of course, examples of individuals and organizations who had shown far-sightedness, courage and a seemingly inexhaustible generosity of spirit. Whether it was the heroic acts of the men from the army, the National Disaster Response Force, the Indo-Tibetan Border Police, or the complete service and dedication shown by volunteers from the Delhi Sikh Gurudwara Management Committee, there was plenty to suggest that we are still a society with caring and selfless members.

But the wounds on the collective psyche sustained by losing so many while they were on pilgrimage, on a mission to meet God, will seep in silently for years to come.

Devotion to God has its own logic, often ridiculed by non-believers, but very apparent to those who consider God as their ultimate parent/protector/provider. By this logic, acts that are performed to earn some merit in His eyes, as pilgrimages invariably are, come with an inherent level of discomfort, or suffering. This is the rationale for fasting during Navaratri or Mahashivaratri, of climbing the steep steps of a mountain for a darshan. When your lungs are bursting in the first leg of the climb to Tirupati, before you have reached Kali Gopuram, a grim determination takes hold. 'I will do this!' may be the prevailing thought. Later, on the last leg, with the end of the climb visible a short distance away, an inner prayer is more likely to be, 'Dear God, please let me complete this! Don't let me breathe my last now.' Such a humble supplication, seeing as it involves the complete destruction of the agency of oneself, achieves the end of an experience like the climb to Sri Venkateswara, the reigning deity at Tirupati. Pilgrims know and accept this.

They also accept rubbing shoulders with thousands of others, enduring more pushing, jostling and being herded than they have occasion to do anywhere else, accepting all this as an inevitable side-effect of the fulfilling moment of darshan, an encounter with the divine that will bring them the assurance that He is looking after their affairs with particular care, at least for another twelve months. Sprained ankles, fractures, lost belongings, even heart attacks for some, all these are taken in stride by many devotees who have suffered them while on pilgrimage. 'God is giving me these minor losses to shield me from even greater ones!' a pilgrim may reason. Or, 'He has given me such a comfortable life. If I cannot bear even this much pain for Him, then of what use are my body and the comforts He has blessed me with?'

The idea of suffering as an offering is an idea that fits perfectly into the frame of devotional logic.

But the scale of that suffering for the pilgrims in Uttarakhand in June 2013, for the native population of this ecologically fragile Himalayan state, and for the rescuers who toiled tirelessly to bring their fellow citizens to safety surpassed anything previously seen and defied all such homely logic.

For His worshippers, God or Bhagwanji can be both loved and feared. Most ideas about Him fall under one or the other category.

'Why me, dear God? Why did this happen to me? Did you not love me enough to spare me this trauma?'

Everyone who has passed agonizing hours in the dark and cold, waiting to be rescued, separated from loved ones, unsure of whether they would reach home again can be pardoned for a dilution of their faith. Among those who managed to return, and their family members at home, there are many who will never venture again on pilgrimage. At least this is what some newspapers have reported.

There are others who are determined to return when they can, as soon as the pilgrimage routes have been restored, regardless of the losses they have borne. The anguished cry of 'Why me?', that seems to rail against the unfairness of God, is actually a very routine part of a devotee's dialogue with God. Such a cry always produces results when it comes out of great suffering — the answer may arrive in unexpected ways for the grieving heart, yet it inevitably strengthens their will to live. Those who declare that their faith remains strong even in the midst of the present devastation probably make these assertions out of the experience of such insights.

'When human greed, corruption and ambition have crossed all limits, God dispenses justice in such frightening ways...'

Karmic retribution is an idea with deep roots in most devotees' imagination. Even those who do not go about their daily activities fearing the awful presence of an unforgiving God at their shoulders, accept and recognize Him as the only true source of ultimate Justice. Tilting somewhat towards the 'Fear' school of belief, there are devotees who consider that the present disaster is nature and God's way of showing His extreme displeasure with the way we have treated mountains, rivers, forests and people. In fact, couched in more scientific and politically correct terms, this is the dominant idea that emerges even in debates across our television channels.

*   *   *   *   *   *   *

A couple of weeks after the rains had wreaked havoc in the towns of Kedarnath and Gaurikund, I had my first glimpse of what the famed jyotirlinga, described in the beginning chapter of this book, looked like after the onslaught of water, silt and rocks. A photograph in the *Indian Express* showed the tip of the Kedarnath Shivalinga, just the top eight inches or so, rising above a mass of grey silt, and still adorned (perhaps with the rescue personnel) with the distinctive bilva offering of three leaflets. The temple and its icon have endured, just as the faith of millions and the democratic fibre of our country will.

But this endurance cannot be taken for granted, or have any meaning without our personal engagement with it.

The days following the Uttarakhand floods threw us all into complete emotional turmoil. The sheer numbers of the dead and injured were horrifying. At any time, even a fortnight after commencing of rescue operations, the television ticker was telling us how thousands still needed to be evacuated from Badrinath. On 25 June, when an Indian Air Force helicopter carrying men who had worked day and night to rescue trapped people crashed, killing everyone on board, it seemed the most grotesque extension of an unrelenting horror. The nation's loss in the Garhwal Himalayas overtook all other disasters at sites of faith — the mountainside deaths of pilgrims on the trail to Naina Devi in 2008, the stampede deaths at the Kumbh Mela in February 2013, the burning of the yagasala, a structure built for rituals, at the Brihadeeswar temple in 2009, all seemed minuscule in comparison.

Even before rescue operations in Uttarakhand had concluded, thousands of pilgrims were already preparing for another arduous trek in another mountainous region — the annual Amarnath yatra. I was left pondering on many of the themes and questions that have emerged at different times in the narrative of this book. As I thought of the pilgrims I had met on so many journeys, and the difficulties they endure, it struck me that, more than prayer, what the faithful of our country need today is to ensure that their fellow humans deliver on the promises they make, particularly during elections. With some apology to an old slogan from the feminist movement, it is perfectly obvious to me that 'The spiritual is political'.

Scharada Dubey
July, 2013

Bibliography

Briggs, George Weston. 1989. *Gorakhnath and the Kanphata Yogis*. Delhi: Motilal Banarsidass.

Pandit, Dr B.N. 1977. *Aspects of Kashmir Saivism*.
Delhi: Utpal Publications.

Pattanaik, Devdutt. 2011. *7 Secrets of Shiva*.
New Delhi: Westland.

Ramana, Maharshi. 2000. *Arunachala: Ocean of Grace Divine*.
Thiruvannamalai: Sri Ramanasramam.

Ramanujan, A.K. (trans.). 1973. *Speaking of Siva*.
New Delhi: Penguin Classics.

Sankshipt Shiv Purana. Gorakhpur: Geeta Press, 44th edition.

Sekkizhaar. 1985. *Periya Puranam*, condensed English
version by G. Vanmikanathan. Mylapur, Madras:
Sri Ramakrishna Math.

Sontheimer, Gunther-Dietz and Hermann Kulke (eds). 2005.
Hinduism Reconsidered. Delhi: Manohar Publishers.